MAPS FOR THE JOURNEY

Finding your way around the Bible

Edgar Wille

The Baca Press

Maps for the Journey: Finding Your Way Around the Bible

ISBN 0-9537419-0-7

Copyright © Edgar Wille 2000

Published by The Baca Press 2000
24 Durrants Road, Berkhamsted,
Hertfordshire HP4 3PF

Typeset in Perpetua by M Rules
Printed and bound in Great Britain

Born in 1923, Edgar Wille was brought up in the Christadelphian faith. Although he parted company with them in the 1970s, he says he will always be grateful for the Biblical grounding he received among them, not least from his father. He spent ten years in farming and over thirty years in marketing and personnel management with British Coal. Currently he is programme director in Central and Eastern Europe for Ashridge Management College. For this he was awarded the OBE in January 1999. He has written a number of management books and one on the Holy Spirit. He is a church warden and lay reader at St Clement's Anglican Church in Prague.

Also by Edgar Wille

The Holy Spirit

Quality: Achieving Excellence

Making Change Work
(with P. Hodgson)

People Development and
Improved Business Performance

Ethics at the Heart of the Business

The Computer in Personnel Work
(with V. Hammond)

The Computer and Business Unity
(with R. A. Hitchcock)

For my children,
Ruth, David and Marion,
and their families

Contents

	Foreword	xi
1	Approaching the Bible	1
2	Beginnings: *Genesis*	11
3	Towards a Promised Land: *Exodus*	20
4	Laws, Statistics and Principles: *Leviticus, Numbers and Deuteronomy*	28
5	Conquest and Settlement: *Joshua and Judges*	39
6	The Rise of the Monarchy: *Ruth, 1 Samuel, 2 Samuel*	48
7	The Divided Kingdom: *1 Kings, 2 Kings, 1 Chronicles, 2 Chronicles*	54
8	The End of the Exile: *Ezra, Nehemiah and Esther*	61
9	Why Do Bad Things Happen To Good People?: *Job*	69
10	Israel's Hymn Book: *Psalms*	75
11	Wisdom: *Proverbs*	82
12	The Preacher: *Ecclesiastes*	91

13	In Praise of Romance: *The Song of Songs*	101
14	Isaiah of Jerusalem: *Isaiah*	109
15	The Second Isaiah: *Isaiah continued*	121
16	Prophet of Sorrow and Joy: *Jeremiah and Lamentations*	130
17	The Living Visual Aid: *Ezekiel*	149
18	Brave and Wise: *Daniel*	159
19	Denunciation and Hope From an Eloquent Trio: *Hosea, Joel and Amos*	171
20	Six Minor Prophets: *Obadiah, Jonah, Micah, Nahum, Habakkuk and Zephaniah*	180
21	The Prophets of the Return: *Haggai, Zechariah and Malachi*	190
22	A Bridge Between the Testaments	198
23	Three Connected Gospels: *Matthew, Mark and Luke*	205
24	The Ministry of Jesus in Galilee: *Matthew*	210
25	The Road to the Cross: *Matthew*	229
26	Unique Contributions: *Mark and Luke*	239
27	The Death and Resurrection of Jesus: *Matthew, Mark, Luke and John*	252
28	Divinity and Humanity Blended in Jesus: *John*	263
29	Christ's Other Self – The Holy Spirit: *John*	276
30	Bringing the Good News From Jerusalem to Rome – Unlocking the Doors: *Acts of the Apostles*	288
31	Bringing the Good News From Jerusalem to Rome – To the Ends of the Earth: *Acts of the Apostles*	301
32	Paul Explains the Gospel: *Romans*	313

33	Troubles in Corinth: *1 Corinthians*	332
34	Paul Shares His Heart: *2 Corinthians*	346
35	Paul Gets Tough: *Galatians*	355
36	The Message of Unity: *Ephesians*	367
37	A Warm-Hearted Thank-You Letter: *Philippians*	376
38	Rescued From the Power of Darkness: *Colossians and Philemon*	385
39	Letters to an Infant Church: *1 Thessalonians, 2 Thessalonians*	396
40	Pastoral Epistles: *1 Timothy, 2 Timothy and Titus*	403
41	A New Way: *Hebrews*	415
42	The One God: *James*	426
43	The General Epistles: *1 Peter, 2 Peter, 1 John, 2 John, 3 John and Jude*	435
44	A Christian Opera: *Revelation*	447

Afterword	457
Further Reading	459
Key Dates	461

Foreword

This books aims to help people who may not be familiar with it to gain a broad overview of the collection of books we call the Bible. This is not a book of profound theology – just an aid to intelligent reading. This is not a book that tells you what you should believe – it simply gives some assistance in the process of making up your own mind and following this in action that you feel in your heart is appropriate. The first chapter says more about the specific objectives of this attempt to place every book of the Bible in a context that will aid understanding.

The editorial work of my grandson Andrew Wille has been invaluable, ensuring a smoother style and clearer expression. My thanks also to Clare Britton, who improved many of the chapters. I have also been encouraged to pursue the work by John Heptonstall and other colleagues at Ashridge Management College, who insisted on having copies of earlier drafts and maintained pressure on me to finish the task. Members of St Clement's Anglican Church in Prague have also encouraged me, as have Ian and Averil McHaffie and other members of the Christadelphian community with whom I maintain fraternal relations.

This book could not have been written without the benefit of wide reading of theological and Biblical scholars and popularisers of all perspectives. They have entered into the texture of my thinking and I may quote them without realising it. If I have done so I ask them not to regard this as a breach of copyright, but as part of a collective effort to help all kinds of people understand the Bible better. I am aware that reading the writing of N.T. (Tom) Wright has influenced me considerably, along with the likes of C.F.D. Moule, C.H. Dodd, John Robinson, John McQuarrie, J.D.G. Dunn and many others. Tom Wright was kind enough to read Chapter 22 sympathetically.

I offer the book prayerfully in the hope that it will stimulate the spiritual growth of those who are Christians and encourage those who are not Christians to consider carefully whether there might be something in the Bible that could enhance their lives.

Edgar Wille
August 1999

1

Approaching the Bible

This introductory chapter is the first meeting point for the readers, the Bible writers and the helper (for this is all I can be). I will tell you why I felt moved to write; you may have some first thoughts about what you want to get out of this book. Ideas on what you might do as a result of our journey together may follow later, though they will be your ideas, not mine, even if, sometimes, they coincide.

A number of my friends, Christian and non-Christian, have said that they would like to be able to read the Bible and understand what it is aiming to say. Some of them are church-goers who only hear selections read in lessons and would like to have an overall picture of what is being said and why. Others recognise that the Bible is great literature, and sense a gap in their education because they can't make much sense of it. Friends in the former communist states, where religion was discouraged, never developed a familiarity with it and would now like to correct that. Others sense that it might help to clarify the meaning of life, or suggest a 'greater purpose'.

For whatever reason they come to the Bible, many people find themselves confused or soon running into difficulties when they start reading it. This may result from the apparent lack of consistency in the Bible, or what seem to be outdated scientific concepts, or moral dilemmas based on behaviour far removed from what we thought Jesus Christ stood for. At first reading much of the material is also rather boring, such as the long lists of family genealogies and detailed descriptions of ancient rites and ceremonies. The Bible certainly appears to be a book that contains material of variable levels.

Two Connected Libraries

In fact the Bible is not a book but a library; you might even say it is two libraries connected by a door. The two libraries are the Old Testament and the New Testament, and Jesus Christ is the door that leads from one to the other. He is the central figure of the whole Bible, even where he is not mentioned and even before he came on to the scene, though that needs careful consideration and we shall examine it later.

Another problem is that to understand any one part of the Bible, you really need to understand all of the rest, but if you wait till you have done that, you will never get started. It may be easier to say that the more you understand of any one part, the more you will understand the rest. Understanding, as in all subjects, is progressive. This is what gives any kind of study its excitement as a journey of discovery. And of course the Bible does claim to be able to give understanding that will make an enormous difference to your life, so it is worth persevering to find out whether its claims work for you.

The fact that all parts of the Bible are interdependent affects the presentation of this book, which offers a broad outline of what you will read in the Bible. Each part will link with others, though I seek to make each understandable in its own right. Gradually, I hope you will create your own connections. After all, this is how we learn anything. We have an experience; reflect on it; develop a little theory; try out the theory; and then it enters into our next experience, right through life, from a child learning that a hot stove can hurt when touched to the older person coping patiently with problems of life.

Your Path Through the Bible

The Bible is not necessarily a book where you start at the beginning and work through till you get to the end, chapter by chapter. There is no right place to start, and a certain amount of jumping about may be beneficial. The same goes for this book too.

A full understanding of later parts of the Bible often requires knowledge of earlier sections. On the other hand, if you think an earlier part represents the final truth of a matter, you may be surprised at a later stage. In the New Testament one writer tells us that the Old Testament (the Jewish Scriptures) can make us wise and affect our destiny if we read it with the story of Jesus Christ in mind (2 Timothy 3:15).

Therefore I do not suggest that you read the books of the Bible in the order in which they appear. Among other things you would have to wait a long while for Jesus Christ to appear on the scene and to make greater sense of all that went before. But this book follows the order of the Bible itself. I do this only for ease of reference so that you can keep in touch with the whole picture in broad terms, while going into greater detail with individual books in any order that suits you. My chapters will summarise each book of the Bible with more detail, or less, depending on how straightforward it is.

When I suggest that you may like to examine a particular

point, I shall use the traditional reference system, by which the chapter and verse are numbered to help you find specific parts of the text. The reference above points you to the Book of – or more precisely, the Second Letter to – Timothy, Chapter 3, verse 15. Whatever version of the Bible you are using, it is doubtless divided into such numbered chapters and verses. It wasn't written like that: the system was added centuries afterwards so that people could find the part being referred to in any discussion or reading. One story tells of a soldier, many centuries after Christ, having to undertake a very long journey in France; to while away the time he divided the New Testament into chapters and verses.

The Methodology of This Book

I write as if the reader is coming fresh to the Bible. Sometimes you may say, 'Oh everyone knows that'; at other times you may say, 'Well, I never knew that before.' I have taken the risk that you may sometimes think I am not giving you credit for your existing knowledge.

I am trying to avoid saying what you ought to believe about the Bible. Obviously I have my own views, and I will not hide them. But my aim is to help you collect enough information about the Bible to be able to make some kind of sense of it – but it will be *your* sense. You will come to your own conclusions and make your own decisions as to what you should do about it all. There has been far too much spiritual dictatorship in the history of religion, and although the God we read about in the Bible, and see represented in Jesus Christ, does claim some authority, it is one he does not impose. In the Bible you are offered freedom to choose, though this freedom comes with a warning that important consequences may arise from your choices.

As we proceed, I shall share some of the various views that have been put forward by scholarly students of the Bible, but only in a broad manner, mainly to help you recognise that there are alternative ways of looking at some of the text. I don't want to write an academic treatise where the power of the message can easily get submerged in a mass of detail of interest only to specialists. In every subject such people are needed to bring their expertise to bear on the text, so long as someone can present their information clearly, but, in the end we must remain free to make our own decisions and not be discouraged by debates that are often highly speculative and go into overwhelming minutiae.

Basically we must allow the Bible to tell us its own story – or stories – on its own terms. We should enjoy reading it in that way, first gaining an idea of what the various writers were trying to say, whether we agree with them or not, whether we like what is being said or not. Often we will have to reserve judgement to a later stage, and always we should be ready to have an earlier understanding modified by a later one. This is why I think of it as a journey of discovery.

The Importance of Story

The idea of story is an important one. The Bible is not, in the main, a volume of philosophy. It tells a story, which is in turn composed of many shorter individual stories. We reap most benefit if we read them for enjoyment in the first instance. We shouldn't hurry to decide what is being taught: just enjoy the story as you would any other. You find yourself taking sides, liking the heroes and disliking the villains, and often trying to make up your mind which are which. Later, you begin to see that there is often a deeper underlying message in the story.

We need not even be concerned whether the story was literally true. So many people have been daunted by supposing the Bible all came down from heaven and is literally and infallibly true: a final revelation. As you read, don't assume that the Bible is demanding that you believe that the creation happened exactly that way in six days of twenty-four hours each, or that Jonah was really swallowed by a whale to be vomited up later to continue his life. It is best to reserve judgement and enjoy the story and perhaps find a glimmer of its real meaning.

Sometimes you may wonder why the Bible is written so indirectly. If it is really important to give meaning to our lives, would it not have been better to have a straightforward book of rules and clear explanations so that we would know exactly where we stood and did not have to do any thinking? God would do all the work for us and we would be bored puppets or robots. And what a way of learning! Who, apart from lawyers, ever found a volume of the laws of a country exciting?

In addition to the strong use of the story and stories, the Bible gives us moving poetry, pithy proverbs, wonderful songs, brilliant verbal cartoons, stirring speeches, sad laments, rational arguments, humour and wit, magnificent debates, personal letters, diaries of journeys, even a love song. There is an endless variety, and the fact that numerous different opinions are expressed by different actors in the great drama adds to the richness of our experience as we read. Yes, it could have been simpler – but would we have been excited by it and would we have been influenced as powerfully? It is a library of books, written by human authors, whom many believe God inspired not to provide an infallible scientific treatise but to lead us to an understanding of God in a way that involves us in much careful thinking.

Translations of the Bible

There are many versions of the Bible. We have to recognise that the Old Testament was mainly written in Hebrew and the New Testament in Greek. Few of us would get far without a translator. I believe that the best translation is the Revised English Bible (1989). Fluent in style, its English is particularly apt for worship.

Very close to it are the New American Bible (revised 1986), which is a Roman Catholic translation, and the New Revised Standard Version Bible (1989). All translation depends in some measure upon interpretation, but these versions appear, in the main, to avoid writing in their prejudices. This is less true of an otherwise very smooth and popular translation, the New International Version (NIV 1984).

These translations will serve well. If you want to study in depth it is a good idea to have several translations as a comparison of versions often brings out the richness of the meaning.

Anyone who has learned a foreign language will be aware of the difficulty of expressing ideas in another tongue; often the equivalents are not exact. This need not raise concern. In certain cases there are difficulties of finding the original text, but that really matters only if you are engaging in deep academic study where subtle distinctions may be important. We are aiming to gain a first familiarity with the Bible.

Principles of Interpretation

In some ways the reading of the Bible needs to be approached like reading any piece of literature. We need to ask:

- What is the writer saying?
- What does the text actually mean? How can I avoid reading my own ideas into it?

- What caused him to write? What is the context? (Some detective work will probably be involved.)
- Was the writer consistent? Or was he involved in an inner debate about the experiences he was sharing? Did his understanding develop? (And it is 'he'. The liberating effect of the New Testament on women had not yet begun to take effect. Apart from one or two songs, there are few women authors in the Bible.)
- If the writer claims he is giving a message from God, are there any clues about how he received it? Is it most likely that he heard the voice of God in his heart, and was it possible for him to misinterpret some of it?

These and many other questions arise. The writers of the Bible are people, with human reactions, contradictions, misunderstandings, optimism and pessimism, common to mankind. Earlier generations of Christians used often to treat Bible writers as puppets or stenographers, taking down the words that God dictated to them. A little reflection shows this is not the case. God could hardly say to one of the people who wrote the Psalms, for example, 'I want you to say how sad you are because it feels as if I have deserted you.' They wrote sad thoughts, because they felt them.

The prophets were people who tried to interpret the times. They were not essentially foretellers of the future. They were puzzled, burdened, encouraged and discouraged as they sought to understand and contribute to their times. They often engaged in dialogue with God, and invite us to join them. We call this prayer. The channel is open for anyone. Anyone can say, 'God, if you exist and if you are there and if you can do anything about it, help me understand what I am reading.' Jesus commended a man who said, 'Lord I believe! Help my unbelief!'

Maps for the Journey

I described reading the Bible as a journey of discovery. Even if you don't know where the journey will end, a map helps. Christopher Columbus had a map showing what were then called the Indies. What he didn't know was that the undiscovered America lay between him and his goal. Voyages of discovery always offer surprises.

So here I offer you some maps for your journey. They do not include all the harbours, peninsulas, estuaries, islands and other features that you will discover for yourself. Nor do they show all the wind directions and sea currents that will challenge you along the way. They simply outline the continents and oceans to give you some idea of where you are going.

Speaking plainly, each chapter contains a brief sketch of the main theme of each book of the Bible, including a short description of its context. The main purpose is to give you a broad picture that you can keep referring back to until you have created your own picture. If you read these map chapters right through now, don't try to remember them all; they won't run away from the pages. Use the chapters of this book initially to establish a feel for how each part contributes to the whole. To return to the discovery metaphor, use them to get the ship heading in the right direction.

We shall take the Old Testament first, with its thirty-nine books, and then the New Testament with its twenty-seven. Some of the books are long, while others are not much more than pamphlets. My chapters will vary in length and coverage. Where a book of the Bible is fairly straightforward narrative, it will need only a broad guide, and several books may be covered in one chapter. Other books of the Bible will call for more detailed coverage, even more than one chapter.

Above all, the ultimate benefit, whatever you are seeking, will come from reading the Bible itself. This book is merely a tool to help harvest that reward.

2

Beginnings

Genesis

We start at the beginning with the Book of Genesis, which means 'beginnings'.

It opens the Pentateuch – the first five books of the Bible. They are traditionally attributed to Moses, though it is unlikely he was responsible for writing them all, particularly the parts that record his own death.

These books, like a number of others in the Bible, were compiled much later from earlier source material. You can spot some different sources for yourself. In Genesis, for example, you can track a source that used the word 'elohim' for God, and it is usually translated as 'God' in English versions. Another source used the word 'Yahweh' as the name of God, usually translated 'Lord' (in capitals) in English versions. The later compiler has skilfully interwoven them into an apparently continuous narrative.

Sometimes such compilers will give their own emphasis, but this is inevitable in any historical writing. It does not detract from the basic soundness of the original material, even though this may contain some symbolism as well as plain facts. For our purposes of reading the Bible on its own terms, this compilation issue need not greatly concern us, other than to recognise that the text of the Bible underwent a complex process before reaching its present form.

The Creator God

The first eleven chapters of Genesis provide the stories of how the people of Israel saw the work of God as the Creator of everything and how the early humans reacted to him and in fact disappointed him, if we can speak of God in that way. These chapters do see God through human eyes. They speak of him as going for a walk in the evening, of feeling he has made a mistake in creating man, of remembering things he needed to do, of coming down to the earth to see what these humans were up to. Scholars call this kind of speech 'anthropomorphism', as it describes God in human terms.

This helps us to understand how all these stories of the origins of the earth and human society need not be taken literally as scientific descriptions. They are instructive, presenting a number of important spiritual truths. You will have to make up your own mind about how far you regard them literally. While some Christians do think of them as hard truth, others see them in a more poetic sense. Both groups of opinion can derive benefit from their interpretations, and they should not fight each other, though rather unfortunately they often do. It must be quite a disappointment to God. (I'm speaking anthropomorphically now.)

In these early chapters we have two versions of creation and particularly of the first humans – presented as a couple, Adam and Eve, whose names meant 'earth' and 'mother'. (The first version is Chapter 1 and the first three verses of Chapter 2; the second is 2:4 onwards.) Many Christians, though believing in a creator God who operated through some evolutionary process, insist that the Bible record portrays God's creative energy as the motivating force behind creation, which was not a spontaneous evolution by an unguided series of accidents and collisions.

You need not discard the science of geology, which has lengthy periods for the formation of the earth, just because Genesis 1 describes a wonderfully vivid drama of the whole activity being carried out in six days of 24 hours. It is concerned with spiritual truths not scientific description, though until relatively recently people interpreted the story more literally.

Paradise Lost

We miss the point of the story of Adam and Eve eating the fruit from the tree of knowledge of good and evil (it does not say it was an apple) if we concentrate our thinking on its literal truth. It speaks of the human search for wisdom disregarding God. This attitude of pride and ambition is not developed by the kind of diet you follow, any more than living forever could be the literal result of eating of the tree of life, with the primitive picture of God having to hurry to stop the newly enlightened man and woman getting to the tree and living forever – immortal 'sinners'.

The idea that the eating of the one fruit sentenced the whole human race to death and cursed the productive capacity of the earth does not fit with the overall picture of the gracious God in the Bible. As a symbolic picture of the human race resisting God's direction and the connected disbalance in nature, it is a wonderful and poetically true presentation. It is very topical too in an age of environmental concern. Notice the 'curse' says 'thorns and thistles shall it bring forth *to you*', not that God purposely created thorns and thistles to punish humans. Instead they would get out of balance and make life difficult. After all, even a weed is simply a plant out of place.

What is called 'sin' enters into the world through the ambition and pride of the early humans. It has stayed with us ever since. We should note, too, that although Adam and Eve are presented as having lost their naïve innocence after the discovery of sin, there is no suggestion that the sin was anything to do with sex, which they seem to have discovered as a kind of comfort after the alienation of sin.

Violence and Disaster

With the coming of the first family, as Cain and then Abel are born, the story of sin gathers momentum, with the start of religious persecution, by Cain of Abel, and the first murder, based on envy. The human taste for war instead of conciliation develops. Mankind creates a self-sufficient and violent civilisation, where Lamech boasts to his wives (he is not satisfied with one) that he has avenged himself seventy-seven-fold for a mere wound. At the same time, with supplementary traditional information from the Book of Jude in the New Testament, we learn that Enoch, who 'walked with God', protested against the prevalent wickedness. Lamech and Enoch were both seven generations on from Adam. You could say that 'Lamech versus Enoch is the key to world history'.

Then comes the flood, portrayed as sweeping away all the human race except for Noah and his family, with whom a new start is made. The reasons are given in two forms. In Genesis 6:5, the Yahwist source tells us 'The *Lord* (Yahweh) saw that the wickedness of man was great in the earth and that every imagination of the thoughts of his heart was only evil continually.' In 6:11, the Elohist source puts it 'now the earth was corrupt in God's (Elohim's) sight and the earth was filled with violence'.

We are being given a spiritual verdict on human behaviour, not a scientific description of some major geological catastrophe. It is hardly credible that the whole globe was submerged in water to the mountain tops and that all the animal species were preserved in one boat – the ark – much smaller than a modern ocean liner. Some such disaster did occur; it is confirmed in the records of the Sumerian and other ancient nations and, though relatively local, it was sufficiently disastrous to be the source of the story and, more importantly, to lead to reflection on human wickedness. Though archaeologists still hunt for the ark on Mount Ararat in Turkey, I personally don't expect them to find anything.

The Beginning of Nations

Following up the story of the flood, God is reported as saying that he will never again destroy the human race so totally and appoints the rainbow as a sign in the sky. You can imagine the situation. For the first time since the flood there is a violent rainstorm. Noah and his family are alarmed. Is this the start of another deluge? But then the sun comes out as the rain is subsiding and the rainbow is seen in the clouds. Noah takes comfort and the rainbow becomes, in many parts of the Bible, the symbol of hope when disaster threatens.

After the flood a picture is drawn of a newly developing civilisation, with mighty warriors such as Nimrod and war and conquest and city-building. A decision is made to build a tower to reach up to heaven to demonstrate the new people's strength, but God is described as confusing their tongues so that they couldn't communicate with each other. This was said to be the creation of the many languages that still impede communication in the world. The science of linguistics would not accept this as a literal explanation, but the story contains a very true insight on the role of the diversity of language in the creation of misunderstanding among the nations of the world. There is also a continuation of the theme of the pride and self-confidence of humankind, with a related rejection of any idea of depending on God.

These chapters also contain a genealogy of the descendants of Noah as a basis for the origin of the geographical spread of nations.

Abraham and God's Promises

After Genesis 12 the dealings of God with Abraham, Isaac and Jacob commence the story of the race of Israel.

Abraham leaves the valley of the Euphrates, migrating first to Syria and then to Palestine. God promises that he will make of his descendants a great nation with a homeland, under God's protection, making them indestructible, and outlasting all their enemies. The purpose of this blessing, formalised into a covenant, was not for their own selfish enjoyment, but that as a nation they should become a channel for blessing all mankind.

Abraham believes God's promises and his faith is considered by God as the hallmark of righteousness. This attitude earns Abraham the title of the father of the faithful and friend of God. His attitude became the subject of much comment by the prophets and in the New Testament, not least in the letters of Paul to the Romans and to the Galatians.

There are fascinating stories about Abraham: how he defeats city kings to save his nephew Lot, who goes to live in the wicked cities of Sodom and Gomorrah, which despite

Abraham's pleading with God are destroyed by fire. Lot escapes and ends his days in a cave where his daughters make him drunk and, without him knowing what he has done, he becomes the father of their children Moab and Ammon, whose descendants are often at war with Israel in later times.

Abraham's wife, Sarah, not expecting ever to have a son as she approaches ninety, asks Abraham to give her a proxy son by Hagar, her servant girl. This works out badly and Hagar and her son Ishmael are sent away, God promising to make out of the boy a great nation – the core of the Arab nations.

Then Sarah herself, amazingly even in times when people were reported to have lived longer, has a child. She is ninety and Abraham one hundred! He is named Isaac, and God indicates that through his descendants the covenant will be fulfilled. The New Testament continues this thread and says that there was an individual descendant in mind – Jesus – and that in him all nations of the earth would be blessed. Circumcision is introduced as a symbol that the promises do not depend on the physical activity of man, but on the trustworthiness of God's word. Once Jesus had come, the New Testament says circumcision was no longer necessary – only circumcision of the heart was required. These stories are the basis of the Jewish and, ultimately, of the Christian religion.

Apart from having a strong narrative, this is an important section of Genesis, because many later parts of the Bible refer to it. The Israelites often thought that they were God's chosen people because they were superior to other nations, whereas it is made quite clear that they were intended to be the means by which all nations would, ultimately, become part of the family of God. They were chosen for service.

Another famous story tells that Abraham thinks that God wants him to offer up his son Isaac as a sacrifice. He has the knife lifted to kill him, but is stopped at the last moment and a ram is provided for a sacrifice instead. This was generally taken by the early Christian Church as symbolic of the sacrificial death of Jesus. It had a further practical purpose for it is noteworthy that right through the history of Israel, human sacrifice, so prevalent among many ancient religions, is presented as a very evil practice – an 'abomination'.

Isaac and Jacob

Isaac's life is relatively uneventful, but his son, Jacob, is a colourful individual. There is the romantic story of his seven-year courtship of Rachel and 'they seemed to him but a few days because of the love he had for her'. There is also the story of Jacob's dream about a ladder reaching up to heaven and his fight with an angel, after which his name was changed to Israel. An interesting feature of the Biblical record is that its heroes are not presented in a uniformly favourable light. Jacob, for example, isn't always a particularly nice person; he deceives his father and steals his brother Esau's heritage by subterfuge. In other ways he is presented in a better light, though, because he cared about God's promises, whereas the more amiable Esau did not.

From Prison to Prime Minister

Genesis concludes with the story of Joseph, which Andrew Lloyd Webber and Tim Rice turned into the musical play *Joseph's Amazing Technicolor Dreamcoat*. It is a tale of jealousy, attempted murder, seduction resisted and ultimate victory. Joseph rises from slavery to become the second ruler in Egypt, in charge of ensuring that Egypt was prepared for famine by his outstanding management skills. In this capacity he also saves his father's family from death through famine. The scene where he makes himself known to his brothers is very moving, as is his reunion with his father, who had thought him long dead, killed by his brothers' jealousy. The brothers are also concerned, expecting him to avenge himself, but he treats them with magnanimity.

The purpose of the story from the Israelite perspective was to show how in a providential way working behind the scenes God was preserving the descendants of Abraham for their ultimate worldwide role, to be the channel of world blessing in Jesus Christ.

Genesis: A Foundation Book

So Genesis tells many good stories. It challenges you to work out what to take literally and to gain spiritual learning as you feel beneath the surface of the stories for the deeper purpose. This book is also the foundation for much of the teaching in the rest of the Bible, though it is reinterpreted in new and even surprising ways, especially in the New Testament.

3

Towards a Promised Land

Exodus

The descendants of Jacob, who was also called Israel, grow in number and power in Egypt, until some generations later a new Pharaoh or ruler of Egypt begins to fear that they are a potential danger to his state. As a consequence he makes slaves of them in his great building programmes, maybe of some of the still existing Pyramids. The first great outbreak of anti-Semitism occurs when the Israelites are instructed by Pharaoh to kill all their male children to stop the growth of the nation.

Moses the Leader and Pharaoh the Persecutor

Moses is as a result concealed in the bulrushes. He is discovered by Pharaoh's daughter and adopted by her, with his own mother as his nanny. He grows up skilled in Egyptian ways, but also well instructed in the hopes and ideals of Israel, equipped to negotiate with Pharaoh for Israel and to lead his people out of Egypt.

Pharaoh, not wishing to lose his supply of cheap labour, refuses to let them go. There follow the twelve terrible plagues, the last one of which is the death of all the firstborn (children and adults) of the Egyptians. This causes Pharaoh to chase them out, but even then he changes his mind and the story continues as he sends his army to stop their flight. The Israelites safely cross the Sea of Reeds (or the Red Sea – opinions differ), but when Pharaoh's army try the same they are all drowned. The Israelites celebrate with a gala concert, when they gloat over their enemies and yet show appreciation to God for delivering them.

The Problems of God's Rescue Operation

Some of the plagues, and particularly the last one, are so cruel that you cannot imagine that the Being – the God – called in the New Testament 'the God and Father of our Lord Jesus Christ' was responsible for such horrors, though Israel thanked him for it all. This is an example of the many moral dilemmas presented by the Bible. You are left with the feeling that the attribution of the disasters to God perhaps results from the way in which Israel perceived them, rather than God's intention. Undoubtedly there were great disasters in Egypt, though perhaps some of them were natural phenomena, which enabled Israel to escape; conditioned by their times, the Israelites attributed it all to the direct activity of God.

There is a mystery here, because right through the Bible this exodus (which means 'going out') is seen as the work of God. It raises the puzzle of whether God uses bad things that are going to happen anyway to secure ultimately good results. We are drawn into deep philosophy about whether humans have free will or whether God is all-powerful. How can God influence things without robbing humans of the power to choose good and reject evil?

I suggest that initially you should concentrate on reading the story on its own terms. Recognise the problems, even make a note of them, and you may find that, as reading proceeds, you discover answers that satisfy you. Alternatively you may decide that there is so much good in the Bible story as a whole that you will accept temporary ambiguity and uncertainty. Clarity grows as you piece together the jigsaw of connected pieces in the Bible. The New Testament portraits of Jesus Christ particularly help to bring everything together. He is the ultimate centrepiece of the whole story. In him everything holds together and the Old Testament finds its fulfilment and reinterpretation. According to the New Testament, he is the one by whom truth is ultimately measured in the Bible.

The Wilderness Journey Starts

The rest of the Book of Exodus tells what happens as Moses begins to lead over half a million Israelites towards the 'promised land', which takes them forty years to reach. The story is very human. Every time the Israelites run into trouble they complain, blame Moses or blame God. They wish they had never left Egypt. Bad though it was, they complain that the desert is even worse. We are then told how God provides them with a bread-like substance which they called 'manna' (which means 'What is it?') and quails for meat. If they collect more than a certain amount they have to share the excess; on Fridays they have to collect twice the normal daily quota, because none is provided on the next day, the sabbath when work was forbidden.

I do not suggest that God sent double portions of manna on the sabbath or that all the miracles that are reported are miracles. You may think of a natural explanation or reserve judgement till you have read further, including a look at some of the New Testament. Of course it is also possible that the God of which the Bible talks actually does perform miracles. Many Jews and Christians perceived many of the events as beyond the natural.

Exodus continues to tell how water is provided in the desert in response to Israel's complaints. Moses is taught by his father-in-law to delegate, instead of trying to do everything himself. The story is told of success in their first battle against the Amalekites, where Moses keeps his hands up in prayer, and as long as he does so the victory continues.

Meeting God in Sinai

Now we reach one of the greatest episodes to leave its mark on the whole of Jewish and indeed Christian history. The Israelites come to what is described as the barren and forbidding area of Sinai. It is the solemn scene of great storms, with thunder and lightning and a loud trumpet blast, 'so that all the people that were in the camp trembled'. Out of the midst of it God speaks. So frightened are the Israelites that they beg Moses to speak on God's behalf and God graciously obliges.

Before delegating the speaking to Moses, God himself speaks the Ten Commandments, which are still often recited in churches and synagogues (Exodus 20). The first four commandments concern the uniqueness of God, and include keeping the sabbath day as a time of rest from all work. They were not to worship or recognise any other gods. The remaining six dealt with how people should behave honestly and with kindness towards each other: not killing, not committing adultery, not coveting another's possessions, not stealing, not giving false testimony in court and showing honour to one's parents.

Moses then goes up the mountain, where God gives him detailed instructions, expanding on the Ten Commandments and giving behavioural details that are the basis of many modern laws. Their spirit influenced the teaching of Jesus. They include laws regulating slavery, though not at that stage abolishing it. Other laws institute claims against other people for personal injury and damage to property, reflected in most legal systems today and very similar to those of some of the other Middle Eastern nations of the time, such as the code of Hammurabi of Babylon (1700 BC). Theft and burglary are also dealt with, and there are rules about trusts and loans and libel. And, of course, there are religious laws.

Worship Established

God tells Moses how to build a tent of central worship called the tabernacle, with the ark of the covenant as its centrepiece, where the presence of God was represented. It was a box overlaid with gold and containing various holy objects. Details were given of the special clothes to be made for the priests and their assistants and also of animal sacrifices to be offered at the consecration of the priests. In the West it would be considered quite repellent if we had to offer them in our churches.

Exodus 25–31 are not overtly exciting chapters but they are important to an understanding of worship and behaviour in ancient Israel. The first time you read Exodus you might decide to skim-read these chapters, just taking enough notice to get a general idea. In later books of the Bible you may find references which send you back for more detail. One thing worth noting is that some of the sacrifices were completely burnt to represent the offerers giving themselves completely to God. (Paul in his letter to the Romans invites Christians to give themselves as living sacrifices to God.) Other sacrifices were to be eaten by priest and people, with only some parts burnt. These were representative of fellowship – between God and the people, and among people.

The materials for the tabernacle were of rich quality and built or sewn by highly skilled craftsmen. The wooden framework, dividing curtains and a large tent over the whole structure are all described in detail. The tabernacle had both a holy section as well as a most holy section also called the holy of holies. The high priest went into the latter once a year on the Day of Atonement when the national sins were forgiven. The only furniture there was the ark. In the holy place, the more public part of the tabernacle that the priests used daily, was a table for the bread of God's presence as the provider (it was changed each day – 'give us this day our daily bread' in the Lord's prayer), the golden lampstand representing the light that comes from God and the altar of incense, which was a visual representation of the idea of prayer ascending as a sweet smell to God.

Outside, in the court, there was an altar for the daily sacrifices. There was also a laver for priests to wash in, to symbolise moral cleansing (and also for practical purposes with all the animal blood around.)

There are other details. They are referred to often in the prophets and in the New Testament they are used as teaching aids, though no longer required in worship. To understand the Letter to the Hebrews you have to refer to this ancient worship to understand how Christ was regarded by the Church to fulfil the ancient worship and render it redundant.

The Golden Calf

While Moses is on Mount Sinai the Israelites think he will never return, so they construct a golden calf and worship it as a symbol of God or even as an alternative to their God and hold a party, in fact an orgy, breaking many of the Ten Commandments. The brother of Moses, the first high priest, Aaron, is forced into making the calf and, when Moses rebukes him, Aaron produces the lamest excuse of all time: 'I threw their gold into the fire and there came out this calf'! God has to be persuaded by Moses not to destroy them and make a new nation from Moses. God accepts the pleading of Moses, but is said to punish the Israelites with plague.

The Name of God

In a following scene Moses goes up to Mount Sinai to get a second set of the Ten Commandments carved on stone; he had broken the original two tablets in his anger over the golden calf. God proclaims his name, which he had originally revealed to Moses at the burning bush when Moses received his commission to lead Israel. The name is Yahweh, the one who is and will be. This time he declares it as his character: 'Yahweh, Yahweh (sometimes translated as Jehovah); a God merciful and gracious, slow to anger and abounding in steadfast love and faithfulness, forgiving iniquity and transgression and sin'. This is the other side of the God who had so recently frightened the Israelites. Yet he will not clear the guilty. A little puzzle there – how does he forgive, yet he won't clear the guilty?

The rest of Exodus is concerned with the ritual being introduced. Earlier chapters said, 'You shall make.' Most of these chapters say 'And Moses made' or 'They made . . .' Exodus 40 finishes with the 'glory of Yahweh' filling the tabernacle. This glory is said to precede the Israelites as a pillar of cloud by day and of fire by night to guide them through the wilderness.

Also the tabernacle had to be dismantled and carried by nominated Levites on all their journeys

The aim of these laws was to instil into the Israelites a sense of the holiness of God, and the need for this sense to be translated into their behaviour.

4

Laws, Statistics and Principles

Leviticus, Numbers and Deuteronomy

Leviticus is concerned with the detail of social and ritual law. Numbers, as its title suggests, contains statistical information about the Israelites during their wanderings in the wilderness, as well as interesting stories about their progress. Deuteronomy, which may have been compiled much later, aims to describe the principles of the law and Israel's position in the eyes of God.

In your first reading of the Bible you might not put these books at the top of your list for thorough reading, but a 'skim-read' to pick out one or two parts may be helpful when you come to references in other parts of the Bible.

Leviticus: The Legislative Book

This is a book about the laws and rituals that Moses implemented on the basis of his understanding of the will of God. It provides interesting insights if you are studying how the Jewish race gained its unique identity and also if you want to understand those parts of the New Testament where, in many ways, the old law appears to be contradicted or cancelled out, though its basic intentions are maintained.

Ritual Sacrifices

Of the first seven chapters of Leviticus, many are devoted to the system of mainly animal sacrifices to be offered in a variety of situations. It is rather unattractive to the modern mind, yet when you examine it in detail it is a remarkable system of symbols and learning aids. The emphasis is that Yahweh is holy and therefore his people must be holy, or separate, from the other nations in their way of life.

There are whole burnt offerings, cereal offerings, sin offerings, guilt offerings, peace offerings – all called by different names in different translations of the Bible. Some of them were compulsory on a regular basis, others were voluntary or met a particular situation to atone for a sin or to express thankfulness to God for special blessings. Where one ate part of an animal sacrifice, the law was very strict that the blood should not be consumed, because life, believed to be in the blood, was ultimately the possession of God. The rules for all the offerings were extremely precise; you couldn't just follow your own inclinations. Leviticus 8 and 9 describe the ordination ceremonies for the priests.

Ritual Uncleanness

Leviticus 11 details laws about animals that can be eaten and those that are forbidden. It is interesting to try to deduce the basis of decision: animals with cloven hoof and that chewed the cud can alone be eaten. Is it for health reasons, or is it a symbol of surefootedness and the need to mentally chew over one's ideas with care?

If you are squeamish, don't read Leviticus 13; it tells the priests how to identify different forms of leprosy by looking at the scabs and pus. Other illnesses are also described. Instructions are given about sexual behaviour. Every time you have sexual relationships you are left unclean and therefore have to remain outside social contact for a day. Later on the Song of Songs makes it clear that this is not because sex is a bad thing, but to emphasise that it is intended to be quite special, even holy!

Guidance is given on what and who you can touch without being made unclean and the need to be isolated. Bodily functions, childbirth, menstruation or touching a corpse make one ritually unclean. These limits on activities can all be very inconvenient, but they emphasise God's holiness. Many of these laws have beneficial health consequences.

Special Days and Seasons

Leviticus describes the solemn Day of Atonement, when the sins of the nation are confessed and ritually forgiven. They are symbolically placed on the head of a goat, which is then driven with them out into the desert. It was called the 'scapegoat' and has given rise to the word for people taking the blame for any kind of failure, even if they are not responsible.

Laws for keeping the sabbath and doing no work that day are provided. Arrangements are made for three feasts for the whole nation each year. The most serious is the Passover, which commemorates the Israelites' deliverance from Egypt. There are also joyous harvest feasts.

Love Your Neighbour As Yourself

In the middle of the description of rituals there are some gems of permanent moral and spiritual truth. For example,

Jesus taught that you 'should love your neighbour as yourself', but he was quoting from Leviticus 19, which also says that Israelites should not hate their brothers in their heart or bear a grudge against anyone. Generosity to the poor, care about employees, safety regulations and the avoidance of sharp business practice are also described. Honesty in trade is not just recommended, but demanded, though slavery is regulated rather than forbidden. (It was only abolished in the United States when my grandfather was a teenager.)

Chapter 19 is worth a full read the first time you skim Leviticus.

Other regulations institute the year of jubilee every fifty years, involving a complete rest from cultivation of the land and the return of all property to the original owners, because everything is leasehold to avoid families being driven into permanent poverty. Every seven years a land sabbath is observed, with no sowing of crops and people eating only what grew of itself or what they had saved from previous years.

Briefly then, I don't want to give the impression that this book has no value, but simply to suggest that it is not essential to spend too much time on it in your initial reading. You will, however, need a clearer idea of it before reading the letter to the Hebrews in the New Testament.

Numbers and Statistics

Numbers is, as it suggests, a book of statistics, though it is interspersed with good stories.

The first four chapters give the results of a census of the Israelites taken at the beginning of their journey through the desert. Chapter 26 gives the census results at the end of the forty years. Some of the tribes have experienced more disasters than others, which is reflected in the population figures, suggesting a basis of truth in the story. A novelist would hardly have invented these statistics, so we can feel that we are reading something that is historically reliable.

More Laws

There are many more laws in Numbers, including a particularly nasty one about a jealous husband going to the priest, who makes the wife drink some horrible liquid to test whether she has been unfaithful. If she suffers badly she is guilty; if not, she isn't, but in the latter case the husband is not punished for being so unreasonably suspicious. Obviously this was a different age, though not so many centuries ago witch-hunts and trial by ordeal were common in Europe and North America. The only problem is that Numbers assumes that God gave these as instructions.

The tabernacle and its worship is finally established and the feasts are regularised. There are more laws about offerings; regulations for the priesthood are also provided.

Grumbling in the Wilderness

The various interesting stories in the book are mainly connected with the wilderness journeys of the Israelites under the leadership of Moses, found from Chapter 10 onward, though they are interrupted from time to time with legislative information, for example, about silver trumpets for sounding the alarm, tithes for the priests, cleansing after death, inheritance laws (including entitlement for women), vow-taking, regulation (but not prohibition) of looting the enemy in war. It also defines the boundaries of the various tribes.

There are stories of the Israelites complaining about conditions in the desert and the dullness of the food and drink. From time to time, they are punished, on one occasion by fatal snake bites, cured only when the injured look up at a pole with a bronze model of a snake. This story is used in the New Testament as an analogy for looking up to Jesus on the cross to be cured of sin.

Cowardice

A further story describes how the spies go ahead to look at the promised land and return with such an alarming report that the people refuse to proceed into battle. Consequently the Israelites are sentenced to forty years of wandering in the desert until the original generation has died out. When they hear this they go into battle, but are defeated because God has withdrawn his support.

Rebelliousness

There are rebellions against Moses. In one of these, three rebel leaders and their families and possessions are swallowed up in an earthquake and all Israel trembles. Moses' sister accuses him of arrogance and is punished for seven days with leprosy. Moses himself is robbed of the chance of going into the promised land because he loses his temper with Israel and, in bringing water of the rock for them, says, 'Must we bring you this water,' thus taking the credit that belonged to God. It seems harsh on Moses.

Nevertheless these stories are significant. Normally nations glorify their ancient history and dress it up to look glorious and noble. Their heroes are all paragons of perfection, inspiring pride. In contrast, Israelite history is filled with criticism of the nation and its leaders. There is little to be proud of, which suggests that there is some basis of historical truth underlying the stories, even if every detail cannot be substantiated and we ourselves would not attribute to God everything they considered he was responsible for.

Wars in Preparation for Conquest

The latter part of Numbers is concerned with the wars preparing for Israel's entry into the promised land and the plans to divide the land between the twelve tribes. Included here is the attempt to exterminate the Midianites utterly, supposedly at the command of God. In spite of our own, far from unblemished, record in modern days we would regard this as very uncivilised. We have to judge it by the standards of the time, particularly when they kill most of the women as well as the men and male children but are permitted to keep the virgins for themselves!

As they are poised for entry into Palestine, Balaam tries to curse Israel on behalf of the King of Moab. Every time he opens his mouth to curse, a blessing comes out, much to the annoyance of the Moabite king who is paying Balaam good money for his cursing activity. God is ruining Balaam's business venture, and finally Balaam's donkey speaks in human speech to rebuke the prophet. There is a touch of humour in the story because Balaam replies to the donkey rationally, as if he is used to donkeys talking every day.

The poems with which Balaam finally blesses Israel are masterpieces, even in translation.

Deuteronomy, or Second Law

The Book of Deuteronomy, generally supposed to have been written many centuries later, is nevertheless quite instructive if we read it on its own terms as if Moses did make all these farewell speeches before going up Mount Nebo to die.

The speeches of Moses are more directly spiritual in the reward they offer than some of the other books of the Pentateuch. We can apply many of his words to our own behaviour as individuals or communities, though the book is still to be read against the historical background of the whole work of Moses in leading Israel out of Egypt to the borders of the promised land over forty years.

Moses lays great stress on the need for Israel to be faithful in obeying God's commandments, and brings out some of their deeper meaning. He still sees God as the deliverer who requires all the war and bloodshed through which Israel would seize the land of Palestine from its current owners. This perception still affects world affairs, when ultra-religious Jews in Israel turn to these writings to justify their claims to the West Bank and Gaza.

Deeper Meaning

Jesus and the apostles in the New Testament are able to use Deuteronomy in their teaching, often bringing to it new meaning more appropriate to the kind of God Jesus represented.

In Chapter 6, we find the words used by Jews every day in the prayer called the Shema: 'Hear, oh Israel, the Lord our God is one Lord, and you shall love the Lord your God with all your heart and with all your soul and with all your might.' These are words that Jesus quoted in his teaching, particularly with the slant that if there is only one God then he must receive all your love. You don't have to share it with other gods (in our day, gods such as money or ambition).

Moses says that God did not choose the Israelites because they are any better than other nations, but because he loves them for the sake of their ancestors like Abraham, and because he wants to use them as a means of educating and bringing benefit to other nations.

Some of the ideas of Jesus in the Sermon on the Mount have their roots in Deuteronomy, such as the assertion that we shouldn't be obsessed with material things, but trust in God, though we should make our own contribution. Man does not live by bread alone. Moses warns the people of the dangers of prosperity and that they must, in the end, depend on God and not on their own proud strength. He encourages continual reflection on God and his deeds and ways. In the family too, spiritual things should be a topic of frequent conversation. Moses also introduces spiritual significance into the understanding of the ritual, for example, speaking of circumcision of the heart and not just of the flesh.

In Chapter 18 Moses mentions a great prophet to come, whom the disciples said was Jesus.

Some of the social laws of Deuteronomy are in the spirit of Jesus, such as the building of parapets on the roof of one's house so that people won't fall off. If they see their personal enemy's ox or ass straying, they are to take it back to him, even though they don't like him.

Some Ruthless Laws

Some of the laws and rituals are reiterated. The people are constantly warned against the influence of the wicked ways of the inhabitants of Palestine through intermarriage, alliance or friendship. We again see that God as presented here is not really the same in character as the one presented by Jesus. Moses insists that they must totally destroy the Canaanite inhabitants of the land. Genocide without pity, whatever the ways and practices of these nations, can never be justified by anyone who has listened to the teaching of Jesus. Though again, some might say that nations that bombed each other to pieces in various recent wars and still hold stocks of nuclear and chemical weapons are hardly in a position to criticise Israel for being the children of their times. Current worldwide concern about anti-personnel mines is encouraging.

Blessings and Curses

Deuteronomy closes with the farewell to Moses, following a series of blessings upon the Israelites if they are obedient to God and curses if they are disobedient. In their many troubles over the centuries, the Jews have often looked for an explanation of their sufferings in these chapters. How true it is that the Jews have found 'no rest for the sole of their feet' among the nations where they have been scattered for many centuries. How the Jews of the holocaust must have recognised their plight in the words 'at night you shall say would to God it were morning and at morning you will say would to God it were evening'. So-called Christians have often, over the centuries, wrongly used these words to justify the persecution of the Jews as they considered they were helping God to punish them. It shows how easy it is to misinterpret the Bible and as a result initiate great evils.

These chapters suggest that the sufferings of a nation are always the results of sin and that things go well when they are obedient. Care needs to be exercised about accepting this as a universal principle.

The words of Moses in Deuteronomy end with two magnificent poems in praise of God's deliverance of Israel. This sense of duty and purpose in Israel's history is picked up in the New Testament and given a positive twist that we can respond to. The earlier writings provide a basis which can be developed into something more noble, beyond the hatred and vengeance so characteristic of human beings when they have either no sense of a God or else a misconceived idea of what God is like.

At the end of the book, Moses is permitted to look at the promised land from a high mountain, before dying and being buried by God in a secret venue. He is given high praise. The writer says there has never been anyone like him 'whom Yahweh knew face to face'!

5

Conquest and Settlement
Joshua and Judges

Joshua and Judges, covering the period between 1250 and 1000 BC describe how the Israelites find a home for themselves in Palestine, known as Canaan. As they perceive it, this period can be summed up: 'Thus the Lord gave to Israel all the land which he swore to give to their fathers; and having taken possession of it they settled there.' Joshua concentrates on the possession or conquest. Judges concentrates more on the settlement, though it was not particularly settled in fact.

Canaan was predominantly populated by small city states, thirty-one of which are listed in Joshua 12 as being conquered, their kings put to death. Joshua believes he had a commission from God to engage in the genocide of the Canaanites and the picture of the conquest is extremely brutal.

Did God Authorise the Slaughter?
This history is based on the Israelites' belief about God, which was later completely reinterpreted on the basis of the teaching of Jesus and the early Christian Church.

All history is largely a matter of interpretation. Facts are described as writers perceive them. Thus, actions actually taken by human beings were counted as the direct acts of God, who was seen as commanding cruel behaviour towards the enemies of the Israelites, wiping out whole nations or tribes. God was fighting their battles, giving them victory when they obeyed him and defeat when they disobeyed.

These interpretations are part of the story. Conversations between God and the Israelite leaders are reported, where he tells them exactly how to defeat their enemies and often to destroy them completely. In addition, a large number of miracles are reported, by which God is seen to support Israel's military efforts. The basic facts are no doubt largely true but, as they were finally written down some time later, there was scope for the story to grow over time and for relatively natural events to be seen as miracles, outside normal experience. Notable among these is the sun standing still in Joshua 10. An event connected with the appearance of daylight probably occurred, but it is hardly credible that the earth stopped revolving on its axis in the evening in order to extend daylight and make additional slaughter and victory possible.

The main structure of the history has been consistently preserved by the nation of Israel. The fact that so much of it discredits the actions of Israel gives us confidence in its substantial accuracy, though this does not necessarily apply to the interpretations accompanying the narrative. There is a pervasive belief that God controlled all the events, yet we cannot suppose that any such control robbed Israel of freedom to choose. This is a perennial theological problem. How can God be sovereign and yet humans be free to go their own way? This question is explored through further study of the Bible.

In the New Testament, Jesus directly overturns the idea of bloodshed and vengeance as being the will of God. He says, 'You have heard it was said of old, "you shall love your neighbour and hate your enemies", but I say unto you "Love your enemies and pray for your persecutors".' Jesus is not just contradicting one verse of the Old Testament, for no verse orders you to love your neighbour and hate your enemy. He is overturning the whole mood of much of this historical period. He also accepts that God has been at work during those centuries, somehow ensuring that the path was being prepared for Jesus to come and re-evaluate the world and bring the covenant history to a focus in himself.

Joshua Takes Over

Deuteronomy ends with the death of Moses. His assistant Joshua assumes the leadership, takes the Israelites into the promised land and begins to settle them there.

Joshua was a good leader and a man of religious principles. The fact that he believed God had required him to engage in so much slaughter was acceptable for the times. Life was cheap and the way we engage in war nowadays leaves us little scope to criticise him. In relation to God and to his fellow Israelites he was an honourable man, with a determination to obey the one true God as he understood him. And this is an important characteristic of so many Old Testament leaders, one that we can learn from. Their relationship with God was close, though their understanding of him left much to be desired.

Joshua was a true patriot and the fact that Israel survived as a nation or confederation of tribes resulted in no small measure from his leadership. His motto was 'As for me and my house, we will serve the Lord'.

The Walls of Jericho

The story begins with Joshua's commission from God. He arranges that the two and a half tribes with land on the east of the River Jordan shall accompany the other nine and a half in the conquest of the rest of the land and immediately sends spies to gain intelligence of the situation on the other side of the Jordan. They are helped by a Canaanite prostitute and in return promise to save her and her relatives when they seize the city of Jericho. The whole nation of hundreds of thousands then crosses the river, which dries up to permit their passage. (This may be explained as an earthquake.)

Just as they need all their strength, Joshua circumcises all the men and waits for them to recover from the operation. This displays amazing trust in God. He believes that as they are doing what God has commanded there is no danger from their foes.

Next, they march silently round Jericho for six days, going around seven times on the seventh day, and at the end sending up a loud shout and sounding a strident trumpet blast. The walls collapse and they seize and then burn the city, killing everyone except the prostitute's family. They lose their next battle, against a small city called Ai, they draw lots to find out why and find that the leading Israelite Achan has kept some of the riches of Jericho instead of destroying them. For this sin he and his family and his possessions are destroyed. Then Israel wins the battle against Ai, because God's anger has been assuaged. (None of this is 'Christian', but some event like this occurred to help Israel survive.)

The Sun Stands Still!

Chapter 10 describes the Israelite army destroying a confederation of Canaanite cities. God is said to have prolonged the day to enable them to finish the killing of everybody: 'Sun stand thou still.' Again, everyone in these cities – man, woman and child – is killed. Eventually enough of the country has been conquered for everyone to receive their part of the territory as a tribal possession, and Joshua proves to be a good administrator. Several chapters detail very precisely the division of the land, demonstrating that the record is fundamentally factual. No one would bother to invent such details.

Cities where people can flee if they accidentally cause the death of another are appointed in order to protect such people from blood feuds, which were customary in those days. The priestly tribe of Levi are given cities, but no tribal territory; they are required to be among the people.

Scholars who have scrutinised Chapters 12 to 21 with the aid of geography and archaeology have become convinced that Joshua did not actually manage to conquer the whole land. It is clear that his armies could not defeat the well-entrenched people of the coastal areas (including the Philistines, who were going to prove an embarrassment for several centuries). Similarly, the Canaanites were too powerful in the Plain of Esdraelon (in the north central area of the country) for Joshua to defeat them.

It seems, therefore, that the Israelites settled in the mostly hilly regions of the south, centre and north of the country. The area around Jerusalem was not captured. Chapter 1 clarifies this by describing the Canaanite tribes that the Israelites failed to drive out, and Chapters 2 and 3 explain this by saying that God did not drive out these enemies, but left them there as a test for Israel to see whether they would keep clear of the idolatry of their neighbours and to give them practice in war! Elsewhere it was said that the occupation occurred slowly as there were too few Israelites to cultivate the land and the wild beasts would multiply, making it unmanageable for them.

Joshua's Faith

The saga ends with farewell words from Joshua before he dies at the age of 110. He warns them to obey and 'incline their hearts toward God'. Israel's thorough involvement in the ruthlessness of the times does not make this book pleasant reading, but nevertheless we should not overlook his faith despite the limitations of their understanding in those days.

Many fundamentalist Christians justify Joshua's ruthlessness on the grounds that the Canaanites were so terribly wicked that there was no other way for Israel to survive. They claim that in the Old Testament it was acceptable to behave in this way; then Christ changed the rules. I find it impossible to believe in such a cruel God, who required such murderous activity. Visualise what actually happened. See the shouting Israelites, breaking into homes and plunging their swords into nursing mothers and little babies. How brutalising it must have been for the Israelites. They would have to have been heartless and pitiless to carry it out.

The Bible is a record of blots on the history of Israel as well as its successes. And our present job is to try to understand it and then, when we have an idea of both Old and New Testaments, to form our personal view of the nature of God as seen in the life of Jesus Christ.

The Tribal Judges

The Book of Judges is very much in the same mould as the Book of Joshua in its depiction of ruthless warlike behaviour. It is sub-Christian, part of the history of the race used by God to prepare the way for Christ, as much through the lessons of their errors as their other achievements.

The Book of Judges makes better reading than the previous book. Its stories contain more variety. Although we cannot approve of the methods of some of the heroes, their deeds capture some grudging admiration from us.

After Joshua and his colleagues die, the next generation is less determined to follow the course that Joshua has set out for them. As you read the Book of Judges you may think that it is describing events covering the whole nation, but in fact the story describes the actions of individual tribes and parts of the nation. One part of the nation would decline from the worship of Yahweh and consequently God would send enemies against them, not to kill them all, but to 'oppress them', dominate them, tax them heavily and generally make life unpleasant. Subsequently the oppressed Israelites would connect their troubles with their disobedience to God and express sorrow. Then, so the story goes, God would raise up deliverers, who would release them from their suffering. This was a continuous cycle (see Judges 2).

Hence there is Ehud, who assassinates the King of Moab in his private rooms and escapes to lead a successful revolt and become the leader or Judge of Israel. (There is a touch of grim humour in the story; the Moabite palace officials do not discover the murder for some time because, seeing the locked doors, they think he is in the toilet.)

Then there is Jabin, a Canaanite king who has oppressed another section of the people, involved in disobeying God. Deborah the prophetess stings Israel into revolt (her name means the 'bee'). The Canaanites are defeated and their commander, Sisera, is murdered with a tent peg through his head at the hands of the woman Jael, who lures him into her tent as he is running away. Deborah sings a song about this victory. It is exceedingly vengeful, though good poetry.

Next the Midianites oppress all, or some, of Israel. An angel inspires Gideon to take a lead in a revolt. With 300 men initially armed only with lamps and trumpets he panics the Midianites into defeat. During the night, at a signal from Gideon, they break the pots that obscure the light from their lamps, scream out at the tops of their voices 'the Sword of the Lord and of Gideon' and blow trumpets. The sudden noise and flash of lights frighten the Midianites into imagining that a mighty force is attacking them and they try to escape as quickly as possible, killing each other in their terror. Several other tribes then join in the chase. Gideon refuses to accept kingship as a reward for his leadership; he is content to remain a judge.

The next hero is Jephthah, who defeats the Ammonites after first offering them a chance to withdraw. Before the battle he vows rashly that whoever comes out first to meet him after the victory that he is convinced will ensue will be offered up by him as a sacrifice to God in gratitude for divine help. His daughter is the unlucky person. After a delay of a couple of months he fulfils his vow. Handel set the story to music.

After this comes the story of the famous strong man Samson. His abnormal strength enables him to walk off with the gates of a city when the Philistines think they have him trapped. He sends foxes into the cornfields of enemies with their tails on fire. He slaughters a thousand men with the jawbone of a donkey. The secret of his strength is said to lie in his long hair, which is never cut because of a religious vow. The Philistines persuade Delilah to wheedle the secret out of him, by weeping, 'If you loved me you would tell me.' (Saint-Saëns puts this disclosure to music, in the famous aria 'Softly awakes my heart'.) The Philistines capture Samson and put out his eyes. Then one day, when they have him on display in their temple by way of entertainment, he takes hold of the pillars of the temple and shatters the whole edifice, killing more in the moment of his death than in all his life. Dying, he attributes this last victory to God.

The Book of Judges finishes with a sorry tale illustrating the depths to which Israel has sunk since the days of Joshua. It is described as a time when there is no king in Israel and every man 'did that which was right in his own eyes'. A man's concubine is murdered. He cuts up her corpse and calls all the tribes out on a battle of revenge on the Benjamites who have done the evil deed: 25,100 (so exact) Benjamites are killed. The other tribes swear that they will not allow their daughters to marry any of the 600 who survived. But this would mean the end of the tribe. Eventually they hold a feast and allow the Benjamites to seize a wife each from the girls who dance at the festivities.

The tone of the Book of Judges is not greatly edifying, though these heroes in their own way showed great courage and faith in God. The book has its place in the Bible as part of the unfolding of the history of Israel. It is not there to be admired.

6

The Rise of the Monarchy
Ruth, 1 Samuel, 2 Samuel

Your People Shall Be My People

The Book of Ruth and the two Books of Samuel cover the story of the rise of David, the greatest king of Israel.

Ruth is a beautiful rural idyll of love and romance with very businesslike undertones. Contrasted with the blood and vengeance of the last two books the Book of Ruth brings some relief.

It describes how the Moabite widow of an Israelite refuses to return to Moab after her husband's death. She says to Naomi, her mother-in-law, 'Your people shall be my people, and your God my God.' This non-Israelite joins Israel. There follows a story of rustic beauty, set in the cornfields at the time of harvest, with Ruth finding a new husband, with some scheming by Naomi. He is much older than Ruth and he is very moved by the fact that she is willing to marry him. She attracts his attention by lying at his feet when he is sleeping for the night on the threshing floor. It is bold, but no naughtiness happens and he duly marries her as soon as he has cleared up some legal matters.

Why have the Jews preserved the book and why has the Christian Church welcomed it? Ruth was the great-grandmother of King David, who was the ancestor of Jesus, of whom the angel said the words so often read at Christmas time: 'The Lord God shall give unto him the throne of his father David.'

This short book also presents a picture of high principles, as indicated by the loyalty that Ruth shows to her mother-in-law Naomi. It is one of a number of cases in the Bible where non-Israelites adopt the faith of Israel.

Samuel is Given to the Lord

The two Books of Samuel take us into a more settled period of Israel's history and revolve mostly around the life and reign of David, the man chosen as king and the famous ancestor of Jesus. At the centre of the story of David are promises God made to him that he would found a dynasty, the most illustrious member of which would lead Israel to final victory. The New Testament applies this to Jesus, though in rather unexpected ways.

First, however, we have the story of Samuel and his relationship with Saul, the first king of Israel. The record starts with a woman who is unable to have a child and is very upset by the taunts of her husband's other wife. Then she promises to give her child to God if only God will give her one. Samuel is born and when still a boy he enters the service of the priest Eli at the tabernacle.

Here the young Samuel receives from God a message of disaster impending to Israel from the Philistines who still occupy much of the sea coast (what we would now call the Gaza strip). Eli and his two irreligious sons die and the sacred ark is captured by the enemy, but it causes so many disasters in their land that the Philistines send it back to Israel on a cart pulled by two cows who left their calves without protest.

Give Us a King That We May Be Like the Nations

Samuel becomes the Judge of Israel and is greatly upset when Israel asks for a king in order 'to be like the other nations'. Samuel wants God to be their sole king. But God agrees they can have a king and the impressive Saul is appointed. Saul has some military success, but Samuel never fully favours him and threatens him with removal from the throne because he offers sacrifices himself and later does not destroy all the Amalekites.

Secretly, Samuel, believing himself to be under instructions from God, anoints the young shepherd David as future king. The older sons of Jesse are not chosen 'Because the Lord sees not as man sees' as Samuel puts it.

Saul, depressed by his failures and his apparent rejection, falls into a deep depression and appoints young David as his armour bearer and court musician, hoping David's skilful harp-playing will lift his spirits.

Then all of the Israelites are horrified at the arrival of the nine-foot-tall Goliath challenging them to send a champion to fight with him. None of the leaders will risk it. Young David volunteers. Armed with just a sling and a stone he kills the giant, after which Israel gains a great victory over the Philistines.

David on the Run

David is praised everywhere as a great hero. Saul becomes jealous when he hears himself compared unfavourably with David, and he tries to kill the young man on several occasions, once when David is playing the harp to him. The javelin Saul throws misses him, but David has to flee into the wilderness where he becomes an outlaw leading a band of misfits. The second half of the First Book of Samuel tells the story of his adventures while on the run from Saul.

One particularly memorable event occurs when Saul enters a cave to answer the call of nature. David and his men are in the recesses of the cave and David could kill Saul. David quietly cuts off a piece of Saul's temporarily discarded outer garment and retreats to the shadows. Saul dresses and leaves the cave. When he is a safe distance away, David appears with the piece of clothing, suggesting the idea that since Saul is still alive he need not fear David. Temporarily Saul is full of remorse, though David doesn't trust himself to him. On another occasion Saul is out searching for David with a view to killing him. David comes across him, asleep undefended in a hillside camp. He slips in and takes Saul's spear and next day he reveals what he has done by shouting across the valley. Saul is again temporarily sorry.

How are the Mighty Fallen?

Saul becomes increasingly sick in mind and eventually dies in battle, thoroughly defeated by the Philistines.

The spooky tale of the last night of Saul's life describes his visit to a spiritualist medium, the witch of Endor. The story of the delightful and innocent friendship between David and Saul's son Jonathan relates how Jonathan is quite happy not to succeed his father as king and is content for David to be king. However Jonathan also dies in the battle. David weeps for Saul and Jonathan in a very moving lament, which opens the second book of Samuel, beginning, 'How are the mighty fallen.'

David is acclaimed king by the southern tribes and after a civil war with the descendants of Saul he becomes king over all twelve tribes. The civil war has many further examples of a spirit of hatred and vengeance that is the opposite of the spirit of Jesus, but, again, David is a child of his times. He shows shafts of generosity and kindness from time to time.

God's Covenant with David

In the forty years of his reign, David defeats all the enemies of Israel and builds an empire that stretches from the Sinai region to the Euphrates River in Syria. It is the high water mark of Israel's national existence and it enables David's son Solomon to commence his reign with a strong kingdom held in respect by other nations.

A crucial episode is the promise that God is recorded as making to David (2 Samuel 7). David feels it is time for God to have a permanent temple, instead of the temporary tent structure known as the tabernacle. He expresses his intention to build such a temple, but a message comes that he will not be allowed to because he has been a man of war. (This reason is given in the Book of Chronicles.) God then promises that he will build a house for David, by which he means a dynasty of rulers, a permanent kingdom. God promises to be a father to the dynasty, which will be 'his son'. They will have to suffer for their sins, but they will never be wiped out.

The New Testament applies the promise ultimately to Jesus Christ, who will establish the Kingdom of God and reign on David's throne. Its political and military aspects are to be reinterpreted in a spiritual, but none the less real, direction, associated with the death and resurrection of Jesus and what is described as his 'sitting at the right hand of God'.

David's Crime

The record is very frank about the heroes of the Bible. It does not hide their faults and thus suggests that the truth is being told. So we have the story of how David sees the beautiful Bathsheba having a bath in her house, sends for her and makes love to her. She becomes pregnant. A scandal is about to burst. Consequently David arranges for her husband, an army general, to be placed in the hottest part of the battle, so that he will be killed. The king then marries Bathsheba. The prophet Nathan comes to David with the case of a rich man who stole a poor man's only lamb and asks for a judgement. Angrily, David says the rich man deserves to die. Nathan dramatically replies, 'You are the man.' David breaks down with remorse and asks God's forgiveness. The child dies and in due course Bathsheba has another son – Solomon.

David finds little peace in his domestic circle. Stories of incest and murder among his sons give him great sorrow, particularly the loss of his son Absalom, over whom he mourns with such eloquence: 'If only I could have died instead of you.' For a time David has to flee from his country because of Absalom's revolt but he is welcomed back and in his last years devotes great attention to preparing the design and the materials for the temple that Solomon will build.

7

The Divided Kingdom

1 Kings, 2 Kings, 1 Chronicles, 2 Chronicles

The two Books of Kings tell the story of the kingdom that became divided into the ten tribes (called Israel) and the two tribes (called Judah). The descriptions are further confused because the whole undivided nation is also called Israel. The two Books of Kings take the history of Israel up to the capture of Judah by Nebuchadnezzar, King of Babylon, in 587 BC and the temporary end of the monarchy. The two Books of Chronicles cover broadly the same period, though from the perspective of the two tribes of Judah. They also describe the return from exile in Babylon.

The early part of 1 Kings sees the death of David and the stabilisation of the monarchy under Solomon with a certain amount of ruthlessness. The kingdom becomes prosperous and develops a large bureaucracy, a taxation system, a standing army and a large harem as home for all the queens Solomon marries as a way of making alliances with surrounding nations. Socially his policies are oppressive, though no one starves.

Solomon's reputation for wisdom spreads all over the Middle East. The Queen of Sheba comes to tap his wisdom, for example.

Solomon's Achievements and Failures

Solomon's main achievement is the building of the temple for God, into which he puts boundless energy and skill. Precise details are given, and a profound prayer that he utters at the dedication of the temple is reported in full. It is relatively advanced in its thinking, recognising that God is too great to live in a temple built with the hands of men, and presenting a personal God who wants a relationship with the human race, or at least with Israel. It was a unique concept of God and was part of the preparation for even more developed perspectives from Jesus later on.

Solomon is ultimately led astray by the many foreign women in his harem – 700 wives, all princesses, and 300 subordinate wives or concubines. He erects shrines for them so that they can worship their national gods and he joins in this false worship himself. The kingdom begins to be assailed by enemies and its glory starts to fade.

The Division

After Solomon's death, the kingdom splits. Ten tribes, known thereafter as Israel, revolt against Solomon's son Rehoboam, who manages to retain only the two known as the kingdom of Judah. The story from then on moves between the two kingdoms. The ten tribes of Israel never hold strongly to the worship of God. Their first king, Jeroboam, initiates the worship of a calf god to represent the true God and subsequent kings worship the various local gods or 'baals'. Some of the kings of Judah are reasonably good. Among them are: Asa who worships the true God and removes the queen mother for worshipping idols; Jehoshaphat who introduces reforms in Judah; Hezekiah who shows great faith and courage against the Assyrian invaders and takes reform further; and Josiah, the young king who, after his servants discover what is probably the Book of Deuteronomy in the temple, makes the people of Judah obey its requirements. This takes us well into the Second Book of Kings. The period from Solomon to the Babylonian captivity runs from approximately 940–587 BC.

Ahab, Elijah and Elisha

Starting in 1 Kings and continuing in 2 Kings, there is the extended story of the weak King Ahab of Israel and his wicked foreign wife Jezebel, who wishes to institute the worship of Baal in place of Yahweh. The stories of the two prophets Elijah and Elisha in their opposition to Ahab and his successors make fascinating reading. There is the great contest between Elijah and the prophets of Baal on Mount Carmel, which Elijah wins when fire comes down from heaven, according to the record. Whether or not you take it all as described depends on your own viewpoint, but the main outline rings true, particularly Elijah's taunting of the priests of Baal to shout louder as perhaps their god is asleep or has gone hunting! Mendelssohn wrote an oratorio that graphically presents the episode. There is also the story of how Jezebel stole the vineyard of Naboth for Ahab, who eventually dies in battle.

Elijah is taken up into heaven and Elisha carries on the work. Elisha works a number of miracles, including the raising from the dead of a young boy, healing the leprosy of a Syrian general and feeding 100 people with a few loaves. He also anoints a ruthless general Jehu to destroy the dynasty of Ahab and become the king of Israel. Jehu carries out this task with a great enthusiasm, for which the prophet Hosea criticises him (in contrast to the vengeance we have been seeing). Jehu also arranges for Queen Jezebel to be killed – thrown out of the window by her servants (the defenestration at Jezreel). Her daughter-in-law, Athaliah, tries to seize the kingdom and she too is killed.

The Ten Tribes Deported to Assyria

Jeroboam II, the last descendant of Jehu, builds up the prosperity of Israel, the ten tribes, and creates a large empire. However its success is only temporary and a few years later the ten tribes are carried away to be captives in the Assyrian empire. Other non-Israelite tribes are sent to colonise the land of Israel. They become known as the Samaritans and they semi-adopt the religion of Israel, a position that still existed in the time of Jesus, when he talks with a Samaritan woman at a well and when he tells the parable of the good Samaritan. But the Jews and the Samaritans were never on good terms.

Judah Deported into Babylon

Following the accounts of Hezekiah and Josiah, the good kings of Judah, who institute many religious reforms, the two Books of Kings end with Judah being carried off into captivity in Babylon, where they remain for some seventy years, and from which some never return.

These books illustrate the wide sweep of Israel and Judah's history under the monarchy. They provide fascinating stories and are vital to the total picture of Israel, which ultimately leads into the unexpected finale in the life, death and resurrection of Jesus Christ as reported in the New Testament. Further significance of these books and of the two following ones of Chronicles lies in the context they provide for understanding the prophets in the last part of the Old Testament.

The First Book of Chronicles

Much of the material in this book is not recommended for reading unless – or until – one is really deep into the study of the Bible. The first nine chapters give very detailed genealogical tables of all twelve tribes of Israel. Stories are tucked into the narrative and the detail gives credibility to the history. Who would bother to invent such boring detail?

The remaining twenty chapters of 1 Chronicles retell the story of David with added detail. We learn how David prepares the design and gathers the materials for the temple that Solomon his son would build. There are some impressive prayers and speeches, showing the nobler side of the nation's religion and King David's fundamentally spiritual character.

The Second Book of Chronicles

2 Chronicles details how Solomon actually builds the temple, including exact measurements and descriptions of the furniture. His prayers and his speeches are also reported. These give an idea of Israel's religion at its most developed and perhaps at its pinnacle, though already it was showing signs of becoming bureaucratic and mechanistic.

The succeeding reigns of the kings of Judah are described with a perspective differing from that of the Book of Kings, emphasising temple and worship and rather more personal detail. Asa, Jehoshaphat, Hezekiah and Josiah stand out again.

Asa removes the idolatrous and semi-idolatrous worship of Judah and when hopelessly outnumbered in battle by the million troops of Ethiopia, cries: 'Oh Lord there is none like you to help, we rely on you and in your name we have come against this multitude; you are our God; let not man prevail against you.' In 1975, I myself stood at Mareshah in Israel, where this battle occurred, and it all became very real for me – 2,700 years of time simply vanished.

Cameos of Faith

In 2 Chronicles there are many little cameos, such as the following: a prophet tells Asa: 'If you seek God he will be found by you; if you forsake him he will forsake you' (15:2). Jehoshaphat sends a team of princes around Judah to run seminars to teach the people how to obey God (17:9). The same king, facing defeat in battle, says: 'We do not know what to do, but our eyes are upon you, oh Lord' (20:12). These little prayers show men of loyalty to their God despite being people of their times in military and social matters.

A phrase concerning these kings occasionally occurs: Amaziah 'did what was right in the sight of the Lord, but not wholeheartedly' (25:2). In other words it is possible to do the right things, but from the wrong motives.

Cameos of Evil

In 2 Chronicles we also learn about bad kings of Judah, such as Ahaz, who changes the altar of God in the temple and has one introduced on a Syrian pattern merely to please the king of Syria. Similarly business tycoons nowadays do things that are not right in order to gain business advantage. In several thousand years some things haven't changed much. Manasseh, son of Hezekiah, was as bad as his father was good. Unfortunately he reigned fifty-five years, which represented a long period of his poor influence and led to the final corruption of Judah. The fact that he personally repented and reformed towards the end of his life could not undo the harm that he had done.

Hezekiah and the Assyrians

In 2 Chronicles there is more detail about Hezekiah's defence of Jerusalem against the Assyrians and the plague that finally defeats them. Before their sudden enforced departure, when the Assyrians are besieging Jerusalem, there is the story of the Assyrian spokesman who stood in a prominent place and shouted in Hebrew so that the people could hear that they were in a hopeless position. Hezekiah's officers asked him not to speak in Hebrew. But the Assyrian said, 'It is the ordinary people that I have come to speak to' and so he stepped forward to address them directly in a manner evocative of modern propaganda wars, only without the microphone.

Josiah's reformation also covers the mass celebration of the Passover feast he inaugurated. A vivid description is given of finding the Book of Deuteronomy among the rubbish in the temple. Josiah reads it and recognises that it spells their doom, because the recent behaviour of Judah is so condemned. This leads to his attempt to improve things, but it is cut short when he is killed in battle.

The book concludes with Judah first becoming captive in Babylon and then returning some seventy years later, under the edict of King Cyrus of Persia, a believer in religious tolerance, who instructs the Jews to return and rebuild the temple that Nebuchadnezzar has destroyed. Of this we shall learn more when we consider the prophet Jeremiah.

We have covered a wide range of history in this chapter. Our summary gives a bird's eye view of more than 300 years of the life of the nation. When we read the words of the prophets we have both a background and a sense of the national history that provided the context for the ministry of Jesus.

8

The End of the Exile

Ezra, Nehemiah and Esther

In 2 Chronicles we leave the Jews receiving permission from the Persian ruler Cyrus to return to their land and rebuild the temple and city. We now look at the two books that expand the story, Ezra and Nehemiah. The Book of Ezra starts with the deeds of Joshua, the priest, and Zerubbabel, a member of the royal house of David.

Joshua and Zerubbabel

Along with permission to return to Jerusalem by a decree in 538 BC, Cyrus also gives the Jews all the golden and silver bowls that Babylon had seized seventy years earlier from the temple – 5,469 of them, exactly counted! Chapter 2 of Ezra lists all the families who accepted the offer to return: 42,360 individuals plus 7,337 servants, a 200-strong choir, 736 horses, 245 mules, 435 camels and 6,720 donkeys. Such detail suggests that the story is based on fact.

Joshua and Zerubbabel lead the people in setting up the

altar and offering sacrifices on it and in the second year they start to build the temple. There is a celebration when the foundation is laid. The young people shout for joy but the elders weep because it is so small compared with the previous glory.

Local non-Jewish people want to join in but the Jews, maintaining their exclusive attitude, do not let them. The rejected local people write to the new Persian king and stop the building. The prophets Haggai and Zechariah, both of whom have later books named after them, encourage the Jewish people and a letter is sent to the king of Persia, lodging an appeal. As a result they have permission to resume building the temple and even receive a subsidy from the king's treasury. In due course they finish the temple and celebrate the Passover with great enthusiasm.

Ezra the Reformer

In Chapter 7, Ezra enters the scene. This is possibly seventy years after the return from exile and we are unsure whether Ezra or Nehemiah came first. Ezra devotes himself to the study of God's law and is now permitted to leave Babylon and teach the Jews the proper ways of keeping the law. The Persian king, a new one yet again, gives a generous donation to help Ezra in the work and exempts all the priests and Levites from taxation. He also authorises Ezra to appoint judges and magistrates and to enforce God's law in the land.

There follow more lists of Jews who return with Ezra from Babylon. Ezra establishes Levites in the service of the temple and organises the equipment for the temple, and a great religious festival is held. Then he discovers that many Jews have intermarried with the people of the land, with the danger of corrupting their religious loyalty. He utters a very impressive prayer to God, as recorded in Chapter 9, which recapitulates the history of their sins and produces in the people a mood of contrition.

The next steps show sincerity on Ezra's part, but are rather unfeeling and drastic. He insists that all the men who have married foreign wives should divorce them. There is a full legal hearing so perhaps there are exceptions, and fair arrangements are made for the maintenance of the divorced wives and the families. Nevertheless it is tough and not justified by the law itself. For these hearings the people stand in the open for three days in the pouring rain, trembling 'over the matter in hand and because it was raining'. The story finishes with a complete list of the men who had to divorce their foreign wives.

Nehemiah the Administrator

In the book bearing his name, Nehemiah's story is linked with that of Ezra and Ezra reappears in it. Whichever of them arrived first, Ezra and Nehemiah ultimately worked together.

Nehemiah is the cupbearer to the Persian king and he hears one day that the wall of Jerusalem is broken down and things are looking bad. He weeps and prays and even looks sad in the presence of the king, which was a dangerous thing to do. The king asks him what's wrong and the story comes pouring out. The king gives him permission and supplies to go and rebuild the walls of Jerusalem.

He arrives at Jerusalem and mobilises the people for the rebuilding work, aristocrats and women as well as working men. Chapter 3 lists them all and tells us what bit of the wall was allocated to their hands. It's all very realistic, even describing one group who are lazy and 'did not put their neck to the work of the Lord'. But on the whole 'the people had a mind to the work'.

Local non-Jewish inhabitants object to these activities and taunt the Jews. The builders therefore have to build with a trowel in one hand and a weapon in the other. The enemies try many tricks to impede the work, but the wall is completed in a total of fifty-two days. And the enemies give up.

If the work of building is difficult, the job of being governor is even more so. The people are a mixed crowd of rich and poor. The rich are exploiting the poor, charging high interest rates for loans and getting people to mortgage their land and property. Nehemiah puts a stop to this and is in a strong moral position anyway, because he declines to take any salary for the job and doesn't even draw his legitimate expenses. Chapter 7 is another of those unreadable lists of all people involved, though it conveys the reality of the events.

Ezra's Six-Hour Sermon

Ezra now reappears in the record and works with Nehemiah, concentrating on aspects of worship. He gathers all the people together and Chapter 8 tells us how he and the Levites read from the law books of Moses all the requirements of God. The people stand listening to Ezra's sermon, which lasts from daybreak to midday, followed by a celebration at the end of the day. Ezra also explains what he has been reading. It impresses the people deeply and they begin to weep, because they realise how they are failing to live up to the high standards of God. But Nehemiah cheers them up. 'The joy of the Lord shall be your strength,' he declares, telling them to organise parties, especially for the poor. They also institute some of the old Jewish feasts, which have not been kept for years. There is great rejoicing.

Then they realise they are not finished yet. There is more to attend to before the people can regard themselves as true and obedient worshippers of God. A solemn meeting is called at which Ezra again preaches lengthily and prays eloquently, recapitulating the history of Israel and involving the whole population in a solemn covenant to re-enter the true service of God. This includes resuming the tithes of their produce to be given to God and a promise that they will not marry the neighbouring non-Jewish people (Chapter 9).

The Nation Stabilised

More lists describe the leaders who sign the covenant and the religious and administrative appointments to secure good government. The last chapter records the tough line taken by Nehemiah to coerce the people to follow the law and be just to each other. He restores the keeping of the sabbath and threatens the foreign traders who try to do business there. If you don't go away, 'I will lay my hands on you.'

This period of Israel's history was crucial. It established the Jewish community back in the land, not with full independence and without a king, but with the opportunity to build and strengthen their national existence. Not least was this important because it meant there was a Jewish nation in Palestine among whom Jesus was born some 400 years later. And it was a nation that no longer favoured the worship of false gods even if it was in danger of becoming somewhat mechanistic in its worship of the true God.

Esther Wins the Beauty Contest

A fascinating story is told in the Book of Esther. It never explicitly mentions the name of God, but he is perceived as present everywhere, influencing affairs on behalf of his people. It shows things working out for the survival of Israel, even if the actions taken are far removed from the principles of Jesus Christ. A strange phenomenon is witnessed: Christ's mission is only possible because the Jews are not annihilated in the period described in the Book of Esther. One of the Psalms says that God makes the works of men praise him, even when he doesn't approve of their deeds. He works round the situation to fit it in with his own long-term intentions, yet without obliterating their free will.

The story opens with a 180-day feast thrown by the king of Persia for all his leading men and allies. Following it he runs a garden party for the ordinary people of his capital. On the last day, when everyone is thoroughly drunk, he demands that his chief wife, Queen Vashti, should come out and show off her beauty to the admiring and no doubt lustful gaze of the population. As a woman of some principle, she refuses and is therefore dismissed, particularly to prevent the women of the empire from thinking that they can disobey their husbands. The chief men fear an outbreak of feminism. Thus by law every man is to be lord in his own household.

A beauty contest is organised for a replacement for the deposed queen. A young Jewess enters and wins after the statutory beautification period of twelve months. Her name is Esther. She does not reveal that she is a Jewess. Her uncle and guardian Mordecai hears of a plot to assassinate the king and notifies the authorities. It is recorded in the court papers. Then a courtier named Haman worms his way into the king's favour and is given great power. Mordecai won't bow down to him and, as a result, Haman arranges with the king that all Jews are to be destroyed on a certain date, because they are different from all other citizens, having different laws and customs and therefore constituting a threat to the nation's stability.

The Jews Threatened With Annihilation

Instructions are issued for this slaughter. Mordecai points out to Esther that as a Jewess she will not escape and that her special position enables her to try to influence the king. She points out that to visit the king is to risk death, unless he holds out his sceptre. Normally the queen could only enter his presence when sent for. Mordecai hints at God's involvement and says, 'Who knows, perhaps you have come to your position for this very purpose.' She becomes bold and agrees, 'If I perish I perish.'

Esther approaches and is welcomed by the king. She invites him and Haman to dinner that day. They go, and are invited to another dinner the next day. Meanwhile Haman is full of joy at this rise in his position. One thing still bothers him though: the refusal by Mordecai the Jew to bow down to him. So he arranges to have some gallows built with a view to a public hanging for Mordecai at the first opportunity.

That night, however, the king cannot sleep and sends for the court records to be read to him, to see if they cause drowsiness. Instead they arouse his interest and the part is reached where Mordecai the Jew uncovers the assassination plot. The king asks whether he has been rewarded and sends for Haman to ask his advice. He frames his question, 'What shall be done for the man the king delights to honour?' Haman thinks he is referring to him and proceeds to suggest the most extravagant rewards, proposing that the man to be honoured should be paraded through the street wearing the royal crown and robes, on the best horse, led by the most senior minister and with a royal proclamation made in the town square.

Haman's Humiliation

'Right,' says the king. 'Go and do all that to Mordecai and don't miss any of it out.' What a shock to Haman: was there ever such a rapid fall? Obviously the king saw through Haman's ambitions.

At the arranged banquet, Esther asks for her life and that of her people with considerable skill. The king is concerned. 'Who would dare do such a thing?' 'This wicked Haman,' she replies. He falls on the queen's couch begging for mercy. The king interprets this as an attempt at rape and orders Haman to be executed on the very gallows he had prepared for Mordecai. Poetic justice indeed!

The Jews Delivered

Persian law could not be cancelled. The king gives the Jews permission to prepare and be ready to defend themselves against their enemies. Mordecai is appointed prime minister in place of Haman and everyone is frightened of the Jews. The Jews use the execution day as an opportunity to slaughter all their enemies and they have an extra day from the king to complete the work. 75,000 enemies are killed, but the Jews do not take up the offer of plunder. The ten sons of Haman are also hanged on his gallows.

The feast of Purim is set up to commemorate the deliverance of the Jews. In spite of its vengeful tone and the fact that it does not rise to the spirit of Jesus, it has a strong narrative. Something like it undoubtedly happened and contributed significantly to the fact that the Jewish people were not annihilated and were still around a few centuries later to be the subjects of the ministry of Jesus.

9

Why Do Bad Things Happen To Good People?

Job

The story of Job has some of the most sublime poetry in the Bible and an outstanding debate on why suffering comes to good people as well as bad. Job is the first book of what is called the Wisdom literature of Israel, which also includes Proverbs, Ecclesiastes and parts of other books. These books are less concerned with the history of Israel as the basis of God's relationship with mankind, and more interested in the meaning of life for the individual.

The reading of Job is challenging; detailed study may wait until more straightforward parts of the Bible have been understood. Develop an awareness of its events for the moment, including a recognition of its magnificent poetry, which comes through even in translation.

The Book of Job can't be a literal account. People do not sit and talk profound philosophy in perfect poetry for many days in real life. And God would hardly bargain with a member of the heavenly court, if there is such an organisation. I believe it is a religious drama, based on real characters, to examine the relationship of God to human suffering as applied to a real case.

The book doesn't find an answer; that has to wait till the New Testament, where we read that 'Jesus was made perfect through suffering'.

The Book of Job starts with God presenting Job as someone who is really good and who would remain so whatever problems he faced. The person called Satan, or the Adversary (for that is what Satan means), challenges this and is given authority to test it out.

Job loses his family, except his wife, in a series of disasters. All his property is lost and he faces ruin. Still he doesn't blame God. The Adversary applies further pressure and Job is subjected to a loathsome bodily disease, a form of leprosy. Even then he refuses to blame God. 'If we accept good from God shall we not also accept evil?'

The Debate

Three friends, Eliphaz, Bildad and Zophar, come to commiserate. They sit speechless for a whole week. It probably started off as the silence of shock and sympathy, but as they sit there day after day, perhaps they begin to develop theories about why it has all happened and initiate their unjust path of criticism of Job.

Job breaks the silence and curses the day he was born. Why did God give him life and let him still live? Eliphaz says, 'You used to give comfort to others. Now you're in trouble you can't take it.' He continues with the unsound principle that nobody innocent really suffers permanently, so everything will be all right. Job responds by affirming his personal integrity and appealing to God to stop persecuting him and using him for target practice. Job is quite outspoken but even at the end God doesn't rebuke Job for arguing with him.

The friends steadily increase their criticism of Job. Their unkindness knows no bounds: 'Your sons must have been wicked or they would not have died'; 'God is punishing you less than you deserve.' Job responds that God punishes the wicked and the righteous alike, and demands that God will appear so that he can cross-examine him as in a court of law.

The friends continue their theme. 'No human being is good before God. So you are blaspheming, Job, in calling God to account.' Job attacks his friends for their unkindness. They are sticking to their traditional doctrine and are like many religious people, who do not accept their responsibility to think for themselves but simply assume that their traditional beliefs are beyond question. Such beliefs can destroy sympathy and human kindness.

Job logically destroys their theories, saying that many people who are thoroughly wicked live to a great age in prosperity. Eventually Eliphaz becomes so driven by his theories that he invents sins Job is supposed to have committed. 'Job, you have been unkind and heartless; you have sent widows away instead of helping them; you must repent of all your wickedness.'

Job finds their help even worse than all his troubles. They are trying to rob him of his very character. But he holds to his integrity and is determined to maintain his belief in God, however unjustly he feels God has treated him. He describes in vivid terms the good achievements of his life and challenges God to answer him and say if this is not true. He asks for the chance to plead his good deeds in the court of God.

The Young Man Elihu

First Elihu, a younger man, has his say. He is not very impressed by the three friends and thinks Job is justifying himself too much. He suggests that sometimes suffering has a beneficial effect in making us better people. It can discipline us to greater obedience. He sticks with the creed that if you suffer it must be punishment for your sins, but the sin of which he accuses Job is his lack of reverence towards God by continually demanding that God answer him.

At this point the clouds gather and a storm is imminent. Elihu uses it as an example of the power of God, who cannot be argued with. He calls on Job to recognise the wonderful works of God and stop arguing with him.

God Answers

Finally, as Job has requested God does answer out of the storm clouds. But what a strange answer. He picks up Elihu's argument and asks Job where he was when he, God, created everything. There are magnificent descriptions of snow, rain, the whale and strange animals such as crocodiles, who seem to have no purpose. And still God gives no real answer. Job has challenged God to reveal himself. God has replied with an exposition of the greatness of God in the works of creation.

Job's questions have not been answered, but for him it is enough, for in the presence of God they are forgotten. It is here that the final message of the book lies. Two great scholars, Oesterley and Robinson, expressed it in 1930: 'Questions may agitate the mind of man, problems may torture his spirit, but when once he has seen God, when once he has stood before him, and begun to know him, the questions and the problems begin to vanish. There is something deeper than reason, more convincing than logical argument. In the light of experience others may cry with Job "I have heard of you with the hearing of the ear, but now mine eye sees you."'

Before the might of God Job recognises his ignorance: 'I

spoke of things too wonderful for me. I yield and repent in dust and ashes.'

The friends sit there smugly, thinking that God is backing them up, but God is angry with them because they have not spoken correctly about him and have stuck to an unthinking religious creed. He commends Job as having a much deeper understanding of God than they had. He has maintained his integrity and his conviction that suffering was not God's punishment for his wickedness. The friends had not shown love to Job, but like so many religious people had been cruel to their neighbour by sticking to their theories of God. God turns the tables on them by saying he will only accept them, these people who thought they were so much better than Job, if Job acts as their priest and offers a sacrifice for them.

The story is rounded off with the restoration of Job's fortunes. Overall it doesn't fully answer the problem of suffering and evil, but it is a marvellous drama that constantly challenges us to think for ourselves and enter into debate with God.

The Lessons of Job

Every time I read the Book of Job, particularly if with a group of other open-minded people, I see it in a somewhat different light and learn some different lessons. This time the main lesson I have learned is that God approves of our curiosity and our wanting to know the meaning of things. And that he doesn't worry too much if we get it wrong. He prefers that to religious dogmatism, where we think we have all the answers.

Too often people stop thinking and asking questions on the grounds that our minds were never meant to understand. As one writer said: 'Fortunately our little minds were meant to question things. A great curiosity ought to exist concerning divine things. Man was intended to argue with God.' If this is true, it acts as a balance to much of the apparent onesidedness of some perspectives that people derive from the Bible.

Job challenges much of what is said in various books of the Old Testament, where there is often an assumption that the prosperity or disasters of the nation are the rewards and punishments for their behaviour. Certainly they saw it that way in many of the statements of the prophets, and possibly it kept them alert, but after the Book of Job one is careful about treating this as an unchallengeable doctrine. We are taught to reflect rather than have standard packages that answer everything.

This book has helped many people in dark days of their lives, when God seemed absent and like Job they have refused to surrender either their integrity or their belief in God. It also helps us to be more content with the fact that even if we are not total agnostics, we are inevitably agnostic on many matters; we may not know, but we carry on searching. As far as the question of suffering is concerned we have to wait for Jesus in the New Testament to get nearer to an answer.

10

Israel's Hymn Book

Psalms

The Book of Psalms presents yet another form of Biblical literature, consisting of devotional writings and songs of thanksgiving and petition to be used in public worship of God and in private prayer. Considerable reference is made to the story of Israel, though no new events are presented. Instead we are helped to make sense of history and of Israel's attitude to it. It also opens us to the inner thinking of the devout Israelite about God. We can begin to understand, even if, through Christ, we no longer think in the same terms, for example about enemies.

The Nearness of God

The Psalms give us an insight into how faithful Israelites interpreted God's activity. Even if they at times pictured it in overly human terms and thought of him as adopting contemporary attitudes, for example in the wholesale destruction of enemies, they felt he was personally involved in the affairs of the nation and indeed of their own lives. Ultimately this extended to a recognition that he was involved in the affairs of all mankind.

From the Psalms we see how faithful Israelites felt God was personally near to them, taking a fatherly interest in them. Their lives were jointly run with God. Despite many of the primitive thoughts of the time, which we have not outgrown even as we approach the third millennium, they express a personal closeness to God. As the Psalms were designed for public worship they also express a sense of community, that human beings are not isolated islands.

This was very different from the attitude of the other nations. The gods, of which they had many, were not the personal heads of a family, but distant, fickle and easily angered, so that they had to be placated, even with human sacrifice or with sexual orgies, complete with temple prostitutes. They were not beings in whom you could place personal trust. Israel's approach was different. Although they shared many of the primitive ideas of the time about retribution on enemies and rewards and punishments in this life, they worshipped a personal God, whom they could even love. They breathed a religious atmosphere in which they grew close to God, while showing respect and reverence. This aspect of the Old Testament should be focused on, rather than the areas where Jesus Christ has taken us on to a higher plane. The basically right attitude to God is already planted in the older writings.

This is not a matter of theology but simply one of fact. When we read the Psalms we are sharing the experience of how people felt about their God. It is also interesting that, side by side with the respect they showed God, they also felt free to complain to him and even argue with him, almost criticising him and, like Job, demanding an explanation of his slowness in delivering them from their troubles. They praised or thanked him for his 'unfailing love' (a Hebrew word 'chesed') and they saw this in the simple things of personal daily life as well as in the profound issues of national life. As a well-known theologian, Claus Westerman, comments, the Psalms speak about God in a very human manner: 'How long will you forget me? How long will you hide your face from me?' He says that 'it is precisely these human questions which indicate the genuineness of a relationship with God in which joy, happiness, freedom, and health can only be understood as dependent upon God's attention to and participation in human life'.

The Subject Matter of the Psalms

The Psalms depict the life of the individual and the community in its endless variety, in its depths and heights, in seas and mountains, with trees, animals and fields, reflecting the individual's joys and sorrows between birth and death, with toil and celebration, sleeping and waking, sickness and recovery, failure and success, despair and comfort. They also reflect the life of people trying to obey God in the midst of others who did not care about him or were even positively opposed to him, referred to as evil-doers.

Scholars have divided the Psalms into five main categories:

- community psalms of lament (e.g. Psalms 44, 74, 79, 80, 83, 89)
- individual psalms of lament (e.g. Psalms 3–7, 10–14, 16–17, 22–3, 25–8, 31, 35–6, 38–43, 51–9, 61–4, 69, 71, 73, 86, 88, 102, 109, 130)
- community psalms of narrative praise (e.g. Psalms 18, parts of 66, 81, 85, 93, 106, 124, 126, 128, 129, 149)

- individual psalms of narrative praise (e.g. Psalms 9, 19–24, 30, 92, 116, 138)
- hymns of descriptive praise (e.g. Psalms 8, 29, 33, 65, 100, 103, 104, 111, 113, 117, 134–6, 139, 145–150)

As you read the Psalms you will find that they often combine several of these categories. There is no need for a mechanistic analysis, but an awareness of the categories helps the reader to identify the mood of the Psalmist or of the people singing the Psalm.

Problems Shared with God

The Psalms of lament are about pouring out sorrow to God. The Psalms of praise are joy and thankfulness poured out to God. Both are divided into categories of individual and communal, the communal ones often being part of a liturgy in worship, with people responding to the choir. The Psalms of the first four of the categories tended to be responses to specific experiences, whereas the fifth category of Psalms was of a more general character, praising God for his general activity.

Many of the Psalms, especially those of lament, do not specify the events that called them forth but regard them as the symptoms of the joy or sorrow of which they were singing. Their words express their beliefs and emotions about their relationship with God, rather than the details of specific events. This is what has given the Psalms their appeal. Anyone, in any era of history, can take the structure of thought in such Psalms and slot into it the particular variables of their own experience, collective or individual. And they can do this without robbing the Psalm of its original context in the history of Israel.

Often the problem of being brought before God emphasises the disturbance of the wholeness of life, particularly of the relationships that are the essence of being alive. The lament is concerned with the relationship with God, the self and others. It often creates a reversal, with the complaint being turned into trust as confidence grows in the saying.

The Poetry of the Psalms

The Psalms have a poetic form, though this is different from Western poetry. Its basis is parallelism with either:

- almost exact repetition of the same idea:
  Bless the Lord, oh my soul,
  and all that is within me bless his holy name.
- bringing out another aspect of the same idea:
  Bless the Lord, oh my soul,
  and forget not all his benefits.
- or contrast:
  All day long the wicked covets,
  but the righteous gives and does not hold back.

Certain rhythmic aspects are lost in translation, but nevertheless a kind of rhythmic emphasis comes through in the parallelism.

The Circumstances of Their Composition

The Psalms are often referred to as the Psalms of David, though they were not collected together in their present form until long after King David's time. There is little doubt that he gave great impetus to the writing of Psalms and King Saul employed him as a court musician long before he became king. Psalms were also composed previous to his time, such as the Song of

Moses in Exodus 15 and the Song of Deborah in Judges 5. Equally, many of the Psalms are clearly written by later composers.

Many of the Psalms have inscriptions at the head of them, stating the occasion that caused them to be written. It is not certain whether these are all reliable, but they convey a sense of the circumstance that may have brought them forth. An interesting set are Psalms 120–34, called in the King James version (English) songs of ascents, sung by pilgrims as they went up to Jerusalem. Many of the Psalms are attributed to various guilds of singers attached to the temple, such as the sons of Korah and Asaph. Some Psalms are known as royal Psalms because they are the kind that would be sung at a coronation. Psalms 2, 72, 101 and 110 are examples.

The Spirit of the Psalms

The scope for detailed exposition of individual Psalms is infinite and would require more than one lifetime. I would re-emphasise here that when you read a Psalm you should bear in mind that they were primarily meant for use in worship, though many of them are worded so that they can be seen as both speaking on behalf of the community and also speaking from the heart of the individual. Even a familiar Psalm, such as Psalm 23, can present God as the guiding shepherd of the community or church, yet at the same time be perfectly appropriate for use in personal and private devotion.

Another important point is that there is little doubt that Jesus used the Psalms in his personal devotion and the early Christian Church applied many of them to him. When applying Psalms to Jesus it is important to remember that there is an element of adaptation. It is the spirit of the Psalm, or of part of it, that is being fulfilled in Jesus. Parts of the Psalm will not apply to Jesus, such as a Psalm that expresses sorrow but then goes on to ask for vengeance instead of forgiveness for his enemies. The first six verses of Psalm 109 perfectly describe the experiences of Jesus, but he would not go on to ask God to make children fatherless, as this Psalm does.

Some of the Psalms that are made to refer to Jesus in the New Testament also speak of his sins (e.g. Psalms 38 and 40). The Church would have accepted this of Jesus only in the sense of his bearing our sins and taking them away. Jesus himself used the words of Psalm 22 on the cross.

A Reading Plan for the Psalms

I suggest that you do not read all 150 Psalms at one go, one after the other over a few days. It is better to absorb them one or two at a time in between other reading. Give yourself time to reflect on the one you have just read. In doing this you may be learning about prayer, for this is what the Psalms were a form of.

The exercise itself of writing this short chapter has enhanced my own awareness of the power and beauty of the Psalms. Above all it has helped me to see that in spite of holding ideas that through the influence of Jesus we could not now accept (such as revenge and total destruction of enemies), the people who wrote the Psalms were closer to God than we usually are in the rush of the twentieth and twenty-first centuries. Reflecting on their history and, surely, receiving impulses from a higher power, led them to a mood where God was a living and hourly reality.

This attitude is very explicit. If we read the Psalms receptively their mood may influence our own thinking, even if initially we simply read them as beautiful poems.

11

Wisdom

Proverbs

While the Book of Psalms is intimately related to the history of Israel, the Book of Proverbs is more of a philosophical book, searching for wisdom in understanding and managing life with all its problems. It belongs to what is often called the Wisdom literature of the Bible, along with the Book of Ecclesiastes (also known as 'The Preacher').

There are at least two other Wisdom books that failed to be regarded as 'holy scripture' when the Jews were deciding which books they recognised. The Book of Sirach (Ecclesiasticus) and the Wisdom of Solomon are part of the second eleven of holy writings, known as the Apocrypha. These writings are recognised by the Roman Catholic Church as equal to the other books of the Bible. The mainstream Protestant churches recognise them as of value, but not equal to the rest of what is called the 'canon' of scripture. They do have many similarities, for example, with the Book of Proverbs.

Approaching Proverbs

The Book of Proverbs does not lend itself easily to being mapped. It consists largely of individual sentences that put principles of good behaviour into a few, easily memorised words. Through the old King James (1611) translation of the Bible they entered, with slight adaptations, into the ordinary speech of British people and are often quoted by people unaware of their Biblical origin. Some examples are:

- 'Spare the rod and spoil the child.'
- 'Hope deferred makes the heart sick.'
- 'A soft answer turns away wrath.'
- 'Train up a child in the way he should go, and when he is old he will not depart from it.'
- 'Labour not to be rich.'
- 'A word fitly spoken is like apples of gold in pictures of silver.'
- 'Where there is no vision the people perish.'
- 'Pride goes before a fall.'

The Book of Proverbs consists of various collections of such proverbs amassed over a wide period. Some are attributed to Solomon, and there is general agreement that many of the proverbs go back a long time. Three collections are mentioned in the text: from Chapters 1–9, 10–24, and 25–9. The book is rounded off with two short thematic selections in two chapters, the second of which describes the ideal wife as seen in those times.

Mental indigestion would probably ensue if you read them right through at a few sittings. It is easier to read a few at a time and think about them. They are not necessarily consistent with one another. They are situational, and the listener has to decide to which situations they apply. A good example is 'Answer a fool according to his folly' followed by 'Answer not a fool according to his folly'. Your choice depends on whether you think you can help the fool to become wise. If not, you may have to meet him on his own level.

This dual approach may explain why misfortune sometimes is seen as punishment and other times as a means of being helped to learn. Quite frequently, however, it is assumed that correct behaviour brings its own reward in this life. This is not always the case. People will take advantage of kindness and fairness. On the other hand, in the field of business a number of writers of books and articles on business ethics have pointed out that integrity, honesty and fairness can contribute to profitable business, based on gaining a respectable reputation with the customers.

Another feature worthy of comment is that the proverbs are poetic in their format. Particularly they use the device of parallelism, where the thought is repeated in different words, often by the use of contrasts, giving the opposite idea in the second half of the verse or section.

'Hear my son'

A certain amount of continuity is found in the first part of the book, up to and including Chapter 9. The writer is giving instruction to his son, based on the idea that all wisdom is founded on the fear of God. The word 'fear' does not mean being frightened of God, but showing him respect. Wisdom is presented as a woman who appeals to people to listen to her and avoid dire consequences.

In Chapter 8 the woman Wisdom poetically expresses what she has to offer. Her speech is not crooked or twisted. Listening to her will lead to good outcomes; Wisdom brings real honour and prosperity. The poem goes on to say that God's work of creation was based on Wisdom. She planned it and urged it into being as the creative force. To follow Wisdom means a continual feast. A wise person will heed criticism and learn from it.

Wisdom is contrasted with the foolish woman. There is a double meaning here. Not only does the foolish woman stand for those who think only of present pleasure and live for the moment but she at the same time warns young men against sexual misbehaviour and entanglements in promiscuity. The foolish woman is being used as a symbol for hedonism as a way of thought and life.

Situational Proverbs

The rest of the book has less continuity. We have a series of wittily expressed observations about behaviour and its direct consequences. Most of them do not express the whole truth but are applicable in a particular situation. Wisdom has to decide on the appropriate situation. The proverbs cannot each be quoted as a final word from God to cover all situations. We show no disrespect to God to say that 'this one does not apply to my particular situation at the moment'. Some of the proverbs may strike us as bland truisms; some as profound. They were current in Israel and reflect the atmosphere of the more thoughtful Israelites, whose whole history was lived in an atmosphere that recognised God as a living ever present reality, whatever limitations this view may have had by New Testament standards.

From Chapter 10 onwards of the Book of Proverbs, a few samples may whet the appetite. You will appreciate their depth and wit. Many of the proverbs are relevant to modern business and politics as well as to individual, family and community life.

All Life Displayed

The following are a sample of the proverbs in the book, chosen from various translations for the clearest sense of the meaning:

- 'A rich man's wealth is his strong city; the poverty of the poor is their ruin.' In other words 'the rich get richer and the poor get poorer', a relevant comment on the modern economy.
- 'A wink of the eye causes trouble; a frank rebuke promotes peace.' Be straightforward in our relationships, even if it means being forthright. It is better than deception.
- 'A talebearer gives away secrets; but a trustworthy person respects a confidence.' A plain statement, but it probes our consciences. Which ones are we?
- 'Like a gold ring in a pig's snout is a beautiful woman without good sense.' Look for something beyond appearance when choosing a spouse.
- 'One man gives freely, yet grows the richer; another withholds what he should give, yet ends up in poverty.' This praises generosity.
- 'Better is a man of humble standing who works for himself than one who plays the great man, but lacks bread.' We know the type, don't we? All talk, show and status, but no real substance.
- 'The way of a fool is right in his own eyes, but a wise man listens to advice.' The fool listens only to himself and understands just his own point of view. Nowadays we would talk about the value of teamwork and seeking the best advice.
- 'Wealth hastily gained will dwindle, but those who gather little by little will increase it.' Business enterprises

as well as individuals might do well to think about this advice.
- 'Walk with the wise and learn wisdom; mix with the stupid and come to harm.' There is something here about the choice of close friends.
- 'A simpleton believes every word he hears; a clever person watches every step.' Don't be naïve.
- 'To the downtrodden every day is wretched; but to have a merry heart is a perpetual feast.' This points out the difference between the people who see their glass as half empty and those who see it as half full.
- 'Without counsel plans go wrong, but with many advisers they succeed.' This refers to teamwork again, but we are expected to reflect on the absolute statement and recognise that you can have too many advisers and make no progress.
- 'Better is a dish of vegetables if love goes with it, than a fattened ox eaten amid hatred.' Some business lunches and unhappy domestic scenes are described here!
- 'Those who are greedy for unjust gain make trouble for their households, but those who hate bribes will live.' This is very relevant in these days of corruption in high places; sleaze is denounced.
- 'The righteous think before they answer; but from the mouth of the wicked mischief pours out.' Sometimes people are not listening or weighing up the position; they just want their own say.
- 'Pride goes before disaster, and arrogance before a fall.' This describes men who are so full of self-confidence that they think that normal rules don't apply to them.
- 'A perverse person spreads strife and a whisperer

separates close friends.' This refers to the sort of person who whispers in your ear, 'Have you heard about . . .?'
- 'One who covers up another's offence fosters friendship but one who dwells on disputes alienates a friend.' This is very much the spirit of Jesus.
- 'A friend shows his friendship at all times and a brother is born to share troubles.' Some friends are true friends; you can depend on them.
- 'A reproof makes more impression on a discerning person than a hundred blows on someone who is stupid.' Am I discerning? That's the question being asked.
- 'A cheerful heart is a good medicine; but a downcast spirit saps one's strength.' We have probably experienced both types in everyday life. Which are we?
- 'Even a fool, if he keeps his mouth shut, will seem wise; if he holds his tongue, he will seem intelligent.' A description of advice they would probably be too foolish to listen to.
- 'The foolish have no interest in seeking to understand, but only in expressing their own opinions.' This has wide application, but remember that all these proverbs are asking us to look at ourselves rather than categorising other people.
- 'The one who first states a case seems right until another comes forward to cross-examine him.' You are not going to win an argument just by having the first say. Your reasoning must be able to stand examination.
- 'The sluggard dips his hand into the dish but will not so much as lift it to his mouth.' A wonderful cartoon of laziness!

- 'To draw back from a dispute is honourable, but every fool comes to blows.' Some people think it shows weakness to avoid confrontation; this is far from the case.
- 'Counsel in another's heart is like deep water; but a discerning person will draw it out.' This refers to the skill of eliciting the best and deepest thoughts of others, sometimes called the art of facilitation.
- '"A bad bargain," says the buyer to the seller, but off he goes to brag about it.' Things haven't changed much in 2,800 years!
- 'The sluggard says "There's a lion outside; I shall be killed if I go out on the street."' Lack of courage and laziness often go together. It requires too much effort to face up to the problem.
- A rather longer quotation describes the effects of too much alcohol. It's too realistic to shorten: 'Whose is the misery? Whose the remorse? Whose are the quarrels and the anxiety? Who gets the bruises without knowing why? Whose eyes are bloodshot? Those who linger late over their wine, who are always sampling some new spiced liquor. Do not gulp down the wine, the strong red wine, when the droplets form on the side of the cup. It may flow smoothly but in the end it will bite like a snake and poison like a cobra. Then your eyes will see strange sights, your wits and your speech will be confused; you will become like a man tossing out at sea, like one who clings to the top of the rigging; you say, "If I am struck down, what do I care? If I am overcome, what of it? As soon as I wake up, I shall turn to the wine again." Was there ever a better description of drunkenness with the unspoken suggestion: 'Don't.'

- 'Like a madman shooting at random his deadly darts and lethal arrows, so is the man who deceives another and then says, "It was only a joke."' This concept sounds modern, but people needed to be alerted about it all those centuries ago.

Enjoy and Learn

These are only a small proportion of the whole, but I hope they have illustrated the flavour of the Book of Proverbs: the wit, the humour, the perception of the observation of human behaviour, the warnings, the relevance. Perhaps you found reason to smile at human behaviour, including our own, maybe along with some sense of shame when we recognise ourselves at our worst.

Proverbs may sound like a book of secular ethics, but if you read it closely, or even just skim-read in search of tasty morsels, an awareness will grow that respect for God and fellow man, love of God and love of neighbour, as Moses and Jesus said, underlies it all. The intention is serious; the rebukes are meant to be taken to heart. The book fits into the structure of the Bible as a whole. While we must read it with discrimination as the writers intended, the aim is spiritual. Its listeners should grow closer to the God of Israel.

12

The Preacher

Ecclesiastes

Ecclesiastes emphasises the futility or pointlessness of life when regarded as an end in itself. It looks at life from an earthly point of view – 'under the sun' – not from a heavenly one. It indicates that there is a higher perspective, to fear (respect and worship) God and keep his commandments, but the Preacher's focus is on normal human existence, which he doesn't think is particularly worthwhile.

All is Vanity

The Preacher uses the famous phrase 'Vanity of vanities; all is vanity'. He has another similar phrase: 'vanity and vexation of spirit'. In English vanity has come to mean a concern about your outward appearance, like a young man or woman who is always looking in the mirror to see if they are handsome or beautiful. Its original meaning was 'emptiness' and modern translations offer the word 'futility'. One could perhaps use the word 'pointless'. The Preacher is saying that there is no point in day-to-day, ordinary existence – a very cynical and depressing approach to life.

The second phrase 'vexation of spirit' translates to something like 'chasing after the wind'. All human activity is likened to forever running after the wind, trying to catch it. The Revised English Bible translates 1:14: 'I have seen everything that has been done under the sun; it is all futility and a chasing of the wind.'

Don't assume that the book is not worth reading because it sounds so unpromising. Seen as part of the total message of the Old Testament it is quite revealing. It expresses the incompleteness of human existence, which the New Testament claims is completed in Jesus Christ. Even though it does sound rather cynical it stimulates some sense of proportion about our individual lives. We are each the centre of the universe to ourselves when we think along natural and not spiritual lines. Perhaps we need to learn that we are not really so important, although we should not allow ourselves to feel so powerless and worthless that we make no contribution to worldly affairs.

From Solomon's Perspective

The writer is the 'Preacher' or 'Speaker' as some translations render the word 'Koheleth', which describes one who makes a call to others. He presents himself as the son of David who was king in Jerusalem – in other words, as King Solomon. Solomon was a very learned man and may have written this himself, or he may have commissioned one of his wise courtiers. My feeling is that an Israelite satirist wrote it, using Solomon's experience as a vehicle for his thoughts on life, consequently putting his own words into the lips of Solomon. Modern satirists often do this kind of thing, creating speeches that politicians might make. Everyone knows they are doing this and smiles at the sarcasm that may be woven into the text. Such literary devices make the message more effective. They have been in vogue for thousands of years.

The writer thinks himself into King Solomon's life as the richest, wisest and apparently most prosperous man of those times. He is asking us to consider the man who ought to have been the happiest of all men and ask whether his life was any less futile than anyone else's.

The 'Flow' of Thought

The imagined thought of Solomon begins to flow. The ancients seldom followed a step-by-step logic in their words. They tended to talk in a circular fashion, repeating themselves and returning to elaborate a subject, much as we do in informal conversation. To summarise twelve chapters in a few pages involves much condensation but the following indicates the ebb and flow of the speaking attributed to Solomon.

- What does anyone gain from all their toil? Life is just a cycle; one generation comes as another goes. The sun rises; the sun sets – every day just the same. The wind blows, north, south, east and west. It's the same with the water cycle, sea to clouds, to rain, to rivers, to sea, in a neverending sequence. It all goes on and on and no real satisfaction is to be found. There is nothing new under the sun. It's all happened before. Why should people get excited about things? Nothing we can do will make any difference to the neverending cycle of life.
- I was king in Jerusalem. I tried everything. I tried wine, feasting, women [and plenty of them: 700 wives and 300 second-level wives or concubines]; I engaged in a

great building programme and constructed beautiful gardens and parks; I had gold beyond count; I denied myself no pleasure that I could imagine, from great learning and wisdom, to sexual thrills and folly. And what did it amount to? Nothing! Futility and chasing after the wind.
- Wisdom is better than folly, but both wise men and fools still all end up in the grave! So what's the point? Why all this labour, only to leave it to my son, who may turn out to be a fool [he did]? What is the point of being a workaholic, who can't even sleep for worrying about his plans? It's all futile – vanity.
- Perhaps the ordinary labouring man has the best situation. He eats and drinks and finds enjoyment in his toil without the complexity and disappointment that I, the king, experience. Perhaps he is closer to God.
- You can't really alter things. Everything has a season and a time: 'a time to be born and a time to die; a time to kill and a time to heal; a time to weep and a time to laugh; a time to mourn and a time to dance . . . a time to love and a time to hate; a time for war and a time for peace.' And you can do nothing about it. You do not choose the time.
- God has given our minds a vision of something better; but even that is frustrating because it is only a taste. We don't really understand God. Perhaps it's best to live a simple life, working and gaining simple pleasure, day by day.
- Consider the people in high places, responsible for the administration of justice. What do you find? Corruption and bribery. [Sleaze!]
- What's the point? We humans are no better than the

animals and we all finish up in the same place. Get on with simple living.
- When you consider all the oppression on the earth, it would be better never to have been born. Think about the efforts and skills of people trying to succeed in business, motivated by envy [this critique of the market economy was written hundreds of years before Christ]. Why do people deprive themselves of pleasure in order to make money, even if they have no children to leave it to? Perhaps cooperation is better than competition. 'Two are better than one' [synergy]. Often the wisest people reside in the lower levels of society, and no one takes any notice of them.
- Even religious worship is usually futile. I, Solomon, should know, with all my temple-building and public worship. It is often a matter of showing off with many words and unfulfilled dreams. True reverence is a rare commodity.
- What about bureaucracy? People think they have power, but each person is subject to a higher level of the hierarchy. [In modern terms, 'Little fleas have bigger fleas upon their backs to bite them.']
- The more you acquire, the greater your expenditure. How much of it do you see? There is no real growth. It's so easy to lose your investment in a bad venture. And anyway you can't take your money with you: 'As he came from his mother's womb he shall go again, naked as he came and shall take nothing for all his toil.' It is best to continue with your work, quietly and unambitiously, living each day in simplicity.
- You can have wealth and no happiness. The appetite is never satisfied. It is preferable to have present reality

than restless dreams. Words are often plentiful, but they achieve nothing.
- The day of your death is better than the day of your birth. Mourning is more satisfying than merriment. Sorrow is more realistic than laughter; you might learn something. The old days were no better than today, though people often sigh for them. Being good is no guarantee of prosperity. And you can't rely upon people. One man among a thousand may be trusted upon, perhaps, but I have not found one woman, after all my experience! [Perhaps he was looking for the wrong things . . .]
- We don't know the future, so we can't prepare for it. Often sinners lead apparently happy lives and righteous people miserable ones. There's no fairness. I return to my idea that a simple life is the best way to follow under the sun. One certainty is death; which brings the end of all this striving. [Despite this depressing subject a touch of grim humour enters the matter. I remember the peals of laughter with which an agnostic friend greeted the verse 'He who is joined to the living has hope, for a living dog is better than a dead lion' when we met to read the book of Ecclesiastes.]
- There's luck in life. 'Time and chance happens to all.' Power often lies in the hands of fools. 'The fool wearies himself to death with his exertions, but he doesn't even know the way to the town.' Nevertheless you achieve more if you prepare as best you can, but don't wait for the perfect circumstances.
- 'If a man lives many years let him rejoice in them all; but let him remember that the days of darkness will be many.' [He can't keep out the pessimism, even when he

permits a single ray of optimism as seen in the next comment.] 'Rejoice oh young man in your youth, and let your heart cheer you in the days of your youth; let your heart and your eyes show you the way; but know that for all these things God will bring you into judgement.'

Eventually we reach the twelfth and final chapter. It begins with some positive thinking. 'Remember your creator in the days of your youth,' but the preacher then continues, 'Before the bad times come and the years draw near when you will say "I have no pleasure in them."' For many, extreme old age feels like this, but for many of us our seventies and eighties are fruitful times still. Perhaps it was less so in those days.

Old Age

There follows a remarkable poem on the distresses of extreme old age, symbolized by a town whose industries have ceased to operate. Women grinding the flour stop work because their numbers are few. This refers to the old person's lack of teeth before the days of fillings and dentures. Those who look through the windows can see no longer, indicating the old person's failing sight, now partly surmounted with cataract operations and spectacles. 'The sound of the mill fades, the chirping of the sparrow grows faint and the song birds fall silent' points to the onset of deafness before the days of hearing aids. 'When people are afraid of the steep place and the street is full of terrors': Mobility is a problem for many very old people. 'The blossom whitens on the almond tree' refers to the onset of white hair, though nowadays there are products like 'Grecian 2000', as President Reagan demonstrated.

All these situations exist 'because man goes to his eternal home and the mourners go about the street . . . and the dust returns to the earth . . . and the spirit returns to God who gave it'. This is unlikely to have been a reference to any idea of an afterlife, but points to God withdrawing a person's breath or life force.

As Ecclestiastes approaches its end it recommends the exercise of care in one's reading material, sticking to the writings and sayings that come ultimately from the one shepherd (God). Apply this notion to all the many media forms today and there is much sense there. But beware even of sensible reading and academic and professional study. It too can be futile, chasing after wind, says our speaker. 'One final warning, my son: of making many books there is no end and much study is wearisome to the flesh.' That was true many hundreds of years before Christ. Perhaps we should listen when we are trying to design educational curricula.

The Whole Duty of Man

The whole book is then given its context. 'This is the end of matter: you have heard it all. Fear God and obey his commandments; this sums up the whole duty of man.' But he couldn't leave it there on a positive note: 'For God will bring everything we do to judgement, every secret whether good or bad.'

Perhaps this is positive. If there is to be a Day of Judgement, then there is the suggestion of an afterlife and a hint of what the New Testament more forcefully presents as truth. 'For we must all appear before the judgement seat of Christ': 2 Corinthians 5:10; the New Testament suggests in many places that such a judgement seat does not have to be viewed with terror. It could be a final ironing out of all the confusions and anomalies of life, preparing one appropriately for entering upon the finality of the Kingdom of God, with the opportunity of rejecting the offer.

Simplicity of Life

The Book of Ecclesiastes is a masterpiece of literature. Overall it is less cynical than we may at first think. It aims to provide us with a sense of proportion about life. We tend to think our lives are so important and this in turn manufactures anxiety, as we try to advance our careers, avoid the setbacks that others may seem to be causing, acquire more material goods, want to keep up with our neighbours, desire every kind of pleasure. And we may be willing to impoverish ourselves to achieve this. The rat race; the mad rush; ambition: do they bring happiness?

The Book of Ecclesiastes pours calm on matters by repeatedly recommending the uncomplicated things of life, simple toil and the love of family. There is even a hint that this sense of futility or emptiness applies to life seen 'under the sun' from an earthly perspective, and that beyond this lies a heavenly perspective where futility ceases and the real meaning of existence is discovered. The fact that the Jewish experts before Christ decided that this was holy scripture means that they must have identified something here beyond a cynical analysis of life.

From the point of view of the New Testament all the books of the Old Testament await the final chapter, which is seen as Christ. We need the incomplete insights of the Old Testament to show us the gaps which the Gospel writers and apostles claim that Jesus Christ alone can fill.

I am not asking the reader of these notes necessarily to accept this, but I am offering an understanding of how the Bible sees itself. If the words of the letter to the Ephesians are true, then we have the answer to the apparent futility of everything. 'God has made known to us his secret purpose, in accordance with the plan that he determined beforehand in Christ, to be put into effect when the time was ripe; namely, that the universe, everything in heaven and on earth might be brought into a unity in Christ' (Ephesians 1:9–10).

13

In Praise of Romance

The Song of Songs

Christianity is generally seen to oppose the idea of sex. The Christian ideal, held right through the Bible, in spite of the long passage of time, is for sexual relationships only within the confines of marriage, though there is a fair degree of leniency in cases of transgression. But sex has been the area where so-called religious people make most fuss, seeing sexual sins as more serious than sins such as selfishness, greed and gossip.

In Praise of Love

Yet here in the Song of Songs we have a whole poetic drama devoted to the praise of the love of the sexes. This is in harmony with Eve being provided for Adam because he was lonely (as told from a male point of view). And there are many love stories interwoven with the history of Israel. Jacob served Laban seven years for the hand of Rachel and Genesis touchingly tells us 'and they seemed to him but a few days because of the love he had for her'(29:20). There is the story of Ruth. But there are also stories of rape and adultery.

Here a whole book is devoted to love and sex, quite explicit about its intimacy, which is presented as something quite beautiful. False modesty will not cause me to overlook this aspect. That would be to misrepresent the book. It is not a book for prudes. My rather Victorian father forbade me from reading the book when I was a child, though of course I did when he wasn't looking. (I must add that my own understanding of the Bible stems from his original encouragement though.)

The Song, or drama, always used to be called the Song of Solomon, but its own opening calls it the Song of Songs. It is the story of two lovers who live in the sort of agricultural and pastoral setting recommended by the author of Ecclesiastes. There are numerous references to vineyards and looking after the sheep. Both lovers seem to own vineyards or gardens and the man seems to be a shepherd.

The drama unfolds as a series of declarations in which the lovers seek to outdo each other with the richness of their expressions and the passion of their feelings. A chorus known as the companions or the 'Daughters of Jerusalem' joins in the drama. There is a certain ambiguity about which parts of the Song are spoken as part of the married love of our hero and heroine, and which are part of their courtship, as they don't seem to follow in sequence. This is not particularly important. Whether courting or married, the lovers convey a mood of deep love, which is quite physical, though in a sense in which each appreciates deeply the beauty of the other's body, rather than thinking only of sexual gratification, though they are quite eager for that as well.

It is difficult to construct a map of this Song in the same way as for the historical parts of the Bible. Instead summaries and specimens, using a variety of translations, can be used to bring out the unique language of love, so much more romantic than that to which we are accustomed. Eavesdropping on such lush sentiments may cause us to feel embarrassed.

Faint With Love

The bride begins the expression of love with words to the bridegroom: 'Oh that you would smother me with the kisses of your mouth, for your love is better than wine . . . Take me with you, let us make haste; bring me into your chamber, O King.' [Though it was once thought she was having an affair with King Solomon, her shepherd lover was like a king or a prince to her.]

The choir of companions join: 'Let us rejoice and be glad for you; let us praise . . . your caresses more than rare wine,' to which the Bride responds: 'I am black but beautiful'; this is not a reference to her ethnic origin, but to the fact that she has become extremely sunburnt as she has worked in the fields and some people have spoken insultingly of this. She is missing her lover. 'Tell me, my true love, where you mind your flocks, where you rest them at noon.'

The bridegroom replies by telling her to follow the tracks and bring her young goats along to graze near his sheep. 'I would compare you, my dearest, to a chariot horse of Pharaoh. Your cheeks are lovely, between plaited tresses, your neck with its jewelled chains . . .' This elicits the answer: 'My beloved is for me a sachet of myrrh, lying between my breasts . . .'

The bridegroom becomes quite rhapsodic: 'How beautiful you are my dearest, ah how beautiful, your eyes are like doves.' The Bride is not to be outdone and continues the love talk: 'How beautiful you are, my love and how handsome!'

He continues: 'A lily among thorns is my dearest among

the maidens.' Not too complimentary to the maidens! These words may have been spread out over time, but we may still find it difficult to imagine young couples talking so intensely today. Perhaps we have lost some of our sense of romance. 'Like an apple tree among the trees of the forest so is my beloved among young men. To sit in his shadow is my delight and his fruit is sweet to my taste. He has taken me into the wine garden and given me loving glances . . . I am faint with love. His left arm pillows my head, his right arm is round me . . .'

After further dialogue between the bride and bridegroom the bride responds to his appeal where he says: 'Arise my love, my fair one and come away; for the winter is past; the rain is over and gone; the flowers appear on the earth and the time of singing has come.' They leave to carry out tasks together such as fighting the pests that spoil the vineyard. She sings: 'My beloved is mine and I am his.'

In Chapter 3 the scene changes and we witness the days of their courtship where for some reason the groom has disappeared and she is trying to find him. Eventually she does: 'I held him and would not let him go till I had brought him to my mother's house, to the room of her that conceived me.' She is obviously determined that courtship and its partings must end and that they should embark upon marriage.

Beautiful Without Flaw

The choir sings about one of King Solomon's many weddings, describing its luxury and splendour. But our couple are not interested. In Chapter 8 the bride speaks of the wealth associated with Solomon's vineyards, but expresses her happiness with their one small vineyard and in modern terms says, 'He can keep his.' They had less, but in the true sense they had more.

Most of Chapter 4 is taken up with the bridegroom praising the beauty of his bride, using agricultural similes that seem strange to us, though there is no mistaking the strength of his feelings: 'Your teeth are like a flock of ewes, newly shorn . . . your lips are like a scarlet thread and your mouth is lovely . . . You are beautiful my dearest, beautiful without a flaw . . . You have stolen my heart, you have stolen it my bride, with just one of your eyes, one jewel of your necklace. How beautiful are your breasts, my bride; your love is more fragrant than wine. Your lips drop sweetness like the honeycomb, honey and milk are under your tongue.' He also describes her as a secret locked garden, meaning that she is reserved for him. She invites him into this garden to enjoy its choice fruit – a rather delicate way of expressing what they both obviously want.

In Chapter 5 the bride loses the bridegroom again, or rather she dreams he had come for her but when she wakes he is not there. She makes everyone look for him, for she is faint with love. The companions ask her what is so special about her lover and she describes him in the same kind of extravagant language as he had used. It may sound unusual to our Western ears, but we have to admire its ability to be intimate without being crude. 'His head is gold, finest gold, his locks are like the palm fronds, black as the raven [presumably the gold refers to the preciousness of his mind, not to the colour of his hair]. His arms are golden rods set with topaz, his belly a plaque of ivory adorned with sapphires . . . his mouth is sweetness itself, wholly desirable.'

By the middle of Chapter 6 they seem to be reunited. The groom has to ask her to look the other way because her eyes dazzle him. Then he makes another indirect reference to Solomon: 'There may be three score princesses, four score concubines and young women past counting, but [for me] there is one alone, my dove, my perfect one.'

This is just a selection. The Western mind might not wish to listen to it all, but remember that it is poetry and it is not suggested that Israelite lovers always managed to speak in such lavish terms. The groom continues in Chapter 7: 'How beautiful are your sandalled feet, O Prince's daughter [yet she is only a shepherdess], the curves of your thighs are like ornaments devised by a skilled craftsman, your navel is a rounded goblet that will never lack spiced wine, your belly is a heap of wheat encircled by lilies, your eyes are like the pools in Heshbon, your flowing locks are lustrous black, how beautiful, how entrancing you are, my loved one. You are stately as a palm tree and your breasts are like clusters of fruits. I said, "Let me climb up into the palm to grasp its fronds." May I find your breasts like clusters of grapes on the vine . . . your mouth like fragrant wine, flowing smoothly to meet my caresses, gliding over my lips and teeth.'

Many Waters Cannot Quench Love

They arrange to enter the privacy of the bushes in the vineyard. She says, 'There I will give you my love' and hints that their love will be fruitful, mentioning mandrakes, a symbol of fertility. The mood is summed up by the bridegroom in the final chapter: 'Wear me as a seal over your heart, as a seal upon your arm; for love is strong as death, passion cruel as the grave; it blazes up like a blazing fire, fiercer than any flame; many waters cannot quench love, no flood can sweep it away. If someone were to offer for love all the wealth in his house, it would be laughed to scorn.'

Why was this Song regarded as part of the sacred scriptures? It is obviously more sophisticated than mere pornography, but it is very frank and open. I believe it shows that God made sex and that he intends it be enjoyed; he developed the attraction between the two sexes and approved of their mutual admiration. It is saying that God is not a 'spoil-sport' or 'kill-joy'; God is not prudish. Love and marriage are his gift to humanity. Often it has been corrupted, but this Song tries to restore sex to a higher level, while still allowing it to give pleasure.

Some religious people might think I shouldn't have written this chapter. But the Jews thought that this was what God wanted to say about this important theme. At various times Church leaders have been very doubtful about the Song of Songs and have almost wished that it were not in the Bible. They have tried to treat it as a code book, not talking about human behaviour at all, but about the heavenly joys of fellowship with Christ. In the first instance it must be taken literally. It is meant to show God putting his seal of approval on love, sex and marriage.

The Joy of Love, Sex and Marriage

Since love, sex and marriage are inherently good, various prophets use these subjects to describe the ups and downs of God's relationship with Israel and with humankind in general. The Book of Hosea is devoted to the subject of the unhappy marriage of the prophet and how it ultimately turned out successfully. He then makes it clear that his experiences were a symbol of God's problems with Israel, which he had treated as his wife. Isaiah goes so far as to say to Israel: 'Your maker is your husband.'

Writing to the Ephesians in the New Testament, Paul is recorded as telling husbands to love their wives as Christ loved the Church so that she might be 'holy and without blemish'. This is a reference to the Song of Songs, where the bridegroom says there is no flaw in the bride. Paul says that the Ephesians must take this both literally and physically: 'But it applies to each one of you; the husband must love his wife as his very self and the wife must show reverence for her husband.' It would have been more in the spirit of the Song if the writer had invited the wife to *love* her husband too, rather than *revere* him, but they were children of their times and would have probably found the love of the bride in the Song of Songs too freely expressed.

The Bible writers used love and sex and marriage as symbols of relationships with God, as a 'great and hidden truth'. If these were a symbol of something beautiful, then they must have been beautiful themselves. The Song of Songs says so in no uncertain terms.

14

Isaiah of Jerusalem

Isaiah

The rest of the Old Testament is provided by the prophets. No women have their name attached to any of them, though there were women prophets, such as Deborah, who appears in the Book of Judges.

What is a Prophet?

First we must understand what is meant by a prophet in the context of the Old Testament. Predicting the future is not his primary task, though he may do this, often indicating the inevitable results, as he sees them, of courses of action undertaken by Israel or other nations. Foremost he is someone who announces – tells forth – what he understands of the will of God in certain circumstances. He rebukes the people of Israel for disobeying God's requirements, and also tells them what will happen if they continue to misbehave. He frequently does this in dramatic poetic language, very effective even when translated into other languages from the original Hebrew.

Although many of the prophetic messages may seem gloomy, they are shot through with shafts of light and hope. Despite their sins, the twelve tribes of Israel are still his people, whom God wants to use to bring blessing to the whole of mankind, as he promised to the patriarch Abraham. They may go into exile, but they will return. God will deliver them himself through 'his chosen one'. The prophetic messages created a sense of hope that the deliverer would soon come to Zion (the other name for Jerusalem). This sense of expectation was particularly high when Jesus appeared, though he reinterpreted the general understanding in terms of service and sacrifice, rather than military victory and conquest.

Isaiah is the first of the prophets presented in the Bible, though chronologically he was not the first. A detailed explanation of all sixty-six chapters of the Book of Isaiah would occupy many pages; a broad outline and guide is offered here.

The School of Isaiah

It is doubtful that the whole book was written by one man named Isaiah, hence my use of the term 'the school of Isaiah'. A number of prophets worked in the spirit of Isaiah over several generations. The original Isaiah points to this idea of a school of people learning from him when he speaks in 8:16 of preserving in bound form his teachings among his disciples. They built on his work and were able to apply it in new circumstances. Not everyone agrees with this interpretation; some insist that one Isaiah wrote it all because Jesus describes these writings as the Book of Isaiah – but then so did everyone else.

If read with care, it is possible to see that most of Isaiah from Chapter 40 onwards is written (or spoken, originally) against a different background and with reference to much later events and leaders. It might be argued that God could cause someone to write in 735 BC as if he were living 200 years later, but the Bible itself does not suggest that we should suspend our rational faculties. It is more reasonable to place many of the words in the second half of the Book of Isaiah in the context of the return of the Jews from exile in Babylon.

There is a note of cheerfulness that the exile has ended. King Cyrus of Persia is mentioned a number of times as the agent of God for the deliverance, as one who is well known for what he has carried out and is continuing to do for the Jews. He is mentioned naturally, in a way that wouldn't have made sense to people living 200 years before. Also, they would have had difficulty in recognising their current time as a happy one such as Isaiah 40–55 describes. And they describe it as both coming into existence and being in existence, which would have made no sense in the time of King Hezekiah.

Isaiah of Jerusalem

The original Isaiah, living 750 years before Jesus, was contemporary with King Hezekiah of Judah, mentioned in Chapter 3 of this book, and is generally known nowadays as Isaiah of Jerusalem. In the first verse of his prophecy he lists the kings under whom he served, including Hezekiah's predecessors, Uzziah, Jotham and Ahaz. Isaiah reached high rank in government in the time of Hezekiah, providing support and encouragement to the king when the future of the kingdom was threatened by the Assyrian armies, as described in Chapters 36–9 (as well as the Books of Kings and Chronicles, which provide historical background to the work of Isaiah).

Isaiah of Jerusalem came on the scene at a most critical time in the history of Israel. In 722 BC the ten northern tribes specifically known as Israel were finally defeated by the Assyrians and the bulk of the population were taken into captivity into Assyria (in modern Iraq). The remaining two tribes of Judah struggled on. Isaiah 36–9 tells the story of the siege of Jerusalem, capital of Judah, the courage of King Hezekiah, supported by Isaiah, and what was seen as a miraculous deliverance from the Assyrians, who were decimated by plague. This was about 701 BC.

Isaiah's Commission

Isaiah started his work in 742 BC, when the leper king of Judah, Uzziah, died. Isaiah tells us in Chapter 6 how he received his call in the temple in Jerusalem. He sees a vision of the Lord God, enthroned in glory, which overwhelms him with a sense of the majesty, holiness and greatness of God. This fills his soul and influences his speech and actions. By contrast he also becomes well aware of the pettiness and sinfulness of humans. Between God and man he sees a great abyss. A coal of fire from the altar is brought by an angel to cleanse his lips – i.e. his speech – symbolising his appointment as God's spokesman. He accepts this task, saying, 'Here am I; send me.' God warns him that this is a tough assignment, because the people will not, in general, listen. Great difficulties lie ahead, and only a minority of the people will really respond.

One important factor we have to bear in mind when reading Isaiah and other prophets is that they are poets. They express their messages in highly dramatic and vivid language. They are not writing legal documents or following a logical sequence all the time. Often they are trying to create a mood in which people will understand the spiritual and political dangers to which they are exposed and will seek to move closer to God.

The Crisis in Judah

The Assyrian empire dominated the region throughout Isaiah's ministry. All nations were plotting and scheming to demolish its oppressive power. Isaiah comments on each nation at various times, emphasising their unsuitability as allies of the people of God. Particularly he tries to steer good King Hezekiah away from such entanglements.

Isaiah perceived a crisis that was not only political and military, but also a spiritual emergency that threatened the very foundations of the national character and religion. Alliances brought compromises of principles and the danger of foreign influence in corrupt pagan worship and moral practices. The Davidic dynasty was the bulwark against this and, largely because of Isaiah's efforts, it remained so in the time of Hezekiah.

Isaiah exposed the unscrupulous nobles, corrupt judges and decadent upper classes, as well as trying to stem the foreign coalitions. At one stage (Chapter 20) he walked barefoot and with only a loincloth for three whole years as a sign of mourning for the state of the nation. It must have been a sensational action for such a prominent and senior adviser to the king. Desperate measures were required to meet desperate situations.

Isaiah 1–5 probably belong to the reign of Jotham in Judah (742–35 BC). Isaiah exposes the moral breakdown in the country, especially in the capital, Jerusalem. Such a start for his ministry was, of course, not going to make him popular, but that was not his objective. His insight is profound. He points out that sacrifices of animals in the temple are meaningless if they are not accompanied by appropriate conduct. And what is that? 'Wash and be clean; put away your evil deeds far from my sight; cease to do evil; learn to do good; pursue justice, correct oppression, defend the fatherless, plead for the widow. Come now let us reason together, says the Lord, though your sins are like scarlet, they shall become white as snow.' He intersperses his appeals with pictures of what will happen if they carry on with the bad old ways, as well as predictions of what will happen if they become 'willing and obedient'.

On the one road: disaster, war, misery. On the other: the fulfilment of God's purpose with Israel, with all nations coming to Jerusalem to learn of the ways of God, listen to the way of peace, and 'they shall beat their swords into ploughshares and their spears into pruning hooks; nation shall not lift up sword against nation, neither shall they learn war any more'.

These same chapters rebuke idolatry and speak of the day of trouble when they will realise that these idols are not God and cannot save them. In Chapter 3 he describes the anarchy that stalks the land and presents a wonderful picture of the haughty daughters of Zion, who 'walk with outstretched necks, glancing wantonly with their eyes, mincing along as they go . . .' It sounds something like the models on the catwalk of a modern fashion show, expressing a certain frame of mind far from God. Alongside these sombre comments, he pictures a good time coming, but mainly he offers warning to a society that 'grinds the face of the poor' and is addicted to drunken pleasure and unfair trading. 'Woe to those who call evil good and good evil.' But retribution will come!

Ahaz succeeds Jotham as King of Judah. They are both much troubled by an alliance of the northern ten tribes (in their last flurry of activity before their final defeat) and Syria against Judah. Isaiah appeals to Ahaz to show courage and faith in God, but the weak and indecisive Ahaz turns for help to Assyria, the very nation that will later try to swallow up Judah in the days of his son Hezekiah. Isaiah 6–12 belongs to this period. In his attempt to stimulate Ahaz and the members of the court there are some expressions of a hopeful future in these chapters.

Sons as Signs

Isaiah presents his own children as signs to the king (8:18). Their names are a foretelling that the Syria–Israel alliance will soon end. There was Shear Jashub, whose name meant ' a remnant shall return' – some of Judah would survive the troubles that were coming (Chapter 7). Then there was Maher-shalal-hash-baz (Chapter 8), whose name, meaning 'quick spoils; speedy plunder', spoke of defeat for the northern alliance.

The most famous son born in that time was one called Immanuel (Hebrew spelling), which means 'God with us'. Its initial meaning was probably a reference to the birth of Hezekiah, who later became the channel of God's presence with Judah. The northern alliance would be smashed before this child was old enough to know the difference between good and evil (7:14–16).

In the New Testament these words are applied by Matthew (1:22–3) to the birth of Jesus: 'A virgin shall conceive and bear a son and his name shall be called Emmanuel.' This is regularly read at Christmas time. Originally it obviously wasn't a reference to Jesus and the Hebrew word meant young woman of marriageable age, not virgin (though the Greek translation, the Septuagint, did say 'virgin'). In effect Matthew must be saying that although an Emmanuel was born 700 years earlier in the dynasty of David through whom God was with Israel, here now in Jesus is the real Emmanuel, God with us, of whom the earlier one was a kind of forerunner.

Throughout these six chapters are several hopeful sayings that Christians have applied to Jesus, e.g. 'The people who walked in darkness have seen a great light' and 'For unto us a child is born' (originally Hezekiah of the family of David, as Jesus was) in Chapter 9.

Isaiah also tells Ahaz that the Assyrians with whom he has become friendly will make trouble for Judah, though in the end God will defeat them, after having used them as a rod of punishment (Chapter 10). The Israelite view of God was of one who intervenes in human affairs much more than we normally believe. We have problems with the idea of God as the great puppet master, making nations do what he wants them to do. Most Christians believe God is involved, though they have problems in linking this with freedom and personal responsibility.

Good Times Coming

Chapter 11 presents another picture of the day when final peace would come through a king on David's throne (a branch out of the root of Jesse, the father of King David). It is a lovely image, so different from the turmoil of Isaiah's day. Justice, fairness in judgement, dependability in government filled with the spirit of God will prevail in these happy days. 'And the wolf shall dwell with the lamb, and the leopard shall lie down with the lamb . . . and a little child shall lead them . . . they shall not hurt nor destroy in all my holy mountain, for the earth shall be full of the knowledge of the Lord as the waters cover the sea.'

Chapter 12 similarly speaks of a day when people will draw water out of the wells of salvation with joy. So Isaiah gives two sides of the picture, and many such phrases are picked up in the New Testament and applied to the work of Jesus Christ.

A Mixed Menu of Sorrow and Joy

Hezekiah becomes king in 715 BC and reigns 'on the throne of David' till 687. Isaiah is his close adviser. Even Hezekiah is tempted to save Israel with political schemes, showing friendship to the king of Babylon, a nation which ultimately takes

Judah into exile. Isaiah points out that though Babylon might look like a useful ally in the end they would disappear (Chapters 13 and 14). Isaiah also examines other nations with whom discussions might take place and makes it clear that they offer little progress: Moab in Chapter 16, Syria in Chapter 17, Ethiopia in Chapter 18 and Egypt in Chapters 19 and 20. Other desert countries and tribes are also exposed and their fate is described. Tyre and Sidon (modern-day Lebanon) are threatened with lengthy captivity at the hand of Babylon (Chapter 23).

Chapter 22 describes the panic in Jerusalem when the king of Assyria is besieging the city. Some try to prepare; others see no point in this and say, 'Let us eat and drink, for tomorrow we die' – the source of the well-known saying: 'Eat and drink and be merry'. Paul in 1 Corinthians 15 in the New Testament quotes it to support the idea that if there is nothing beyond this life, there's not much point in it.

Isaiah of Jerusalem has various other mixed menus of sorrow and joy. In Chapter 24 he has a world being turned upside down, followed in Chapter 25 with a day when death will be destroyed and all tears wiped away. It must have been comforting as a counterbalance to all the bad news he had to offer. This idea of death overcome in Chapter 25 is rare in the Old Testament, where there are few references to the concept of resurrection. Chapter 26 has dead corpses from Israel rising to live: 'Awake and sing you that lie in the dust.'

In Chapter 28 Isaiah defends himself against those who poke fun at his warnings; he promises that God will make them come true, but also confirms that the dynasty of David will survive in words that the New Testament applies to Jesus as the foundation stone of a temple of righteousness and truth. The changeable mood of Isaiah's words reflects the perspectives which divided Judah. As Chapter 29, in criticising the inhabitants of Jerusalem, makes clear, there was much insincere lip service to God: 'This people draw near me with their mouth; they honour me with their lips, while their heart is far from me, and their fear of me is a commandment of men, learned by rote.' This is not unknown in Christian worship today.

Two main groupings were developing in Judah at the end of Isaiah's ministry: one looked for help from Babylon and the other favoured Egypt. Isaiah opposed both and appealed for trust in God and avoidance of foreign alliances, which would have a negative effect on the spiritual life of the nation. Chapter 30 in particular warns them not to seek help from Egypt. Very practically he refers to the history of the past which showed how unreliable Egypt was. She was 'Rahab who sits still' – all talk and no action. Instead 'in calm detachment lies your safety, your strength in quiet trust'. In Chapter 31 he points out that the horses of the Egyptians are flesh and not spirit.

A King Shall Reign in Righteousness

Chapter 32 is full of hope again: 'A king shall reign in righteousness and his ministers rule with justice.' 'Righteousness will yield peace and bring about quiet trust forever. Then my people will live in tranquil country, dwelling undisturbed in peace and security.' Related to the turbulent times of Isaiah, these words in fact have a timeless quality and such passages provide the basis of the New Testament perception of hopes long expressed, at last coming to fulfilment in Jesus Christ.

Many of Isaiah's more cheerful comments are related to the elevation of Hezekiah as a faithful holder of David's crown and convey a sense of certainty that God's promises to David about the permanence of his dynasty are certain to come true. (The New Testament agrees that this happens – in Jesus.) The king is seen as reigning on behalf of God: 'The Lord is our King, he will save us'(33:22). The well-known words ' the desert shall blossom as the rose' come from Chapter 35, speaking of a day when 'the eyes of the blind shall be opened, and the ears of the deaf unstopped; then shall the lame man leap like a hart and the tongue of the dumb sing for joy'. In several places in the gospels this and similar passages are applied to the healing mission of Jesus. Whatever explanations you prefer, there is little doubt that many people claimed to have been so cured by the touch or the command of Jesus and the writers of the New Testament felt they were seeing the hopes of many generations being fulfilled.

The Long View

Isaiah stands out as a contemporary teacher, politician, statesman and preacher, anxious for Judah to avoid the pitfalls of purely human solutions to their problems. He wants them to see God as a living reality, who is truly interested in Israel and, through it, the whole human race, as he promised both Abraham and King David. God would never turn totally from the dynasty of David. Isaiah sees God as one who acts in current affairs, not as a distant and passive philosopher.

But Isaiah is also a man of vision, looking down the corridor of time to a day when God will succeed in bringing peace and harmony to Israel and the human race, though not without their willing cooperation. This perspective gives Isaiah of Jerusalem many gems of poetry, which provide a suitable basis for comment on the work of Jesus as recorded in the New Testament. Of him the angel tells Mary that 'He shall sit on the throne of his father David and reign over the house of Israel for ever'. Isaiah makes a significant contribution to the linking of the Old and New Testaments.

Although Isaiah of Jerusalem is an extremely influential figure, the second Isaiah is even more important. The works attributed to him are the writings of a member or members of the school of Isaiah, about 200 years later when the Jews were returning from exile.

15

The Second Isaiah

Isaiah

We now move on a century and a half to the end of the exile. Between 606 and 582 BC most of the Jews were taken into exile in Babylon. About 539 BC Cyrus, the new Persian king, decreed that the Jews could go back to Judah and rebuild their temple in Jerusalem and settle there again.

At least Chapters 40–55 of what we know as the prophecy of Isaiah were spoken and written in the period immediately before and after this end of the exile. The author's name is unknown and he is therefore usually called Deutero-Isaiah, which simply means 'Second Isaiah'. He speaks in the spirit of Isaiah and was doubtless a member of the school of disciples whom the original Isaiah of Jerusalem had referred to and who had kept copies of what Isaiah had said.

Chapters 56–66 of the book possibly originate with the same period and author, though many believe that they come from later members of the school of Isaiah. To make the distinction, the section of these final chapters is often referred to as the work of 'Trito-Isaiah', which simply means 'Third Isaiah'. This is not greatly important, as the mood of the second half of the book is largely similar and is not dependent on specific details of history other than the return from exile.

Return From Exile

Isaiah 40 presents the idea of a herald announcing the imminent end of the exile and the return to Zion or Jerusalem. The opening words 'Comfort ye, comfort ye my people' (King James version) will be familiar to those who know Handel's oratorio *The Messiah* where they are used as descriptive of the salvation and comfort brought by Jesus according to the Gospel message of the New Testament, which freely uses a number of references to this part of the Book of Isaiah. However powerful the links with the New Testament, initially the context was the return from exile in the sixth century before Christ. As we grow to understand how parts of the Old Testament are reapplied or adapted in the New Testament, we learn to work with two meanings at once. But if we seek clarity, we have to start with the original.

The return from exile is presented in glowing terms as something more wonderful than it would have really appeared. Times were tough, even with greater freedom. It is seen as the return of God as their king, and they are invited to prepare a highway for the divine king. This would be a metaphor for the preparing of their hearts and minds, as John the Baptist used it in relation to the appearance of Christ in the Gospel story. 'And the glory of the Lord shall be revealed.' Good news is being brought to Jerusalem, 'glad tidings to Zion' in Handel's *Messiah*. Like a shepherd he shall feed his flock.

Then the prophet, as on subsequent occasions, emphasises

the power of the God of Israel, compared with those by whom they had been surrounded in Babylon. Their God was able to achieve his objectives. 'He does not grow faint or weary, his understanding cannot be fathomed' (40:28). Chapter 41 describes in dramatic terms Cyrus as the agent of God for the liberation of Judah.

The Servant Chapters

A new poetic puzzle is presented in Chapter 42. A character called 'my servant' is introduced, remaining for several chapters. Bible students have often debated who this servant is meant to be. Sometimes it is Israel as the ideal representative of God, as in Chapter 44. In Chapter 42 he is an individual who will establish justice in the earth, who is God's chosen one, in whom he delights. This could be a particular leader or the personification of Israel, as if the nation were an individual. The New Testament applies it to Jesus as the final expression both of Israel and of God, who among other things will 'open the eyes of the blind', literally and figuratively (Isaiah 42:7 and Matthew 12:17–21).

Cyrus is also God's servant, shepherd and anointed one (the meaning of the word Christ), his instrument who has made possible a repeat performance of the deliverance when Israel came out of Egypt in the time of Moses. Much of the language in these chapters echoes those earlier events, which lie at the root of Israel's faith and very existence. In Chapters 44 and 45 Cyrus has a high profile and is complimented, though God is seen as the driving force.

Chapters 46 and 47 describe the end of Babylon, captured by Cyrus. And in Chapter 48 Israel is warned not to be too complacent in view of its past record of disobedience to God, from which he has now redeemed them. In this chapter Cyrus is even called God's friend whom he loves (48:14). This echoes God's universal concerns, which are often revealed in Isaiah.

Chapter 49 returns to the servant theme. Here he is Israel (49:3) personified as an individual person called from his mother's womb (also echoed in the New Testament, in relation to Jesus). This servant Israel is also going to be used as 'a light to the nations' so that 'God's light may reach the remotest bounds of the earth'. God never elected Israel for their own sake, but for a channel of blessing to the whole world (focused in Jesus by the New Testament).

In Chapter 50 the servant seems more like an individual, who in 50:4–9 speaks of his dependence on God and the sorrow his mission has brought him. This was the experience of many prophets during the sinful history of all twelve tribes, notably Jeremiah, in the closing days of the kingdom.

Chapters 51 and 52 look back over the sinful and sad history of Israel, but now God is bringing them joy and gladness, forgiving them and bringing them into the fullness of his fellowship. A well-known chorus in the poem is 'How beautiful upon the mountains are the feet of him who brings glad tidings to Zion . . . saying your God is King.' This is quoted by Paul in the New Testament epistle to the Romans (10:15) and applied to the preaching about Jesus by the apostles.

At the end of Chapter 52 the servant is in poor physical shape. His form is so disfigured that he hardly looks like a man. This is a reference to suffering in some way being the price of salvation. It is difficult to know exactly what it – and Chapter 53 – meant in their original context. Perhaps it is a price paid by the prophets who had tried to bring Israel back to God, reminding that without their faith Israel might not even have survived to the day of deliverance it is now enjoying.

The Suffering Servant

Chapter 53 continues with a description of the experiences of this servant prophet figure. Again Handel puts them to music in *The Messiah*. 'He was despised and rejected, a man of sorrows and acquainted with grief.' His suffering is presented as representative, on behalf of all Israel: 'Surely he has borne our griefs and carried our sorrows . . . he was wounded for our transgressions . . . bruised for our iniquities . . . and with his stripes we are healed . . . the Lord has laid on him the iniquity of us all . . . like a lamb who is led to the slaughter he opened not his mouth.'

Already we find ourselves thinking that these words apply to Jesus Christ and his sufferings more realistically than to anyone else. In the New Testament this chapter has a profound effect on thinking about the suffering and death of Christ. Meaning was found in this great tragedy by words from Isaiah 53, such as 'He shall bear their sins . . . he made himself an offering for sin . . . the righteous one, my servant, shall make many to be accounted righteous . . . he poured out his soul unto death and was numbered with the transgressors . . . he bore the sin of many and won pardon for their offences.' Add to this the reference to Jesus making his grave with the rich and in the end being alive, after dying, able to see the beneficial consequence of his sacrifice: 'He shall see the fruit of the travail of his soul and be satisfied.'

Isaiah 53 had a profound effect on Jesus himself and on the early Christian Church. It makes greater sense when applied to Jesus rather than any contemporary of the Book of Isaiah. Its original context for the first time is worth remembering and thinking about, particularly when we read the New Testament. This Book of Isaiah could be more powerful writing than we have ever realised.

God Remarries Israel

The beauty of Isaiah continues in Chapter 54. Israel is symbolised with the idea of a marriage that in some way has failed. She has been left deserted as if she is a widow. But her maker is her husband; although he has divorced her for a time, with tender affection he brings her home again and says his love will never fail. (This reminds us of the Song of Songs.) He will protect her and they will have a large family of children who will be 'taught by God'. She is likened to a city with bejewelled walls and buildings. This poetry is taken up in the end of the last book of the Bible, Revelation, where the bride of Christ, the Church, is likened to a city with every kind of precious stone used in its construction.

These chapters of the Second Isaiah end with an appeal to the Jews, now in their own land, to collect water, wine and milk for free, as God's gift. Jesus develops this idea in John 4 when he offers the everlasting water to the Samaritan woman at the well.

'Seek the Lord while he may be found,' cries the prophet, who goes on to speak of God as a forgiving God, pointing out that forgiveness is not the norm of humans. 'My thoughts are not your thoughts, neither are my ways your ways, for as the heaven is higher than the earth so are my ways higher than your ways and my thoughts higher than your thoughts.' This is said specifically of God's quality of forgiveness, opposed to man's preference for revenge. We have now moved on from the times of Joshua and the Judges, when genocide was deemed to accord with the will of God, towards the direction of the love of God that Jesus makes plain.

The Third Section of the Book of Isaiah

The chapters of the third section of Isaiah continue in the mood of the Second Isaiah, though the criticism of those who do not keep the sabbath and of leaders who are lazy does not seem to belong to the time of the return from exile, but to a later lull in the national enthusiasm, when people need to be stirred up to continue building 'the house of prayer for all nations'. This opening of the temple to all nations is an advance in thinking. Parts of Chapter 56 and all of Chapter 57 seem to belong to the time when Isaiah of Jerusalem was rebuking the people in the time of King Ahaz, but it also contains hope of reform.

Chapter 58 belongs to the same grouping, though its definition of fasting is quite advanced. The fast that God wants, says the prophet, is the sharing of their bread with the hungry and the bringing of the homeless into their houses. He promises permanent honour and joy to an Israel with this spirit. Chapter 59 also contains sharp criticism of an earlier time. It nevertheless holds out hope of forgiveness if Israel repents, when the redeemer comes to Zion and puts his spirit on the former sinners.

Chapter 60 portrays a day of glory for Zion, when she shall be a light to the world, though there is a touch of triumphalism here: nations have to pay homage to Israel, recognising their own inferiority. Isaiah 61 is an individual statement of one who says 'the spirit of the Lord is upon me, because the Lord has anointed [christened] me, to bring glad tidings to the poor, to heal the broken-hearted, to proclaim liberty to the captives, to proclaim the year of the Lord's favour'. After this mission to the afflicted the rest of the chapter sees Israel as a priestly nation helping to transform the attitudes of all other nations, making righteousness the norm of mankind. This is a high view of Israel being chosen by God not for her own benefit but as a channel of his activity for the whole world.

In Luke 4, Jesus quotes this chapter in the synagogue in Nazareth. After the reference to proclaiming the year of the

Lord's favour, he says, 'This day this scripture is fulfilled in your ears.' He claims to be in himself what Israel ought to have been but very rarely approached. A major job of prophets was to maintain this ideal before Israel. Jesus claimed to be the true embodiment of the ideal, so in its messages for its own days the Old Testament was providing a foundation on which, in the New Testament, the message of Jesus and his apostles could build.

Looking Beyond the Present

Isaiah 62 continues the hopeful message of joy for Jerusalem becoming salvation for the world. 'Tell the daughter of Zion: behold your deliverance comes, his reward is with him, his recompense before him.' With the personalisation in the use of the word 'him' and 'his', it is evident that these prophecies pointed to a particular person leading the ultimate deliverance for Israel and mankind from all their troubles. And from many other sources as well as the Bible, we know that when Jesus was born Israel was full of expectation that a Messiah would come. In claiming to fulfil these expectations Jesus changed some of the actual formats, though not the intensity of the expectations.

The links between the Old and New Testament give you the raw material to arrive at your own conclusions. All parts of what we know as the Book of Isaiah contribute to our understanding of the Bible as a whole; clues in one part link with clues from another to open up great possibilities in the search for truth of every kind: physical, historical and spiritual.

The last three chapters of the book similarly look beyond themselves. Three key references are used in the New Testament:

- 'Since the beginning of the world, men have not heard,

nor perceived by the ear, neither has the eye seen, what he has prepared for them that love him.' This idea of the future exceeding what we could possibly imagine is quoted by Paul in 1 Corinthians 2:9.
- 'I am ready to be sought by those who did not ask for me.' This is used by Paul in Romans 10:20 to show that God always intended non-Jews to share the promises he had originally revealed to the Jews.
- Speaking of physical temples, the last chapter of Isaiah moves on to a higher level: 'What is the house that you would build for me? This is the man to whom I will look; he that is of humble and contrite heart and trembles [with excitement] at my word.' God wants a temple made up of responsive people. This is quoted by the martyr Stephen, as recorded in Acts 7, in a speech just before his execution, because of his reinterpretation of the history of Israel and the message of the prophets.

Several times these closing chapters of Isaiah refer to a new heaven and a new earth, meaning a new order of things rather than a new physical universe. The idea is picked up several times in the New Testament, especially right at the end of the Bible, in Revelation.

16

Prophet of Sorrow and Joy

Jeremiah and Lamentations

Jeremiah is often used as a nickname for a pessimist, someone long-faced and grim, who can never see the bright side of a situation. It is in fact a libel on the prophet Jeremiah, who was the author of some of the most hopeful pictures of the future in the whole of the Bible. Like all the prophets he offered criticism and rebuke of the uncontrolled and godless ways of the inhabitants of Judah, but his was a glowing faith, confident that divine harmony would prevail in the end in Israel and the whole world.

Jeremiah was not only a teacher, but also a leader who tried to persuade successive governments to change their policies to what he saw as the will of God. As a result he landed himself in trouble. He was active in the closing half-century of the kingdom of Judah (the two tribes). Born about 650 BC, he disappears in Egypt, where he had been forcibly taken, around about 580 BC.

Born of a priestly family in the little village of Anathoth, near

Jerusalem, Jeremiah was called to his task in his early twenties, in the thirteenth year of King Josiah, the reformer, who tried to bring Judah back to the law as expressed in the Book of Deuteronomy, which had been found during the cleaning of the temple in the reign of King Josiah.

Jeremiah's Call

The first chapter tells us the story of Jeremiah's call to service. He becomes conscious of an inner voice from God to be a prophet. He is convinced that before he was born this destiny was determined for him. Despite this strong conviction he is unhappy. He feels inadequate, a feeling that comes upon him frequently throughout his career, although he always keeps going. In his prayers he recognises this strong sense that God is calling him, but declares, 'Ah Lord God, I am not skilled in speaking; I am too young.'

In the record it sounds like a conversation direct with God, but it seems more likely to be a matter of his reflection as he wrestles with an inner conviction. Many people have experienced this sense of a power greater than themselves compelling them forward, even against their own human inclinations. Such an inner sense drove Albert Schweitzer into the jungles of West Africa as a medical missionary, leaving behind successful careers in theology and music.

Jeremiah's inner sense of God begins to banish his fear; his insight into the needs of the time clarifies and he sees the spirit of God, not his personal eloquence, energise his words. These words will have power and influence political affairs. He feels God is saying to him: 'This day I am giving you authority over nations and kingdoms to uproot and to pull down, to destroy and to demolish, to build and to plant.'

While thinking in this way he has a simple experience which

convinces him of his duty. In the garden he sees an almond tree (or *shaqed*) and his mind makes a connection with another Hebrew word, *shoqed*, which means 'watcher'. The play on words impresses him and he suddenly recognises that he is being called to be a watcher for God over Israel.

As he actively watches the affairs of Judah and the nations, Jeremiah begins to recognise more clearly the threat from the nations who would come from the north and create dire trouble for his people. He sees this as punishment for their wickedness in 'forsaking God'. He feels God is saying to him, 'Brace yourself, Jeremiah; stand up and speak to them; tell them everything I bid you; when you confront them do not let your spirit break . . . though they attack you they shall not prevail, for I shall be with you to keep you safe. This is the word of the Lord.'

This opening chapter of Jeremiah's prophecy sets the scene for so many of the things which happen in his dramatic life and gives the background for the inner turmoil he so frequently experienced. I believe it also helps us to realise that although God is represented as being at work in the activities of the prophets, this is far removed from magic and wizardry. It all happens with a degree of normality. Things in the Bible do not belong totally to another type of existence, not available now. The supernatural can appear quite natural.

Public Ministry Begins

In the early chapters Jeremiah begins his public mission in the reign of good King Josiah, who at an early age had tried to get Judah back to the true service of God. The prophet presents much of his teaching in the form of a direct appeal from God. In Chapter 2, God appeals to Israel as if he were a husband who had been deserted by his bride (the mood of the Song of

Songs). God says, 'I remember the devotion of your youth, your love as a bride, how you followed me through the wilderness' – a reference to the making of the Sinai Covenant at the time of Moses, even in those early days generously overlooking the golden calf and other weaknesses.

The idea of Israel being unfaithful to her marriage vows to God frequently recurs in the words of Jeremiah: 'You have picked your way so well in search of lovers, that even wanton women could learn from you'. They are accused of prostitution and adultery, both literal and spiritual (Chapter 3); yet God is portrayed as appealing 'Come back apostate Israel; I shall no longer frown on you, for my love is unfailing; I shall not keep my anger forever.' And when they do return they will attract all nations to the worship of God (3:17).

'What did your fathers find wrong with me that they went far from me?' (2:5). This presents a wonderful concept of a God who is patient and caring and tries to understand human weakness. It may express God in human terms, but it shows that the Old Testament concepts of God are not just negative and angry.

'My people have rejected me, a fountain of living water and have hewn out for themselves cracked cisterns which can hold no water' (2:13). This is echoed in the New Testament, when Jesus presents himself in John 4 as the source of living water. In the context of Jeremiah it leads to the political situation of two parties, one saying that Judah should seek alliance with Egypt and the other saying they should make friends with Assyria. He expresses this in poetic terms: 'Why should you make off to Egypt to drink the waters of the Nile; or why make off to Assyria to drink the waters of the Euphrates.'

A Reflective Man

Jeremiah is frequently tormented by the difficulty of understanding the behaviour of Israel and the ways of God. He often takes the traditional view that God will punish the wicked and reward the righteous, which as we saw in the Book of Job is open to doubt. From time to time he gains another insight, such as 'It is your own wickedness that will punish you' (2:19). Many actions, such as political manoeuvring, can bring about their own defeat, though we understand that they can also be seen as the punishment of God.

Sometimes God is seen as erecting a wall round the people when they are being responsive to him. Some held the idea that if the holy spirit of God really dwells within a people it will create a kind of force field to hold back the enemy or any other disaster. We need not necessarily accept this idea, but simply see how it made sense to some people. This view led Jeremiah in his interventions in the politics of Judah to oppose both pro-Egyptian and pro-Assyrian parties and occupy the middle ground of depending on God, an approach that had been taken several generations earlier by Isaiah of Jerusalem.

Jeremiah often presents disasters as opportunities for reflection and repentance. This is described as 'taking correction' (2:30), but the prophet complains that they did not take it or learn from it. He was often tormented by the effort to understand what God was doing, rather like the man who said to Jesus, 'Lord I believe; help me in my unbelief!' Jeremiah asks in 12:1–2, 'Why does the way of the wicked prosper and the treacherous live at ease?' and at times he asks God to take vengeance on them. At other times he asks forgiveness on their behalf.

His confusion adds to the sorrow and the heavy weight of responsibility he feels. This is illustrated in 17:16: 'I have not pressed you to send evil, nor have I desired the day of disaster.' In 17:18 he does just that: 'Bring upon them the day of evil; destroy them with double destruction.'

On another occasion, when there are plots to silence him, Jeremiah reminds God how he had pleaded with him not to be angry with the people. But now: 'Deliver their children to famine and let their wives become childless and widowed . . . Forgive not all their iniquity' (18:21–3).

Of course Jeremiah supported the Josiah reformation, but he maintained his rebuke of Judah, because it had not come back to God 'in sincerity, but only in pretence' (3:10). The people had 'spoken, but they had done all the evil they could' (3:5). They did not match their words with action. He tried talking to the poor, but they could not understand, then he talked to the great but they didn't want to understand (5:4–5).

The Religion of the Heart

Jeremiah tries to get to the heart of religion at this time by telling the people of Judah that one day they will not be concerned about the ark of the covenant hidden in the inner shrine of the temple. They themselves will be God's dwelling place along with representatives of all nations (3:16–17). People must have gasped in surprise, particularly as Josiah was busy re-establishing the temple worship. This was a very New Testament message.

A major problem for Jeremiah, throughout his sixty years as a prophet, lay with other prophets giving contrary messages, claiming they came from God. They proclaimed peace when there was no peace, and people preferred them. 'The prophets prophesy falsely and the priests rule at their direction and the people love to have it so'(5:31; 6:14).

Continually the prophet protests about the observance of

religion externally without corresponding internal change. 'Don't think just because you have the temple all is well,' says Jeremiah as he stands at the gate of the temple. 'Amend your ways and your doings.' He also tells them that they have made the temple a den of thieves, as they used it for commercial gain out of the sacrifices (8:11, quoted by Jesus in Matthew 21, when he turns the moneychangers out of the temple). There is much reference to the greed of many in Judah, and their unconcern for the poor. They should glory in the ways of a God who loves, and respect justice and fair dealing (9:23–4).

In Jeremiah one can get tired of the constant denunciation, though relief comes in the many gems of spiritual wisdom interspersed throughout. If one uses some imagination, it is possible to see the prophet standing by the temple gate or in the marketplace or on a street corner. The text can come alive. The audience would shout insults and perhaps throw stones at him. He did not have an easy task, particularly as he was a basically shy man. There were death threats too, as at 11:21, even at the early stage of his ministry.

Acted Parables

Some of Jeremiah's preaching is dramatic, using acted parables. He is told to bury underwear beneath a rock near the River Euphrates. After a time he digs it up and it is completely rotten. Israel was like a garment clinging intimately to God; they had ended this close relationship and buried it, and it had rotted (Chapter 13).

In Chapters 18 and 19 he first goes to a potter's workshop and sees how the potter can start again and reshape a pot when it has lost its shape while he is working with soft clay. God can do the same with Israel if it remains soft. Then he takes a pot after it has been baked and demonstrates in the potter's field that if it is not accomplished correctly then nothing can be done to fix it. It is hard-baked, like Israel.

From Chapter 21 onwards we see Jeremiah under the later kings, Jehoahaz (or Shallum), Jehoiakim, Jehoiachin (or Jechoniah or Coniah) and Zedekiah, when the kingdom of Judah is slipping into its death throes. The writings are not in order but feel as if they were blown off a table by a strong wind and assembled in a random order

Jeremiah in Danger

Jehoiakim reigned eleven years. He was placed on the throne by the Pharaoh of Egypt to act as a buffer against Babylon, and was totally impervious to spiritual reasoning. He disliked Jeremiah's denunciations. In Chapter 22 the prophet launches a biting attack on this king. While trouble and poverty were everywhere, Jehoiakim concentrated on building his palace and living a life of luxury, 'though your cedar is so splendid, does that prove you are a king? Think of your father (Josiah); he dealt justly and fairly, he upheld the cause of the lowly and poor; did not this show he knew me? says the Lord'(22:15–16).

Dramatic stories describe Jeremiah's impact. Chapter 26 pictures him in the temple court, denouncing the behaviour of the king and people. The princes then propose the death sentence on Jeremiah. He stands up to them, repeats his accusations and appeals to them to repent. Certain elders discuss precedents where previous prophets were not executed for saying unpopular things. Jeremiah is ultimately acquitted and for the moment goes free.

Another grave attack on King Jehoiakim draws attention to the Rechabites, a family that has promised its ancestor that it would not drink alcohol or adopt an urban way of life. He then tries to shame Judah for not being faithful to God their father in contrast with the dutiful sons of Rechab (Chapter 35).

Chapter 36 tells the story of how Jeremiah asks his secretary Baruch to write up the speeches that the prophet has made so far and read them to the people in the temple area. Baruch does this; the courtiers tell him to hide and make sure Jeremiah does as well. They deliver the scroll to King Jehoiakim who, sitting before the fire in the winter house, has it read to him, three or four columns at a time, with all his sins and those of Judah listed, along with appeals to change their ways. At the end of each section the king tears them off with a knife and throws them into the fire with sheer contempt for the prophet and disbelief that he represented God! Baruch and Jeremiah hear what has happened and Baruch gets the job of rewriting all the words, with Jeremiah dictating, and this time 'many similar words were added to them'.

Jehoiakim would never like a prophet who foretold that he would die unlamented 'with the burial of an ass he shall be buried, dragged and cast forth beyond the gates of Jerusalem' (23:18,19). Jeremiah also told him that Judah would experience some seventy years of captivity at the hand of Babylon. All the other nations of the region would suffer too until finally Babylon itself would be eclipsed (as happened when Cyrus the Persian achieved ascendancy). Chapter 25 describes the threat of the captivity.

Jedoiachin succeeds to the kingship, but after three months he gives himself up to Nebuchadnezzar, king of Babylon. In 597 BC he is taken into captivity in Babylon along with the cream of the nation. They are treated well and in Chapter 29 Jeremiah sends a letter to these captives in Babylon, telling them not to plot to return but to settle down in Babylon, for that generation will not return to Judah. One of the Jewish leaders in Babylon writes reporting Jeremiah to the Jerusalem authorities for his unpatriotic letter and asking that he be punished and placed in the stocks.

Zedekiah, the Spineless King

Jehoiachin's uncle, Zedekiah, is subsequently made vassal king by Nebuchadnezzar on a promise of submissive behaviour. He is a spineless man who bends in every direction, depending on who frightens him most at any moment. Jeremiah becomes outspoken: the only sensible course is to submit to Babylon and not to fight or hope that Egypt will help. He claims that this is what God wants. But he is seen as an unpatriotic man and a traitor, and narrowly escapes death on several occasions.

From the beginning Zedekiah involves himself in a conspiracy against Babylon with the kings of a number of neighbouring states. They come from Moab, Edom, Ammon, Tyre and Sidon to Jerusalem, which serves as the hub of the planning. Jeremiah places a yoke on his shoulders to illustrate the ideas of service and submission and in a high-profile protest walks around Jerusalem as all the ambassadors arrive. He directly addresses them and Zedekiah, telling them that they must submit to Babylon and cease their plotting. This is regarded as defeatism, placing his mother country in a negative light with its neighbours. He tells them if they do not listen to him they will be defeated by the king of Babylon.

An alternative prophet, Hananiah, announces that the captives in Babylon will return in two years with all the vessels of the temple worship. Jeremiah publicly contradicts this, whereupon the false prophet breaks the yoke that Jeremiah is still wearing. Jeremiah some time later reaffirms that Hananiah has spoken falsely and there will be no speedy end to the captivity, adding, 'And you Hananiah will be dead this very year.' And according to the record he is! 'In the seventh month the prophet Hananiah died' (Chapter 28). No explanation is given. Perhaps Jeremiah knew Hananiah had a terminal illness.

The vacillation of Zedekiah is illustrated in Chapter 37. The Babylonians have begun to besiege Jerusalem and Zedekiah asks Jeremiah to pray for him and the people. Jeremiah sticks to his insistence that there will be no change in the immediate future, and that they might as well end their resistance right now. Babylonian troops withdraw from the city for a while when there comes a temporary threat that Egypt might enter the fray. In the fright of the initial siege, Zedekiah decides to obey the law of God and orders the release of all Jewish slaves, in accordance with the law of Moses. As soon as the Babylonian threat is withdrawn Zedekiah reneges and takes the slaves back into servitude. In Chapter 34, Jeremiah severely rebukes the king, not only as a law breaker, but as a covenant breaker and deceiver. He assures Zedekiah that he, the king, will die in captivity himself, though not be executed. (This was fulfilled, though his eyes were put out too.)

Imprisoned as a Traitor

Jeremiah uses the temporary withdrawal of the Babylonian army to attend to personal affairs in the village of his birth three miles away. As he leaves he is arrested as a deserter and accused of defecting to the Babylonians. He is given a summary trial and imprisoned in a dungeon after receiving a beating. Zedekiah sends secretly to Jeremiah to ask him to come to his quarters and tell him if there was any message from the Lord. We see yet again the indecisive nature of the king. A message says that Zedekiah will go into captivity. No change. Zedekiah instructs him that if anyone finds out about the meeting he is to say that he has asked to be kept in a better prison. And in fact Jeremiah is moved and as long as there is any bread in the besieged city he is given a loaf a day from the bakers' street.

From this better prison Jeremiah continues to send messages saying that the king should surrender to the Babylonians. The princes and nobles ask for the death sentence for Jeremiah as he is weakening the morale of the army (Chapter 38). Zedekiah weakly says that there is nothing he can do to stop them, so they let him down by ropes into a cistern in the palace court where there is no water, only mud. And Jeremiah sinks into the mud.

Another hero enters the drama. Ebed Melech, an Ethiopian employed in some position of trust in the palace, reports to the king that Jeremiah will die if nothing is done. With his characteristic lack of any purpose the king tells Ebed Melech to take three men and ropes and haul the prophet out before he dies. The story is related in extreme detail. Ebed Melech finds some old clothes so that Jeremiah can put them under his armpits to stop the ropes from hurting him; such minor incidental detail suggests that we are reading about a real happening. So we can imagine the scene, with the men pulling against the suction of the mud, followed by the sudden release of pressure. Jeremiah comes out of the mud and is hauled to the surface.

Zedekiah then again meets Jeremiah secretly. If only he has some of the prophet's courage, he might save the situation. Again he asks Jeremiah for the plain truth and swears not to punish him if it is unpalatable. Which it is! With a combination of spiritual insight and political wisdom, Jeremiah can see that if the king does not surrender nothing but disaster faces the city and the state. The king keeps his promise so long as Jeremiah does not reveal the true nature of the discussion. He returns to a reasonable prison until the Babylonian army finally capture the city in 587 BC and, as Chapter 39 indicates, Zedekiah suffers as predicted. The palace and the temple are burnt down and many of the people are placed in captivity. A blind, bereaved king lives out his days far from home.

Jerusalem Captured

Nebuchadnezzar gives instructions that Jeremiah is to be granted special treatment. For once, his faithfulness gives him the advantage, because Babylon sees him as an ally. They know he has long been counselling surrender. 'My country right or wrong' has not been his motto. He is allowed to live among the remaining people in the land and city with special protection from Gedaliah, governor of the province of Judah. Ebed Melech is also treated favourably. The Jews who fled into neighbouring countries return and form a core social group in the land that allows for a reasonable existence (Chapter 40).

But not for long. Gedaliah is a trusting man who does not believe that there is a plot to kill him when he is warned, so he is assassinated by Ishmael, who wants power in the truncated state. He in turn is forced to flee for his life in a battle led by Johanan, who has warned Gedaliah (Chapter 41). There follows a great debate about the safety of Jews remaining in Judah (Chapter 42). Jeremiah appeals to them to settle in their land and remain free of political entanglement. All will be well. Although the leaders had asked for Jeremiah's advice, they respond by telling him he is a liar and that he has not given them the will of God.

Jeremiah Disappears in Egypt

Jeremiah appeals to the people not to go down to Egypt, but his advice is ignored and they avoid being taken to Babylon as they supposed. Down in Egypt Jeremiah still does not stop (Chapters 43 and 44). He rebukes the people for having gone and denounces their adoption of Egyptian ways, in conflict with the ways of the God of Israel; they even participate in Egyptian idol worship. The Jews turn against him, saying that worshipping the God of Israel has done them little good; things were much better when they worshipped the foreign gods, so they will return to that. He warns them that it will all end in tragedy when the Babylonians defeat the Egyptians.

At that point Jeremiah disappears from history, forthright and unpopular, faithful and determined as ever, even though it conflicted with his personal temperament. He is a character from whom we can take encouragement to persist in a noble cause we believe in, even if we suffer and it goes against the grain of our character. A bonus from reading this kind of history is that we can gain insight into the running of our own lives by meeting characters like Jeremiah in whom we find admirable qualities. The Bible is not basically a book of moralising, but has good and bad examples that can influence us.

The 'Confessions' of Jeremiah

The inner suffering of Jeremiah in defence of his principles is illustrated in a series of laments, scattered throughout the book, and in the short book of the Lamentations of Jeremiah, in which he wrestles with his conscience and complains to God, yet reaffirms his determination. As a personality he really comes alive in these outbursts, which are often called the 'Confessions of Jeremiah'. Such personal pictures of a prophet guide us towards a view of what the Bible claims to be: an aid to understanding God through the experiences of men as they relate to him and try to comprehend him. The Bible does not claim to be a book sent down from heaven in which every word enshrines an eternal truth, else how could we have a prophet complaining and even arguing with God and expressing his independent thoughts? The Bible is much richer in helping us to interpret our own experiences when we see that it embraces human freedom and is not just a solid blast of divine authority and dictation.

Summaries of the confessions follow:

- From Jeremiah 4:19 onwards the prophet is distressed about the prospect of disaster to his people in Judah. The intensity of this sorrow is touchingly expressed: 'Oh, how I writhe in anguish; how my heart throbs, I cannot keep silence.'
- 'There is no cure for my grief; I am sick at heart . . . I am wounded by my people's wound; I go about in mourning, overcome with horror' (8:18). As Chapter 9 begins: 'Would that my head were a spring of water, my eyes a fountain of tears, that I might weep day and night for the slain of my people.' This is the spirit of love, contrasted with the hate that often develops in religious disagreements.
- On the other hand, in 11:18–20 Jeremiah learns that people of his home town Anathoth are plotting to kill him, even in the early part of his ministry, and asks God, 'Let me see your vengeance upon them.' It is very human to present contradictory emotions. Similar requests for vengeance are found from 18:19 onwards. Jeremiah asks God to remember how he used to plead for these people in his prayers, so now he asks God to kill off them and their families .
- In 15:10: 'Alas my mother that you ever bore me, a man doomed to strife, with the whole world against me . . . everyone abuses me.' He continues to say how he loved God's words at one time, even though it has

brought him little happiness. He even accuses God of being like a stream whose water supply is unreliable, but then he concludes that God will still save and deliver him. This seesaw of response to God is realistic, and is more encouraging than if all these prophets were perfect. In 20:14–18 he curses the day he was born. Why did not his mother's womb become his grave? 'Why did I come from the womb to see only sorrow and toil, to end my days in shame?'

- 23:9: 'Within my breast my heart gives way, there is no strength in my bones; because of the Lord, because of his holy words I have become like a drunken man.'
- Lamentations 1:12: 'Is it nothing to you who pass by? Look and see if there is any sorrow like mine.' It is not always clear in Lamentations whether Jeremiah is speaking himself as a bearer of Israel's sins and troubles, or whether it is a poetic device to make Israel speak for itself: 1:21: 'Hear how I groan, there is none to comfort me'; 2:11: 'My eyes are blinded with tears; my soul writhes in anguish'; 3:1: 'I am the man who has seen affliction, under the rod of the wrath of the Lord'.
- Lamentations 3 lists at some length how Jeremiah feels that God has mistreated him, but he eventually says: 'The love of God never ceases, his mercies never come to an end; they are new every morning, great is your faithfulness; the Lord, I say, is all I have; therefore I shall wait for him patiently' (3:22–4).

The New Covenant

Despite such sadness and his sensitivity to the sins and the sufferings of his nation, Jeremiah presents perhaps the most glowing picture of hope in the whole of the Old Testament, one that has a vital influence on the New Testament and the future of the Christian Church. At the very time that Jerusalem is surrounded by hostile armies and the temple and worship in Jerusalem are about to be destroyed, he possesses a wonderful sense of a New Covenant to replace everything that has gone before, running from Chapter 30–33. He says that in spite of all the evil, God will have compassion and restore Israel to joy and happiness. He will provide a prince from their own nation who shall represent them before God (a reference to the Davidic dynasty of which Jesus Christ was a member). As a deserted lover, God still declares his love for Israel and determines to build them up and to save at least a remnant (a minority). He will give them gladness for sorrow. 'I will satisfy the weary soul.'

Then from 31:31 onwards come some of the most significant words of the Old Testament:

> The days are coming, says the Lord, when I shall establish a New Covenant with the people of Israel and Judah. It shall not be like the covenant I made with their forefathers when I took them by the hand to lead them out of Egypt, a covenant which they broke, though I was patient with them. For this is the covenant I shall establish with the Israelites after those days, says the Lord: I shall set my law within them, writing it on their hearts; I shall be their God and they will be my people. No longer need they teach one another, neighbour or brother, to know the Lord; all of them high and low alike, will know me, says the Lord, for I shall forgive their wrongdoing, and their sin I will call to mind no more.

This passage moves on from vengeance and punishment to inner reformation and forgiveness. It is quoted in the New Testament, used many times and extracted from its political, territorial basis to speak of the mission claimed by the apostles for Jesus, to make available repentance, forgiveness and salvation for everybody. It is the key passage describing the New Testament, for the phrase New Testament really means 'New Covenant', as Old Testament really means 'Old Covenant'. Jeremiah is led to perceive the highest level of spiritual truth in the darkest of days.

Other interesting parts of the Book of Jeremiah are not particularly related to a specific time of his ministry. Chapters 46–51 foretell the tragic destinies of all the nations around Judah, who would fall victim to Babylon before Babylon herself fell before Persia and enabled the Jews to return from exile. Jeremiah expresses his faith in this return from exile by buying a field in the middle of the siege (Chapter 32). He speaks of this as a symbol of God's everlasting covenant. Although it is formed with Israel, by implication it will ultimately be for all people.

Jeremiah in the Sistine Chapel

The story of Jeremiah is sad, adventurous, dramatic and full of deep significance. His personality was summed up for me when I sat in the Sistine Chapel in Rome on a quiet day, without crowds of visitors. Michelangelo's ceiling painting sums up the whole ministry of Jeremiah with the brilliance of his art. Jeremiah looked down upon me and seemed to be saying, 'Oh dear, what shall I do about Judah? Why won't they listen? My heart is broken for them.' Then I looked again and he seemed to be saying, 'Oh Israel, I am losing patience with you. Oh God, cannot you punish them once for all; they are past redemption.' Then again I looked and there was a hint of a smile and he seemed to be saying, 'Thank God there will be a good ending to the sorry story of mankind and of Israel. A New Covenant is coming and God will at last manage to have his law written in people's hearts, and will forgive their sins and wrongdoing. There is hope in the end.'

That conversation with Jeremiah, by courtesy of Michelangelo, is among the most memorable moments of my life.

17

The Living Visual Aid

Ezekiel

Ezekiel was a priest taken to Babylon in the Jehoiachin deportation of 597 BC. It was a fairly lenient captivity and as indicated by the letter Jeremiah had written to them (Jeremiah 29), the Judeans were allowed a certain amount of freedom; they could live in their own communities and build houses. Ezekiel was Jeremiah's counterpart within the land of captivity. Some of the deportees would plot to return to Judah, and one of Ezekiel's tasks was to resist this. He made it clear to them that the Babylonians would win. The temple would be destroyed along with the city of Jerusalem.

In the early part of the book Ezekiel reproaches the Judeans for their past and present sins and the inevitable consequences. In 587 BC he was vindicated when Jerusalem falls. Throughout his ministry, Ezekiel was very concerned to help the Jews to learn how they could maintain their spiritual life in captivity, and especially after the temple and its worship was destroyed. He no doubt looked forward to the end of the exile after a generation or two as the restoration of all that Israel stood for or ought to stand for, little realising that it would be a long time away and that in the ministry of Jesus a new approach to restoration from exile would be introduced.

A Vision of God

The prophet's ministry and commissioning starts in a dramatic vision that portrays heaven's control of earth in a very vivid manner (Chapter 1). One should not try to find specific meanings in the four winged creatures of the chariot, with the faces of ox, eagle, man and lion, probably based on the standards of the camp of Israel in the Book of Numbers. They had calf hooves and were surrounded by radiant fire, moving in a strange manner connected with bejewelled wheels. Above this unique chariot he sees the vault of heaven and a brilliant figure representing God. It is an awe-inspiring sight, reflecting the power and holiness of God. This never leaves Ezekiel's mind and he tends to teach on a less human level than Jeremiah.

Ezekiel receives a commission in the vision – to preach to the captive Jews about the sins of the nation, explaining the reason for their deportation. He is to persist in it, whether they will listen or not; he is not to be afraid of their hostility (Chapter 2). Like Jeremiah, he has a sense of being called to a significant mission. In the vision he eats a scroll, inscribed with words of woe for him to absorb and deliver. In no way is it a pleasant meal. The chariot of the winged creatures returns in further visions as he hears himself appointed to be a watchman over Israel. If he fails to warn the people he will be held responsible for their sins, just like an unreliable watchman on the city walls who does not alert the people that the enemy is approaching (Chapter 3 and Chapter 33).

The Dumb Miming Prophet

The vision overwhelms Ezekiel and leaves him in a comalike state for a week. When he comes round he finds he has lost the power of speech, so how can he carry out his task, which involves speaking? He discovers that when he feels impelled to say something by way of teaching the people he can do so, but when his work is done the dumbness returns (Chapter 3:26–7).

This makes him a centre of interest. Whenever he speaks, word gets round that Ezekiel is speaking again and people rush to hear him. He also engages in many visual aids to illustrate his teaching, creating a double source of interest. So in Chapter 4 he makes a model of Jerusalem and depicts a siege taking place, with all the engines of war, playing model war games as many men do nowadays. As Jerusalem was shown as the loser, many people would find this very upsetting as they crowded round the dumb prophet.

Then Ezekiel lies upon his left side for 390 days to bear the sins of the ten tribes of Israel. People go and look and see him still lying on his side (presumably he dealt with essential hygiene when no one was looking, perhaps during the night). One day there is great excitement, with crowds flocking round, as he has turned over on to his right side in order to represent extra penance for the sins of the two tribes of Judah. Every now and then his tongue is loosened and he can explain what he is doing. It would not be difficult to find a psychosomatic explanation for such behaviour. He subsequently becomes rigid for a period, pointing at his model of the siege. During this whole period he eats preprepared rissoles, very strictly rationed to represent the food shortage in Jerusalem. Another visual aid is the eating of bread that has been baked on a fire fuelled by dry human dung. This runs contrary to his priestly principles, but is aimed to bring home the inevitability of the fall of Jerusalem and its distressing circumstances. He then shaves his hair and divides it into three portions to represent three types of fate awaiting the people of Jerusalem (Chapters 5 and 6). In Chapter 8 he experiences a repeat of part of the first vision and he is lifted up by the spirit to look through a hole in the wall at the wicked idolatry of Jerusalem – magic, pornographic art and orgies. In a vision he also sees similar sights in the court of the temple. In Chapter 9 he witnesses a man with writing material making a note of who is going to perish in Jerusalem. One can just imagine how interest would be aroused when from time to time the prophet could speak and explain.

In Chapter 10 he witnesses the full vision of Chapter 1, described as the glory of the Lord leaving Jerusalem. In Chapter 11 he conveys his first gleam of hope, stating that the Jews in exile are preferred to those rebelling in Jerusalem and in due course they will be given 'one heart and a new spirit within them'. This echoes Jeremiah's words about the New Covenant.

Chapter 12 calls Ezekiel a sign man, as he mimes his way through his teaching, where words are available only sparingly. Other subjects of Ezekiel's teaching in successive chapters are denunciations of the use of magic, clairvoyance and mystery religions and a declaration that the seat of idolatry lies in the heart. He describes Israel and Judah's history under symbols of adultery and prostitution – the Song of Songs in reverse (especially in Chapters 16 and 23). In Chapter 17 he opposes those who favour alliances with Egypt and the other nations and in particular the way in which these led Zedekiah to break his oath to the King of Babylon. Promises are to be kept even to enemies. (See also Jeremiah 34.)

Personal Responsibility

Chapter 18 is particularly important, initiating a recognition that people were responsible for their own actions. Children should not be punished for the sins of their parents and parents should not be punished for the sins of their adult children. 'It is the person who sins who shall die.' This is a distinct move forwards from the tribal view that says, even in the Ten Commandments, that God 'visits the iniquities of the fathers upon the children unto the third and fourth generation'. The view that whole families should die with a sinful father, as happened in the case of Achan in the Book of Joshua, is no longer acceptable. Morality is developing side by side with the grim decline. This message is given more than once by Ezekiel and is repeated in Chapter 33.

In the midst of all the denunciation Ezekiel declares that God has no pleasure in the death of the wicked. He would rather that they repent. In Chapter 21, Ezekiel receives detailed instructions to perform a dance in which he slashes a sword over Jerusalem in imagination. His teaching and mimes are a mixture of making clear that although Jerusalem will not escape, individual captives may do so if they heed the prophet's words.

One of the most distasteful experiences of Ezekiel is the death of his wife (Chapter 24). Even this becomes a visual aid. He obviously loved his wife, 'the delight of his eyes', but he is convinced that he is not intended to mourn, believing that God wants him to continue as if nothing has happened, not to weep, not to put on special clothes or eat special food. People are staggered at this apparent lack of feeling. Ezekiel explains to them that this will be the case in Jerusalem, hundreds of miles away in the siege, when bereavement will be a daily occurrence and they will pine away, too preoccupied with their sufferings and mere survival to mourn in the usual way.

These actions and explanations are aimed at making sure that the people in captivity once and for all surrender any idea of returning to Jerusalem in their generation and that they stop plotting to do so. It was probably quite effective for no credible plot was undertaken by the captives.

Speech Returns as Jerusalem Falls

In Chapter 33 we are told that in the twelfth year of the exile a message comes to say that Jerusalem has fallen. Ezekiel's teachings through his mimes and occasional words have been justified. It is now obvious to everyone that plotting is impossible, so Ezekiel rediscovers his voice and is no longer dumb. He turns to new matters.

Chapters 26–32 feature a series of prophecies in high poetry against Tyre and Sidon and Egypt, making it absolutely clear that these nations are doomed as well. In the case of Tyre, once the commercial capital of the ancient world, Chapters 27 and 28 describe in vivid poetry their history, their riches and their pride, which was going to bring them to a sorry end.

A New Heart and a New Spirit

Chapter 34 describes the leaders of Israel as shepherds who had not looked after their sheep properly. This chapter and Psalm 23 are drawn upon by Jesus in much of his teaching about himself as the good shepherd, as in John 10 and elsewhere. Jesus says he will go and search for the sheep that are lost (taking more care for one sheep that is lost than 99 that are safe); God is presented as saying the same in this chapter. It also presents the idea of God providing a shepherd from the dynasty of David to bring peace and prosperity ultimately to the flock of Israel.

The New Testament picks this up and applies it to Jesus. Everything that gives hope in the Old Testament, will in one way or another be brought about by Jesus, though often in a different way from the precise terms described in the Old Testament.

Ezekiel 36 is the counterpart of Jeremiah's words on the New Covenant. God says:

> I will sprinkle clean water on you, and you shall be clean from all your uncleannesses, and from all your idols I will cleanse you. A new heart I will give you and a new spirit I will put within you; and I will take out of your flesh the heart of stone and give you a heart of flesh; and I will put my spirit within you and cause you to walk in my statutes and be careful to observe my ordinances . . . You shall be my people and I will be your God.

The Valley of Dry Bones

Chapter 37 is well known, partly through a much loved American spiritual. It describes Israel coming together bone to bone out of a valley of dry bones. The breath of God enters them and they stand upon their feet, a great army. It is primarily about a national revival and restoration of Israel, which some consider to have been fulfilled in modern Israel, though that state is no closer to the spirituality described in the New Covenant passages than are the nominally Christian nations. The New Testament tends to use this kind of passage as referring to the growth of the Church, where it is true to God. This particular chapter is also applied to the physical resurrection of believers: 'You shall know that I am the Lord when I open your graves and raise you from your graves, O my people. And I will put my spirit within and you shall live.'

This indicates the various sources of many ideas adopted by the Church. Belief in the resurrection is hard to sustain from this verse alone. The New Testament presents a stronger case, though each individual must decide what is credible. I believe it with my own mind, but I also admit that I find it hard to imagine with a conviction that goes beyond reason, a difficulty of faith that an earlier generation didn't seem to encounter.

Extravagant Interpretation

Chapters 38 and 39 of Ezekiel are the bread and butter of Christians who use the Bible as a divine Nostradamus, giving us the details of history before it happens, especially in relation to the end of human history. They describe the forces of Gog and Magog descending on the land of Israel, which is then rescued by God in bloodthirsty massacres of the enemy. Its background came from the short-lived threat to the Middle East from Scythian invaders from Turkey and southern Russia. Many fundamentalist Christians have seen this as a picture of Armageddon and have seen Gog and Magog as the forces of Russia and later of the Soviet Union, entering upon the final war of human history. In spite of the changes in the world and the end of communism, some people still search the Bible for this kind of information, as if it were an almanac giving a detailed preview of history. This draws attention away from the really important issues to which the Bible gives priority. Such use of the Bible frustrates my purpose of trying to help readers find their way around its books and develop the tools for interpretation. I do not hide my own beliefs, but I don't want to force them on anyone, though I make an exception here and warn against this way of approaching the Bible. I believe it is destructive of real and useful understanding.

Ezekiel's New Temple

The last part of Ezekiel is devoted to detailed plans for the rebuilding of the temple when the exile finally ends. It provides quite an impetus to the work of Zerubbabel in rebuilding of the temple. Its measurements are very precise, and it portrays a building not too different from Solomon's temple.

These plans are associated with great idealisation of the future. Ezekiel sees a stream going out from Jerusalem, giving life to the Dead Sea and linking with the Mediterranean. He sees Israel recovering the borders it had at the time of its greatest prosperity under David, and the name of Jerusalem will be 'The Lord is there', a utopia to encourage people after all the suffering. In New Testament terms the temple that really matters is the temple of people for God to live in and affecting the way they behave, as described in the hopes of the Second Isaiah.

The Drama and Spirituality of Ezekiel

Ezekiel may lack the excitement and breadth of Jeremiah, but it describes another brave man convinced of the need to call Israel back to the right course and the service of their God. It illustrates how one needs to use imagination and to read such a book carefully. Notice what is really happening. Many people read the Book of Ezekiel and fail to absorb the fact that he was dumb for much of the time and needed to resort to visual aids, occasionally offering further explanations when his voice returned. As a result the drama and power of Ezekiel's ministry is often overlooked. I imagine Jews in Babylon found him a regular topic of interest and conversation: 'I wonder what Ezekiel is up to today.' Their curiosity may have led them to learning and decision.

The most important truth emerges in Ezekiel 18, taking a leap in spiritual understanding with the recognition that individuals are responsible for their own sins and cannot be treated in racial and tribal packages. This is thoroughly relevant in the modern world.

18

Brave and Wise

Daniel

The Book of Daniel, especially its first half, contains dramatic stories, such as the one about the three young men in the furnace and Daniel in the lions' den, which delighted me as a child, when I loved to read it in a picture book. The stories themselves relate to the period of the exile in Babylon, where Daniel rose to high office under King Nebuchadnezzar. His elevation reflects how Jeremiah and Ezekiel told the exiles to settle down and not to plot their return to Judah; they would stay in captivity for a generation or two (seventy years). Many scholars believe that the Book of Daniel was written in the second century BC but based on real historical individuals of the sixth century BC, with their actions imaginatively recreated.

Whatever the origins of the Book of Daniel, we can read its stories straightforwardly on their own terms. It is useful to know that this book was very popular in the second century BC, when the Jews were being subjected to persecution for sticking to their religion. We can read it from the earlier perspective, but recognise that its greatest benefit came to a later audience.

The Vegetarian Trainees

Daniel begins with a story of men of faith resisting temptation and overcoming adversity. In Chapter 1 we meet Daniel and his three Hebrew friends, known usually by their Babylonian names Shadrach, Meshach and Abednego, early exiles from the time of Jehoiakim (around 606 BC). The Babylonian king decides to grant them three years' training to take up service in the royal court with knowledge of the Babylonian language Chaldean and its literature. They are assigned rich food from the king's table, including certain items forbidden by Jewish law.

Daniel asks the official in charge if they could be excused from this food and drink and be allowed to follow their own simple diet. The official is worried that he will get into trouble if they do not look as fit as the other trainees, but agrees that for a ten-day trial they can eat a vegetarian diet and then review the situation. At the end of the test period they look fitter than any of the colleagues who were eating the king's food, so they are allowed to continue with their own diet, which enables them to be true to their religion. They also excel in their studies, and are top of their class.

Nebuchadnezzar's Dream

In the second chapter, the king of Babylon has a dream that leaves him so troubled that he can't sleep. He assembles all his magicians, sorcerers, exorcists and astrologers to expound its meaning and they ask not unreasonably, 'Tell us the dream and we will tell you its meaning.' He replies that they will just concoct a meaning if he describes the dream, but if they can tell him the dream and its significance he will have confidence in their interpretation. If they can't do this they will be hacked from limb to limb and their houses burned. They remonstrate that no king has ever asked them to perform such a difficult task. Only the gods could do it.

The king falls into an uncontrolled rage and sentences them all to death. When Daniel hears of it, he goes to see the king, asking for some time with a promise that he would describe the dream and provide its interpretation. He returns to his three friends and they all pray. In a dream Daniel receives the answer and in a beautiful prayer thanks God 'who reveals deep mysteries'.

Daniel then asks the executioners to delay the executions and marches off to meet the king. The king asks him if he can really do the job. 'No, I can't,' says Daniel in effect, 'but there is a God of heaven who reveals secrets and he is telling you what will happen in days to come. It's not my wisdom but God's power. In your dream you saw an enormous image of a great warrior; head of gold; breast and arms of silver; belly and thighs of brass; legs of iron; feet a mixture of clay and iron. Then a little stone was cut out of a mountain without hands. It struck the image on the feet and it completely disintegrated. The stone became a great mountain to fill the whole earth.'

'Now for the interpretation,' says Daniel. 'You, O king, are the head of gold. After you will come two other kingdoms inferior to yours (silver and brass), followed by a very strong one which however will be unstable (feet of part iron and part clay). In the unstable days the God of heaven will set up a kingdom which shall break in pieces and destroy all these kingdoms and it shall last forever.'

The king goes down on his knees before Daniel. He gives

him many presents and promotes him to be governor of the province of Babylon, with district authority for his three friends.

The names of the kingdoms are not indicated but when the Book of Daniel was most popular people interpreted it as Babylon being succeeded by Persia and Greece. The fourth kingdom would then be the Seleucid kingdom, which was persecuting them and whose end they greatly desired. The prophets had always spoken of a day of the Lord, when God would amend everything through a king of the dynasty of David (which the New Testament interprets as Jesus, though it doesn't picture him in terms of military might). Whatever disaster Jews or later Christians were facing, they always applied the last kingdom to their own times. The most popular interpretation has been that the Roman Empire is intended, both in its original power and then in its long centuries of decline and fall. But God is not a fortune-teller, and the message is essentially an assurance that ultimately he will sort out the sorry mess of human history, though in such a way that it will not release humans from responsibility.

The interpretation most likely to have been held at the time when the book was finally assembled was influenced by the problems the Jews in the second century BC were experiencing at the hands of the Syrian ruler, Antiochus IV, who persecuted them and tried to destroy their religion. He was king of one of the separate dynasties that carved up the empire of the Greek Alexander the Great when he died without an heir. Two of these dynasties are the subject of Chapter 11: one, called the king of the south, was the dynasty of the Ptolemies, based on Egypt, well known for their patronage of science and the arts. The other was the king of the north, the Seleucid dynasty based in Syria, and very aggressive.

Chapter 11 presents the history of those times in a mysterious way, as if it was written before it happened. Even where prophets claim to foretell the future they never elaborate with such detail as this. Many scholars have therefore concluded that the text of this chapter – and the Book of Daniel as a whole – was finalised in the time of Antiochus IV to encourage the Jews, who were under such severe pressure. It certainly performs that function well. The fragmented nature of the times fits this view. Greece had not finally lost its power, while Rome had not fully gained its ascendancy. Whatever the circumstances, Daniel and his friends still appear to be real historical figures of the period of the exile and we can read the stories in that way.

The story is very real to me. Twenty-three years ago I sat in a restaurant in the ruins of Babylon and told the story of the great image to some Iraqi officials (in the days before Saddam Hussein). They had never heard it, though it happened within a few yards of where we were sitting.

The Three Heroes in the Fiery Furnace

Chapter 3 tells how Nebuchadnezzar contemplates his dream further and decides to defeat it by making his own rule permanent. No breast of silver and belly of brass will follow him, so he builds a huge image, ninety feet high and nine feet broad, made entirely of gold. He gathers together officials and provincial and district rulers and the Babylon city orchestra, and he orders them to prostrate themselves before the image the moment the band begins to play. Hundreds of important people bow down, acknowledging the power of Nebuchadnezzar, but the three friends Shadrach, Meshach and Abednego remain standing (Daniel is not there).

Nebuchadnezzar demands to know the reason for their

disobedience and gives them another chance. They reply, 'If there is a god who can save us from the blazing furnace, it is our God whom we serve; he will deliver us from your majesty's power. But if not, be it known to your majesty that we shall neither serve your gods nor worship the golden image you have set up.'

The king is furious. He orders the furnace to be made seven times hotter and the three men to be hurled in. Its heat is so fierce that it kills the officials who throw them in. Then the king has a tremendous shock when he sees the three men walking about alive in the furnace, joined by a fourth person who looks like a divine being. The king orders them to come out and they do unsinged by fire, without even the smell of smoke on their clothes.

Nebuchadnezzar is so impressed that he issues a decree ordering everyone in his empire never, on pain of death, to say a word against this powerful God, who has saved his servants in such a dramatic way. The three friends are further promoted. Did these remarkable events really happen? Many Jews and Christians believe they did. Others interpret this story as a piece of holy fiction where some true episode has been developed to stimulate enthusiasm for the God of Israel. With all our twentieth-century rationalism, we still enjoy the story.

Nebuchadnezzar's Seven Years of Madness

Daniel also features another unusual factor: what is called apocalyptic writing. This developed particularly in the third and second centuries BC as a somewhat cryptic expression of hope and encouragement in times of persecution. Reality is expressed in a highly poetic and obscure code that people can decipher for reassurances that God's will is triumphing in history. Many of the pictures are serious cartoons, with nations represented as animals and angels serving as God's ministers; natural disasters such as earthquakes, and heavenly objects and eclipses are also employed to represent activity of nations and rulers.

Nebuchadnezzar has another dream of a tree having its top lopped off and of himself becoming mad and eating grass like an ox for seven years. Daniel is called in. Full of anxiety, he tells the king that he is going to be mad for seven years and think and act like an ox, like a beast of the field, until he knows that the 'most high God rules in the kingdoms of men'. Daniel advises him to change his style of life and government, so that maybe the sentence will be delayed.

The king is walking on the palace roof a year later. Looking across the city he exclaims, 'Is not this great Babylon that I have built?' Immediately the madness strikes him and he goes out into the fields. Seven years later he is cured and immediately decrees to the whole empire that they are to pay proper respect to the God of heaven. The seven years were later interpreted apocalyptically as seven long periods of 360 years (each day representing a year), during which men rule in madness, to be succeeded by the Kingdom of God. Even if it is a holy legend it still helped people to have confidence in their God.

The Writing on the Wall

Nebuchadnezzar was succeeded by Belshazzar. During a celebration, using cups and vessels that had been stolen from the Jewish temple, a hand suddenly appears and writes on the wall, 'Mene, mene, tekel, upharsin.' The king is panic-stricken. 'His knees knock one against the other.' Daniel is sent for and offered rich rewards if he can explain it. He tells the king to keep his rewards and goes on to explain that the king and kingdom have been measured (mene), weighed in the balances (tekel) and found wanting (upharsin). Because of Belshazzar's pride and sinfulness, the kingdom will be taken over by the Medes and Persians. That very night Cyrus leads his troops on the drained river bed of the Euphrates and captures the city. Belshazzar is killed. We now say that the writing is on the wall when a government is about to fall.

Daniel in the Lions' Den

Another mentioned king cannot be traced in history, which may result from a mistake in old manuscripts. The essence of the story is that the pagan colleagues of Daniel, who now serve the Persians, see the chance to dispose of him as they notice that he prays every day with his window open towards Jerusalem. They are envious of the favour with which the king regards him, so they persuade the king to issue a decree that anyone who presents a petition to any god or human being other than the king in the next thirty days will be thrown into the lions' den.

Daniel continues as usual. He doesn't even close his window. His enemies ask the king to reaffirm his agreement that the laws of the Medes and Persians cannot be revoked, then tell him about Daniel's prayers. With great sorrow, after trying to overturn his own decree, he has to let Daniel be thrown into the lion pit. And he says to Daniel, 'May your God to whom you pray save you.'

The king stays awake all night. At the first light of dawn he goes down to the lions' den. 'Daniel! Has your God, the living God, been able to save you from the mouth of the lions?' Daniel answers that he is safe and the king is overjoyed, throwing the conspirators into the den, where they are promptly devoured. The king then issues a decree telling everyone to show fear and reverence to Daniel's God.

The Four Beasts

Chapter 7 is apocalyptic. Daniel has a vision of the same four kingdoms as Nebuchadnezzar does in his dream in Chapter 2, though this time they are represented by four beasts: a lion, a bear, a winged leopard with four wings and four heads and a composite wild beast, great and terrible. In the end God's holy ones take over the rule of the earth, and the four wings of the leopard and the four heads speak of the fourfold division of Alexander's empire after his death. From the Jewish point of view, out of that division comes the terrible persecuting power of the fourth beast, seen as Antiochus IV, the Syrian king, the Seleucid dynasty. He changes festivals and religious laws, both of the Greeks and against Jewish conscience, as mentioned in 7: 25. His rule is expected to give way to the Kingdom of God.

Also in the vision Daniel sees a representation of God as the 'Ancient of Days', surrounded by many apocalyptic symbols of force and brilliance. Pictures of this kind, though not to be taken literally, sometimes give us a sense of the solemnity with which the writers expect us to envisage God. One, the Son of Man, comes to the Ancient of Days on the cloud of heavens and was given the everlasting Kingdom. We are told in the New Testament how Jesus called himself the Son of Man and how this passage was applied to him.

The Vision of the Ram and the Goat

Chapter 8 portrays the Persians as a ram, butting towards north, south, east and west. Its two horns represent the union of the Medes and Persians, with the Greek conquerors 'a he goat coming from the west skimming over the earth without touching the ground'. 'It had a prominent horn between its eyes' – no doubt Alexander the Great – and defeats the Persian ram. The prominent horn breaks and the four-fold division of

Alexander's empire occurs. From the Seleucid section, another horn develops. This is a further representation of Antiochus IV and his suppression of the Jewish religion is vividly described in apocalyptic terms. In the end he will be destroyed by the Prince of Princes. Daniel is overcome by the power of the vision and falls sick for a while.

In all these apocalyptic visions, with their mysterious symbols, current events connected with Antiochus IV are described as if they are predictions made in a previous period. It uses the literary device of putting contemporary writing back into the lips of a well-known person from a previous period, in this case Daniel, so the visions sound as if they foretell what was then future. This adds to the emphasis of God's care.

Daniel's Prayers and Heavenly Visions

Chapter 9 describes Daniel studying the Book of Jeremiah, praying and wondering when the exile would end. His prayer is given in full, conveying a sense of the basic spirituality of a man of God in those times. Daniel takes upon himself the sins of the whole nation and asks forgiveness. The angel Gabriel comes and reassures him with further apocalyptic material relating to unknown mysterious time periods, and mentions the forbidding of sacrifice and offering – another reference to Antiochus IV.

Chapter 9 has another meeting between Daniel and an angel, who gives a vision of the glory of God, which puts him into a coma. He is called a 'man greatly beloved'. The angel suggests that history is manipulated by angels, who stand behind events, shaping their course. This presents great philosophical problems, but if we accept a God, we cannot rule out the idea that he holds his hand on the steering wheel of human affairs to ensure that the ultimate outcome will be a situation that gives joy to God and humans without absolving their responsibility.

Chapter 11 is very relevant to all these references to Antiochus IV. In cryptic apocalyptic language the story of the battles between the Ptolemies of Egypt and the Seleucids of Syria is related in extreme detail, describing the numerous marriage alliances and battles. Antiochus is described in 11:31 as setting up the 'Abomination of Desolation' and desecrating the sanctuary. He blasphemes the 'God of Gods' but comes to a bad end. In the New Testament, Jesus uses the chapter to transfer the abomination of desolation to the Romans in his own time. The reapplication of an Old Testament situation to a New Testament one with adaptation of the detail is frequent.

The final chapter also has an apocalyptic flavour, concerned with the climax of history, with what is called the time of the end. Chapter 12 speaks of a time of trouble such as has never before been known, but also of a resurrection to judgement of both the good and the bad. The wise will shine like the stars forever and ever. The book finishes by describing a series of time periods, taking Daniel up to the end of the age. He hears and he does not understand. We are in much the same position, except that we can grasp the message that there is in the mind of God a plan to bring good out of the many evils that have afflicted human history.

The whole book aims to give people hope and determination in staying true to their God, and the two periods it spans are unique. The time of Antiochus IV, with its persecutions and attacks on the religion of Israel, meant that people needed to be sustained in their troubles. These troubles are further described in the Books of the Maccabees, which were never included in the Jewish canon of scripture, but appear in Bibles published for Roman Catholics as well as many editions of the

New Revised Standard translation. It is interesting to read it beside Daniel 11.

There is no doubt that the Jews of the second century BC were much encouraged to consider Daniel and his friends, who refused to eat the king's food, who braved the fiery furnace, who courageously told kings the truth, Daniel who was thrown into the lions' den for his fidelity. Even if an element of fiction creeps into the way these stories were told and despite the mysteries of their apocalyptic sequences, the Book of Daniel had a profound effect some 300 or 400 years after the time of the stories it told. Christians today still draw some courage from the boldness of its characters.

19

Denunciation and Hope From an Eloquent Trio

Hosea, Joel and Amos

The minor prophets are so called possibly because their prophecies are shorter, though perhaps also because none of them rise quite to the national eminence of Isaiah, Jeremiah or Ezekiel, despite being influential in the politics of Israel and Judah. I have chosen to deal with all the books of the Bible in the order in which they appear, so chronologically we have already been moving backwards and forwards between different periods, and this is the case here. This chapter introduces Hosea, Joel and Amos. The first and the third prophesied to the ten tribes in the period 786–746 BC and are directly linked. Joel indicates no particular time, it could have been somewhere around the time of King Josiah in Judah, though a reference to the Greeks could make it much later.

An Unhappy Marriage with a Happy Ending

The Book of Hosea forms an emotional representation of the love of God for Israel. It uses married love in fidelity and in infidelity as a symbol for the relationship of God and his people, giving additional purpose to the presence of the Song of Songs in the Bible, with its praise of sex and marriage. Hosea prophesied in the reign of Jeroboam II in the ten-tribe kingdom. Though a godless king, he brought it to a position of great, though temporary, prosperity, with a large empire that however had no permanent structure.

The book opens with Hosea being told to marry a prostitute, Gomer. In the context of the book it is not clear whether this is a reference to her existing or future profession. It fits the story better if she became a prostitute later, as this links with Israel's original loyalty and subsequent disloyalty to God. He marries her and has three children, all of whom, like Isaiah's children, are given names symbolising the relationship of God with Israel, particularly, at this time, with the ten tribes.

The names were:

- Jezreel, a son whose name means 'whom God shall sow' – the seed. This was a name of hope, linked with the promises about Abraham's seed or descendants, as well as the Valley of Jezreel, where the king's ancestor Jehu had massacred the supporters of his predecessor. God expresses his disapproval of this and will punish the great-grandson for the earlier sins (quite the opposite of Ezekiel 18, though Jeroboam had plenty of sins of his own).
- Lo-Ruhamah, a daughter, whose name means 'not to be pitied', referring to the state of the ten tribes in relation to God.
- Lo-Ammi, a son whose name means 'not my people', describing the divorce between God and the nation.

As with Ezekiel and his signs, this creates great interest.

People hear that Gomer is pregnant and wonder what the name of this child will be.

In Chapter 2, Hosea reveals that his wife has been unfaithful. He describes his sorrow and anger, which then blends, without any particular transition point, into a description of God's feelings about Israel's infidelity. The punishment seems to have the purpose of reform, and there is a picture of ultimate restoration. God woos Israel to regain its love. He says, 'I will allure her' into coming back. This is also portrayed in the personal story of Hosea, who assembles the children and gives two of them new names. Lo-ruhama becomes Ruhamah: 'not to be pitied' becomes 'to be pitied'. Lo-Ammi becomes Ammi: 'Not my people' becomes 'my people'. I can imagine Jezreel wanting to know why his name is not being changed and being told that it is already a name of hope.

In the third chapter we learn that Gomer has left Hosea. He buys her back in the marketplace and places her under home arrest until she proves that she can be trusted. As the book continues he always has a love for her. It would have been a sensation when he bought her back. People would say he was crazy and others that he had broken the law. When criticised he may have said, 'But I love her in spite of everything', which accords with God's basic attitude to Israel.

There follow the outpourings of God's disappointment with his unfaithful wife, Israel. Its crimes are described in some detail: idolatry, lack of love for one's neighbour, unjust government, especially over the poor. The analogy of marital unfaithfulness is maintained. Hosea's own heart is breaking, as he spoke for God. Hosea can sympathise with God and the impact would be considerable, because Gomer's misbehaviour had been widely noticed. Sometimes he also hopes that Judah, the two tribes, will not catch the spirit of the ten.

Chapter 6 shows signs of repentance: 'Come let us return to the Lord . . . Let us press on to know the Lord' (such knowing is a word of intimacy, used sexually in many places in the Bible). God makes it clear through the prophet that he desires 'love, not animal sacrifices' and 'knowledge of God, not burnt offerings'. In the New Testament Jesus quotes this to the leaders who concentrate on the externals of religion.

The king's godlessness is bemoaned and there is rebuke for all the foreign alliances that have brought weak influences into the land. Their deeds will have consequences. As the well-known verse says: 'They sow the wind; they shall reap the whirlwind' (8:7). Agricultural analogies also abound: 'Sow for yourself righteousness, reap the fruit of unfailing love. Break up your fallow ground; it is time to seek the Lord'. (Chapter 10).

Chapter 11 is based on Hosea, the family man, who loved his children. 'It was I who taught Ephraim (another name for the ten tribes) to walk, I took them in my arms; I secured them with reins (such as little children are held by to stop them wandering), I led them with bonds of love; I lifted them like a little child to my cheek; I bent down to feed them.' God goes on to say through the prophet that he really ought to give them up, but he can't as he loves them too much. From his own experiences, the prophet learns his concept of God in a moving way both sad and happy.

The prophecy concludes with a picture of ultimate restoration. We may assume this was true of Hosea and Gomer and it is promised for the nation when it returns to God and flourishes like a vine and has no further dealings with idols. The whole book comprises one of the most personal and tender representations of God in the whole of the Old Testament.

The Years That the Locusts Have Eaten

Terrible damage is often wrought by hordes of locusts in Africa and the Middle East. They literally darken the sky and, when they land, soil, vegetation, crops and houses inside and outside are covered with a seething mass of crawling, almost liquid insect life, When they move on, there is absolutely nothing left to be eaten.

Joel's mission was undertaken at such a time of disaster. So frightful was the scourge that he visualised it as a symbol of the coming 'Day of the Lord', the Day of Judgement for sin. In the face of the advancing catastrophe, Joel summons the people to repent and to turn to the Lord with fasting and weeping. He orders them to call a solemn assembly, where the priests will pray for deliverance. They follow his orders and God is reported as answering their cry, promising to drive away the locusts and bless the land with peace and prosperity.

The description of the locust invasion is very vivid, and the different types and stages of locust are mentioned in 1:4. At the same time there is an implication that human locusts are also being depicted. It is all visualised as the Day of the Lord, a phrase frequently used by prophets for the final outcome of human history, so once more we have the language of analogy and metaphor.

Joel calls the locusts 'God's army', suggesting that they are instruments of correctional education of his people for their sins. In connection with the solemn assembly he has called, he asks the people to tear their hearts and not just their clothes, returning to God with their whole being and not just outwardly. God's response is assured, because he is 'gracious and merciful'. The departure of the locusts, who had come out of the north, is vividly described in the second half of Chapter 2. It is also declared that the relief felt will lead to an unparalleled outpouring of the spirit of God upon everyone, young and old, important and unimportant, whether they are religious authorities or not (2:28–9).

This final passage is used by the apostle Peter on the Day of Pentecost as a parallel to what was happening when ordinary people are described as receiving the gift of the Holy Spirit after hearing Peter's witness to the life, death and resurrection of Jesus. Again, this is not restricted to the religious leaders, who in fact were largely hostile in the story in the Book of Acts (Chapter 2). Peter also says it is the precursor of the Day of the Lord, which Joel goes on to describe in apocalyptic terms, when the sun is darkened and the moon is turned into blood.

The third chapter is another apocalyptic one, describing poetically the Day of the Lord, this end of history, when there is a great battle in the valley of decision and God roars from Zion and the stars cease to shine. God will deliver his people: 'The mountains will drip sweet wine and the hills shall flow with milk and a fountain shall come forth from the house of the Lord.' The enemies will be defeated and 'the Lord will dwell in Zion'.

This book could be fitted in at many times in the history of Israel. It is based on the two tribes, centred on Jerusalem. In the New Testament it would be reinterpreted as the effect of the activity and victory of Jesus Christ. Religious Jews today would see it as a deliverance of their troubled nation, still to happen, a view that feeds their determination to settle in all parts of Palestine, including the Arab areas.

The Prophet Who Didn't Mind His Own Business

Amos was a shepherd at Tekoa, in the land of Judah. He did not belong to a prophetic family, and was not a person of any consequence, as he himself declares in Chapter 7. Instead of minding his own business and staying in Judah, he wanders off to denounce the reign of King Jeroboam II of the ten tribes. He was thus a contemporary of Hosea and indeed of the early days of Isaiah of Jerusalem.

Amos sees through the hollowness of the prosperity of the empire of Jeroboam II and denounces it, using images drawn from his own experience as a herdsman. The book is an anthology of his speeches, with no connection to any specific events except his conflict with the Israelite authorities.

The book has a dramatic beginning. The visiting prophet starts by standing up and proclaiming punishment on the surrounding nations. The Israelites would quite like this. I can hear them saying 'Hurrah' as he told them of God's intentions for Syria, Philistia, Tyre, Edom, Ammon and Moab. They would become positively rapturous when he included Judah, the two tribes, in his diatribes. Then dramatically he launches into the fiercest denunciation of all – against the ten tribes! He exposes their idolatry and unjust ways and describes the doom that faces them. He makes it clear that being chosen by God to be the channel of his truth brings responsibility that they have neglected: 'You only have I known of all the nations of the earth; therefore will I punish you for all your crimes.' He inveighs against the love of luxury in the royal household and foretells an end to it all. He is very forthright as befits his lowly origin, referring to the ladies of the aristocracy as cows of Bashan – not very polite in anyone's language.

Amos particularly denounces the worship of the calves at Bethel, originally set up by the first Jeroboam when he led the revolt against Solomon's son Rehoboam and established the separate kingdom of Israel. He gives them hope if they will change their ways, but doesn't really expect to have much effect on them. He must try, impelled by an energy that he would see as summoned by the call of God.

He rebukes bribery, the enjoyment of luxury at the expense of the poor and the refusal to help the needy. 'Seek good and not evil that you may live . . . Hate evil and love good that justice may prevail at the gate.' He tells them not to long for the Day of the Lord, for they will be its victims. God hates their form of religious worship. They act as if they are worshipping him at the calf shrine at Bethel.

Eventually the authorities can tolerate him no longer. Amaziah, the priest of the shrine at Bethel, tells him to go back to his own country of Judah and mind his own business instead of interfering in the affairs of the ten tribes. In effect, he says, 'This is the king's sanctuary and a royal temple and we can't have you making all this trouble.' Amos points out that he didn't ask for the job; he was no professional prophet, but a poor farmer, living very frugally. It was God who called and sent him (Chapter 7). He then proceeds to prophesy more fiercely. Amaziah's wife will be driven to prostitution in the troubles to come, and Israel shall go into captivity. He continues to describe their greed and dishonesty, how they will sell the poor for a pair of shoes (8:6). The ten tribes themselves will become poor beyond imagination.

Even so the record of his prophecy finishes on a note of hope. They will be sieved out and those that survive the process will be joined to the dynasty of David, when 'I restore the house of David and rebuild it as it was long ago . . . I shall restore the fortunes of my people Israel . . . They shall never again be uprooted.'

This section of Chapter 9 is quoted in a discussion in the Church and Jerusalem as recorded in Acts 15. The Greek translation of the Old Testament (the Septuagint) and the sequences about Israel possessing Edom are used, with a declaration that 'the rest of mankind will seek the Lord.' (Edom is a word linked with Adam, who stands for mankind.) On the basis of this and other reasoning the Church decides that non-Jews can join the Church without having to obey Jewish ritual laws.

Hosea is the prophet who stands for the love of God, despite the unworthiness of people to receive his love and although they must accept correction for their crimes. Joel is the mysterious prophet who uses the plague of locusts to herald the 'Day of the Lord'. And Amos is the courageous farmer who takes on the might of a prosperous kingdom and tells it what it does not want to hear.

Among the arguments, denunciations and threats from all three, there are rays of hope and gems of moral and spiritual truth, which come ringing down the ages with messages that we too can learn.

20

Six Minor Prophets

Obadiah, Jonah, Micah, Nahum, Habakkuk and Zephaniah

Six of the so-called minor prophets take us up to the time when the people of Judah were deported to Babylon. The books are not brought together in chronological order, and some are short one-subject prophecies.

Obadiah Against the Edomites

Obadiah is a one-chapter composition containing one of the sternest prophecies of the Old Testament. We don't know who wrote it or when. It could have been written during the closing days of the kingdom of Judah, when the Edomites, south of the land of Judah, first tried to join with Judah against Babylon and then harassed them when they were in trouble, as other prophecies indicate. During the exile the Edomites occupied southern Judah and on their return from exile they became adversaries to the Jews. Verses 10–14 refer to this unfriendly attitude of the Edomites in gloating over the misfortunes of Judah. Edom is now part of Jordan, most famous for the rock buildings of Petra, which are a considerable tourist attraction. There is reference in verse 3 to its people dwelling in the clefts of the rocks.

Obadiah is not a particularly edifying book. It forms a long, bitter cry for vengeance on Edom, a feature present in most of the prophets to a greater or lesser extent. Jesus turns this on its head in the New Testament and proposes the change of heart of loving your enemies, a long-term approach not so immediately satisfying to barbarous human emotions. We have to bear in mind that the prophets have their limitations and provide part of the gradual education, which, according to the New Testament, finds its pinnacle in Christ.

The prophet promises severe punishment upon Edom and on all the nations (with a play on words between Edom and Adam's similar roots, making a connection with earth and mankind).

In the day of Edom's final disaster things succeed for Israel and Jerusalem becomes a place of holiness and a source of vengeance against Edom. The Israelites will be united as one kingdom and occupy all their former territory. 'Saviours shall ascend Mount Zion to rule the mount of Esau and the Kingdom shall be the Lord's.'

The Man Who Came Back From the Dead

The Book of Jonah is a very instructive spiritual novel. No doubt Jonah did exist. However to argue whether or not a whale really swallowed him is to miss the point of one of the most advanced books in the Old Testament. A piece of holy fiction can be quite illuminating to the reflective mind.

The story is fascinating. God instructs Jonah to preach to the wicked people in Assyria's capital, Nineveh, somewhere in the closing days of the kingdom of Judah. Jonah doesn't want to.

He complains that God is very patient and compassionate and that he will forgive the Ninevites if Jonah's preaching is successful.

Jonah pays his fare and sets sail for Tarshish (in this instance probably near Gibraltar), to go as far as possible in the opposite direction from God's instructions. A great storm blows up and the ship looks as if it will break. All the sailors pray to their gods, but Jonah sleeps through it in the hold. The sailors meanwhile throw a cargo overboard. The captain comes to Jonah and in effect says, 'What are you doing asleep? Get up and call upon your god.'

The sailors hold a lottery to find out who has done something wrong and caused the danger. The lot singles out Jonah. They ask him his personal details: Where do you come from? Where are you going? And he tells them the whole story including his faith, 'I worship Yahweh, the God of heaven, who made the sea and the dry land.' The sailors are frightened. 'They knew that he was fleeing from the Lord, because he had told them.' 'How could Jonah do such a thing?' (The narrative has a superb sense of timing.)

The sea becomes more turbulent and Jonah tells them to throw him overboard. The sailors are decent fellows and don't want to do that, but in the end they have to comply. They ask the forgiveness of Jonah's God and toss him into the sea. Immediately the storm abates.

A large fish or whale with a bigger throat than usual is waiting. It swallows Jonah. Jonah remains alive and conscious in the whale's belly, though it is rather dark, and prays from the whale's belly to God. His prayer is that of a deeply religious man, who is extremely upset that his predicament prevents him from worshipping at the temple in Jerusalem. He describes his experience of nearly drowning before the fish appeared, and he is confident that he will one day worship at the temple again.

'Then the Lord commanded the fish to spew Jonah upon the shore.'

God instructs Jonah to go and preach to Nineveh a second time. No more whale bellies for Jonah. He does as he is told. Surprise! Surprise! The people of Nineveh take him seriously, and put on clothes of sorrow and mourning and repent – even the king and his nobles.

They may have been startled into doing this. Three days hidden in the fish will have made Jonah totally ghostly white. When the people of Nineveh saw him in the streets they would have panicked, thinking a ghost was among them. And when he explained they would say that he was a man who had come back from the dead. Because they believed in his resurrection they believed his message and that God said he would not destroy the city if they repented.

Does this success as a preacher please Jonah? Not one bit. He goes and sulks and complains to God: 'I told you so. I knew you were a gracious and merciful God, slow to anger, rich in mercy. I'd be better off dead than see you forgiving these people.' He sits there overlooking the city to see if God will change his mind and destroy the city that had done so much damage to his nation.

The weather is hot and God very mercifully makes a shrub spring up to supply Jonah with shade. Jonah is pleased, but during the night God sends a worm to kill the plant so he has no protection from the sun that beats down. Again Jonah petulantly wants to die.

'Jonah,' God says, 'you're angry over a plant on which you bestowed no effort. Shouldn't I be concerned over Nineveh, a great city, in which there are one hundred and twenty thousand people who don't know their right hand from their left – and much cattle!' I love that bit about 'much cattle'. God even cares for the animals.

Jonah is a wonderful book defending the love of God against narrow nationalism, prefiguring the New Testament message that people will be saved irrespective of race. The fact that Jonah is seen as the man who has come back from the dead – who has been raised from the dead – links with the New Testament. The belief that Jesus had been raised from the dead was the key to the success of the apostle's teaching. Jesus himself spoke of the sign of the prophet Jonah: 'As the prophet Jonah was in the whale's belly for three days and three nights, so will the son of man (Jesus) be three days and three nights in the heart of the earth' (Matthew 12:40). Jesus was not so much concerned about the three days and three nights, but the sign of the man who came back from the dead (himself) would convince people.

The Man who Influenced a Good King

The prophet Micah lived at the same time as Isaiah of Jerusalem. According to Jeremiah (26:17) he influenced the thinking of the reformer king, Hezekiah of Jerusalem. He came from a little village called Moresheth in the hills of Judah, overlooking the plains of southern Judah, with the sea in the distance.

With energy and eloquence, Micah attacks the wealthy exploiters of the poor, the dishonest merchants, the corrupt judges and irreligious priests. As a countryman he especially blames the cities of Jerusalem and Samaria (capital of the ten tribes) for the decline of truth and righteousness. He tells them what God has in store for them.

Like other prophets he was a man of sign and for some of his time he went about barefoot and naked to emphasise the sorry state of affairs. He walks through the various towns he lists with his indictment of their sins, describing the rich on their luxurious couches planning to cheat people and seize their property, but suggests that a minority will keep aloof from such behaviour.

But most 'hate what is good and love what is evil'. The prophets encourage complacency and the leaders will do anything for a bribe.

Suddenly in Chapter 4 he describes a day when God will bring peace and they shall beat their swords into ploughshares. 'And dwell every man under his own vine and fig tree and none shall make them afraid.' This is identical with Isaiah 2. We don't know which is the original or whether both came from somewhere else. In spite of His rebukes, Micah still sees God as having a future for Israel, as did all the prophets, thus providing the background against which Jesus emerged.

Micah 5 is read in carol services every Christmas. It tells of a ruler who is going to be born in Bethlehem, descended from King David. The Jews generally read this as a prophecy of the Messiah or Anointed One and Matthew certainly presents it as referring to Christ (which means 'Messiah' or 'Anointed').

In a third part of his prophecy Micah reminds the people of the way in which God has cared for them over the centuries. He looks for a response. This leads to the famous words: 'With what shall I come before the Lord . . . Shall I come before him with burnt offerings, with calves a year old? Will the Lord be pleased with thousands of rams . . . He has showed you, O man, what is good; and what does the Lord require of you but to do justice and to love kindness and to walk humbly with your God!' (6:6–8).

This declaration forms one of the finest statements of a pure spiritual religion and way of life in all literature. It is succinct and powerful, another case of a prophet rising above ritual and nationalism to understand the real meaning of loving God and loving your neighbour, the two commandments of which Jesus spoke.

In Chapter 7 he returns to warn the Israelites of all the tribes, especially highlighting the breakdown of the family in 7:6. He finishes on a note of praise to God and hope for the future: 'Who is a God like you, pardoning iniquity [incidentally, Micah means 'Who is like God'] and passing over transgression; he does not retain his anger forever, because he delights in unfailing love. He will again have compassion on us; he will tread our iniquities under foot. You will cast all our sins into the depths of the sea. You will show faithfulness to Jacob and steadfast love to Abraham as you have sworn to our fathers from the days of old.'

Nahum on the Fall of Nineveh

Eventually, despite Jonah's unwilling work, Assyria's capital Nineveh falls to Babylon and this leads to the Babylonian invasion of Judah and the series of deportations of the Jews to Babylon. Nineveh falls in 612 BC and Nahum in his prophecy rejoices at its approaching destruction. It is understandable, even if it does not rise to loving your enemies. The Assyrians were particularly cruel conquerors compared with the Babylonians and the Persians. Every time the Assyrians did any conquering they left behind 'mounds of heads, impaled bodies, enslaved citizens and avaricious looters'.

There is some restraint in Nahum's anger. He asserts that God is a just governor of the world, so he presents God as the great avenger, but also as slow to anger. When he is angry it is blazing anger, but he also offers refuge in the day of distress. He promises that ultimately heralds will bring glad tidings to Zion (as in Isaiah 40 and 52). The second half of the short prophecy of Nahum details the impending fall of Nineveh.

The military descriptions are vivid. You can almost hear the shouting and yelling of the warriors and the massacred people, and feel the roaring of fire as the city burns. When I was about eight years old my father showed me part of the wall of Nineveh in the British Museum. You could still see the marks of fire on it. It made it very real.

A Prophet's Dialogue With God

One of the features that repeatedly comes out in the Old Testament is that we can have a false sense of God as totally unapproachable, although he is reported to have allowed Job, Jeremiah and various Psalm writers and prophets to argue with him. He is presented as wanting them to understand him intelligently. Habakkuk is another example.

Habakkuk was prophesying prior to the Babylonian capture of Jerusalem. He presents a dialogue with God, where he is asking God to explain himself. He actually questions the ways of God and calls Him to account for his government of the world.

Habakkuk starts by complaining of the behaviour of the Jews: violence, strife, law-breaking, injustice. What is God going to do about it?

God replies that he is going to send the Chaldeans – as the Babylonians and Assyrians were also known geographically – to punish the Jews.

But the prophet says that is even worse. The Chaldeans are appallingly cruel and never satisfied. Habakkuk tells God he can't do that, and watches to see what will happen.

God replies that he will punish both the Jews and the

Chaldeans, but the just shall live by faith or 'he who by faith is righteous shall live'. As the prophet continues his denunciation of the sins of both the Chaldeans and the Jews, one can assume that the faithful and righteous people need not only be Jews. This is the use made of this passage by the apostle Paul in the New Testament in his letter to the Romans. Faith in God, not nationality or mere legal righteousness, is what pleases God.

Habakkuk finally writes a splendid Psalm reviewing all the great achievements of God during the history of Israel. It sees him. ultimately repeating them to perfection. Meanwhile the prophet accepts that there's going to be great trouble for Judah, which he will share, but he shows himself a man of faith in the final lines:

> Though the fig tree does not blossom, nor fruit be on the vines, the produce of the olive fail and the fields yield no food, the flock be cut off from the fold and there be no herd in the stalls, yet will I rejoice in the Lord, I will joy in the God of my salvation.

However great the disasters to come, he will stick firm in his faith in God, who will ultimately bring everything to a good end.

Zephaniah and the Day of the Lord

Zephaniah prophesied in the reign of Josiah, the reforming young king of Judah (640–609 BC). He was probably working just before Jeremiah started his mission.

He protests against the worship of false gods and the introduction into the court by the pro-Assyrian party of foreign ways, when Josiah was not old enough to reign for himself. This locates Zephaniah in the early part of Josiah's reign. His speech in the first chapter is very forthright, full of threats of what is going to happen to the false leaders. It provides the text of the Christian hymn found in classic requiems and known as Dies Irae.

Then Zephaniah broadens out to describe the threat of the Chaldeans to all the nations of the area and how Nineveh itself will finally fall.

In the third chapter he further rebukes all the leaders, priests, princes, judges and prophets in Judah, but finishes on a note of hope that in the end a remnant of the people will return to God and to honesty and to joy. God will appear as their saviour and God will renew them in his love. He will bring them home. This would materialise geographically but as interpreted in New Testament terms it would be a matter of coming to God in spirit. Many of these rather tedious prophecies were adapted in the New Testament and made part of the gospel of Christ preached by the Apostles.

Few of the books of the minor prophets would fall at the top of my personal reading list, apart from Jonah. Gems are tucked away in all of them, and they form part of the ongoing story of Israel leading to the New Testament. Micah 6 perhaps has the most beautiful expression of what belief in God means in action.

21

The Prophets of the Return
Haggai, Zechariah and Malachi

A generation or two after the deportation into Babylon, King Cyrus of Persia allowed Judah to return and build the temple, giving back the temple vessels that had been stolen. Zerubbabel and Joshua led the rebuilding of the temple and later Ezra and Nehemiah consolidated the situation.

Rise and Build

Some eighteen years after the return very little progress had been made with the construction of the temple, largely because of the interference of the Samaritans and other neighbours, who at one stage even persuaded the king of Persia to forbid the Jews to proceed, though this had not stopped them building their own houses. Into this situation comes the prophet Haggai.

He points out that Judah is experiencing economic difficulties because it has not been putting God and his temple first.

The temple is a shambles while they 'busy themselves in their houses'.

'You have sown much, but reaped little, you eat but never have enough to satisfy, you drink but never have enough to cheer you, you are clothed but never warm, and he who earns wages puts them into a bag with holes in it.' That last phrase is a wonderful description of the effects of inflation. 'Is it time for you to live in your well-roofed houses, while this house (the temple) lies in ruins?' Haggai urges the people into the hills to collect wood and other materials needed for the building of the temple. Joshua the high priest, Zerubbabel the governor and all the people are stirred by the words of the prophet and they set to work on the building.

Some of the people are demotivated, comparing the temple they are building with the glory of the one that was destroyed by the Babylonians. Haggai encourages them to take heart, because God's house will be filled with glory and in the end all the nations will bring their treasures into it. The temple will be better than the previous one and the land and city will be filled with prosperity and peace. According to the New Testament this wealth is not material, but that of a spiritual temple composed of people who were part of the Church of Christ. The Old and New Testament become interlinked, whether you feel convinced by the connections or not. Handel's *Messiah* uses this passage in the spiritual sense.

Haggai continues by strengthening the resolve of the leaders not to allow foreigners to contaminate the worship for which the temple was being built, then promises that now they have started to put first things first, God will bless them 'from this day forward'.

The prophecy concludes by supporting the authority of Zerubbabel of the royal dynasty of David, though he had not taken the throne. Nevertheless God thought of him very highly, and pays him the very high compliment that he will wear Zerubbabel as a signet ring on his hand. None of the enemies will be able to frustrate his efforts.

The Apocalyptic Visions of Zechariah

Contemporary with Haggai, the prophet Zechariah joins his voice in encouraging the people with a series of mysterious visions associated in many challenging ways with the business of worship in a temple and the problems encountered from enemies. Because some of the messages are coded, the people who hear them are fascinated with cracking the code. Many of them could do this as the code was based in earlier scripture. They were also accustomed to the apocalyptic genre of literature, with its poetic mysteries.

Zechariah begins by pointing out that problems began with the misbehaviour of the previous generations of the Jews, who failed to heed the warnings of the prophets. He then moves on to encouragement. The apocalyptic visions are summarised here.

An angel is seen in a woodland of myrtle trees, talking to a man on a bay horse and accompanied by other horses of various colours. They are described as a patrol that has been going through the earth to report on the state of things to God. They have found the whole world to be at peace and quiet, perhaps because of Persian rule and perhaps also as an expectation of an ultimate situation for the world.

The angel then assumes the task of a surveyor and puts a measuring line over Jerusalem in readiness for building the temple; this gives a sense that God will help the builders and bring comfort to Zion.

In the next vision, four blacksmiths are armed with horns

such as those belonging to a fierce bull to defeat the powers hostile to the Jews.

Another surveyor measures the city to indicate its growth in population and therefore size. The rest of the people still in Babylon are invited to return; they will be safe because God will be like a wall of fire encircling them. 'Sing and rejoice oh daughter of Zion. See. I am coming to dwell among you.'

Joshua the priest is standing in dirty garments following an argument with Satan (which means the Adversary). The clothes are removed and clean priestly robes are put on Joshua, along with a fresh mitre. This is said to also represent the removal of guilt. Joshua and his associates are described as men of sign or of good omen as they stand before an altar containing seven eyes representing the fact that God is all-seeing.

A great mountain in front of Zerubbabel is levelled and becomes a plain. The neighbouring nations who have despised 'the day of small things', as they and some Jews described the activities of temple-building, are defeated. The mountain of difficulty becomes a little molehill. The victory comes not by the strength of man, but by the spirit of God.

The seven-branched lampstand of the temple is seen next. There is an unusual feature. Oil is provided direct from two olive trees piped into the lamp, and just as the olive trees provide the service to the temple, so do Joshua and Zerubbabel serve the nation in its worship. They are two anointed ones, standing by God.

Next a scroll is flying through the air, bearing a curse upon the enemies over whose territory it is flying.

The scroll is followed by a flying barrel containing a woman called 'Wickedness', who is imprisoned by a leaden lid. Two other women with stork's wings pick up the barrel and transport the woman to Babylon. Her wickedness is not wanted in Jerusalem, so they export it to the land of their former captivity.

Another chariot scene follows, where the patrol of horses and chariots reviews the earth to quieten it and to quieten God's spirit. These four horsemen are the basis of the four horsemen of the apocalypse in the Book of Revelation.

A coronation scene sees Zerubbabel crowned. Although a member of the royal family of David, he never occupied the throne, but in principle he is seen as if he were a king. This supports his authority in the eyes of Jews and Joshua is also seen as happy with the arrangement. (The Hebrew text says Joshua is crowned, but it is considered by many scholars to be a miscopying, as a priest would not have a king's coronation.)

By Chapter 7 most of the apocalyptic visions are completed, though another one in Chapter 11 sees the prophet become a shepherd to the Jewish flock. He takes two staves and makes one out of them, to symbolise the rejoining of the ten tribes and the two tribes, of Israel and Judah as one state again.

Chapter 7 presents a text similar to Isaiah 58, where God describes the kind of fast he wants, where people will abstain from treating the poor unjustly and show kindness and compassion to each other.

There is a picture of an ideal future Jerusalem, when boys and girls play in the streets of the city watched over by very old people. At the time of the prophecy, there was a shortage of the very young and the very old in the city, but that would change. The blessings of that time of the full and true return from exile are described: agricultural richness, brotherly harmony, cheerful festivals which other nations would wish to join in. These pictures were seen as long-term pictures of the age of the Messiah, but they gave a sense of destiny and hope, even in the present. They were reinterpreted in the New Testament with Jesus at their heart.

After words against the surrounding enemies, Chapter 9 has a messianic message about the king who shall ride humbly into Jerusalem on an ass. Jesus deliberately fulfilled this prophecy when he entered Jerusalem in the week before his crucifixion. Here and in the following chapter a new order is described for Israel, when they shall be restored.

Chapter 12 has further pictures of Israel victorious, which Jesus demilitarised and made into spiritual victory through the apparent weakness of self-sacrifice. An interesting verse speaks of the Jews mourning over someone whom they had pierced. John 19:37 and Revelation 1:7 apply this to Jesus.

A fountain is opened in Jerusalem to cleanse people from their sin. They will have to experience more discipline before they will be ready for it (Chapter 13). The last chapter describes a final war that subjugates the nations and brings them to the state where they come up to Jerusalem every year to keep the feast of booths (tents or tabernacles). Though it sounds a matter of military compulsion, the New Testament spiritualises such pictures and turns it into the voluntary compulsion of love.

The Messenger of the Covenant

The last book of the Old Testament is by Malachi, whose name means 'my messenger', which may have been his pen name. He is probably on the scene at about 455 BC, during the time of Nehemiah's efforts. Things have started to go downhill again, and he has some pretty tough things to say. It is possible that he prepared the ground for the reforms of Ezra and Nehemiah.

He rebukes the leaders for bringing as sacrifices animals that were no good anyway, blind and lame. The leaders also have an avaricious approach, where they won't act as doorkeepers in the temple for free. One day there will be pure offerings all over the world, which the Church has sometimes interpreted as the Eucharist, commemorating the sacrifice by Jesus of his very life.

The second chapter continues to regret the failure in duty by the priestly tribe of Levi, who were not providing good leadership or clear instruction. They are told that there is little point in making a great show of weeping at the altar, if their heart is not true.

The last chapter is usually considered to have messianic overtones, foretelling the work of Christ. 'The Lord whom you seek shall suddenly come to his temple . . . Who can abide the day of his coming?' 'He shall purify the sons of Levi' is taken by the writers of the Gospels as being most fully fulfilled by the ministry of Jesus against the background of John the Baptist. Handel's *Messiah* set these sentences to great music. The New Testament regards the return of Elijah right at the end of the book as a reference to John the Baptist who came ' in the spirit and power of Elijah'.

Malachi has not had the benefit of the teaching of Jesus and so looks forward to treading the wicked under his feet like an ash footpath. I once wrote in the margin of my Bible: 'I don't want to; Jesus has taught me otherwise.'

After further rebuke for inattention to proper worship the prophet sees the immediate future as lying in the hands of groups of people who would meet together to strengthen each other's faith:

Then they feared the Lord spoke often with one
another; the Lord heeded and heard them and a book of

remembrance was written before him of those who feared the Lord and thought upon his name. And they shall be mine when I make up my jewels [King James Version] . . . And on them shall the Sun of Righteousness arise with healing in its beams.

22

A Bridge Between the Testaments

In Chapter 1 I described the Bible as two libraries connected by a door, the Old and New Testaments linked by Jesus Christ, who leads from the one to the other. Here I use a different metaphor, describing him as a bridge spanning the gulf of time from one epoch to another.

The Essential Themes of the Old Testament

Before studying the New Testament it will be helpful to remind ourselves of the essential themes of the Old Testament. What was the basis of the national and spiritual life that provided the background of the ministry of Jesus? What were the expectations of the Jewish people standing at the New Testament end of the bridge? Did Jesus fulfil those expectations, and if so, how?

The Creator God

The great themes of the Old Testament begin with God as creator. The whole universe is considered as owing its origin to the God of Israel. He is the only true God. While some kind of grudging existence is sometimes allowed to other gods, they are powerless. The picture of them with which Jesus would have grown up was that they were non-existent imaginations of the human mind. 'Hear, oh Israel, the Lord our God is one God' was fundamental to Israel's religion. He was the only God, an integrated being fully self-consistent, covering the whole of existence; different gods were not required to attend to different aspects of life and its environment. And God asked for total allegiance from people.

Sin

People withheld this total allegiance, so the Old Testament is concerned with the theme of sin from the beginning of the Book of Genesis. Sin, very simply, is defined as doing what God has forbidden or not doing what he has requested. This requires clarification. It is not a matter only of obeying or disobeying external rules and regulations, of offering animal sacrifices and carrying out temple ritual, but is a matter of the heart and of attitude. This was as true under the Old Testament as under the New Testament, and was greatly emphasised by the prophets. The Old Testament contained many more external rules, and hence greater scope for mere compliance. This is very relevant to the teaching of Jesus.

Punishment

Associated with sin is the question of punishment. The Old Testament presents a number of problems. Punishment tended to be collective and often covered several generations after the original sins ('to the third and fourth generation of those who hate me' Exodus 20:5), with whole families involved in the punishment of one of its members. We have seen that this was hardly the will of God, but how it was interpreted.

On the other hand, we have also seen how the prophet Ezekiel declared that individuals would be punished for their own sins, not for the sins of others. This view of rewards and punishments was somewhat simplistic, as the Book of Job suggests. Not only bad people suffer; good ones do too. The Book of Isaiah has a picture of a suffering servant who suffers for the sake of others, fulfilled in Jesus, according to the New Testament.

Forgiveness

Also related to the question of sin is the matter of forgiveness, which is prominent in the Old Testament. God declares his name or character to Moses, 'Yahweh, Yahweh, a God compassionate and gracious, long-suffering, ever faithful and true, forgiving iniquity, rebellion and sin, but without acquitting the guilty.' Less mercifully, the writer understood God to go on to declare that he will punish 'children and grandchildren to the third and fourth generation for the iniquity of their fathers'. The main statement, however, describes a God far more prone to forgiveness than the pagan gods. There are many examples of such forgiveness in the Old Testament, another element providing the basis of the teaching of Jesus. Such forgiveness was offered to those of humble hearts, not to those who offered the most animal sacrifices.

Another problem was that the concept of justice underlying the idea of punishment led to the view that Israel's enemies were to be punished with little mercy. In many cases it was seen as the will of God that they should be ruthlessly destroyed. This was something that Jesus changed when he told his followers to love their enemies.

One of the most frequently used Hebrew words to describe

the characteristics of God is 'chesed'. It is variously translated as 'loving kindness', 'covenant love', 'mercy', 'steadfast love' or simply 'love'. This bridging concept leads us to the life and teaching of Jesus.

The Chosen People

Another important Old Testament concept is described theologically as 'election'. This simply means 'choice'. It refers to the fact that the Bible speaks of God as choosing Israel, who thus became known as the chosen people. The prophets often complain that the people of Israel assumed that they were God's chosen people because they were in some way superior to other nations. The Book of Deuteronomy makes it quite clear that Israel was chosen for a mission to be a light and an example to all nations, who would admire the wisdom and understanding of Israel and want to share in it (4:6–8). The insular attitudes often displayed by Israel were a negation of this responsibility. Jesus took it on himself.

The promises made by God to Abraham lay at the root of this duty. God promised to Abraham that in his descendants all nations of the earth would be blessed. These promises were repeated to Isaac and Jacob and much of the teaching of the prophets is rooted in them.

A Good Time Coming

This leads us to the other major theme of the Old Testament of a good time coming, when God would be king over Israel and all the earth, through a representative who would reign on the throne of David and be triumphant for God over all his enemies. He would be God's anointed king. The Hebrew word for anointed is the basis of the term 'Messiah'; the Greek word for anointed is the basis of the title 'Christ'.

Whenever Israel encountered troubles there was always an upsurge of hope that these promises would soon be fulfilled. Things could not always be so full of disaster. God would intervene. When Jesus appeared, it was a time of oppression for the Jews under the Romans. It was not the worst they had known, but there was no sign of independence and God's promises were slow in coming to fulfilment.

We have looked at many of the forms this hope developed in our consideration of the Old Testament, particularly of the prophets. The book named after the prophet Isaiah is particularly rich in pictures of the future prosperity of Israel and, through them, of the whole of humanity. Jeremiah and Ezekiel spoke of a day when God would give Israel a new heart. Pictures are given in Isaiah and Micah of all nations going up to Jerusalem to worship the Lord of Hosts. The Psalms also have many graphic pictures of the day when a king should 'reign in righteousness', and there should 'be a handful of corn in the tops of the mountains' and the ends of the earth should respond to God.

How the Kingdom of God was Interpreted

Mixed up with these pictures of peace and prosperity are images of ruthless warfare thought necessary to defeat the enemies of God and of Israel before the Kingdom of God. The acceptance of God's reign by the world was to be a matter of compulsion and submission by fear, though ultimately it would be accepted with gratitude.

There are many factors in the Old Testament expectations of the kingdom that differ from those of Jesus in the New Testament.

The Jewish contemporaries of Jesus interpreted the Old Testament in a highly political way, as a matter of regaining the independence they had enjoyed in the time of King David. It was based on victory over enemies in some of the fiercest battles of history, in which the slain of the Lord would lie from one end of the earth to the other and 'the Lord himself will come from afar, his anger blazing and his tongue like a devouring fire' (Isaiah 30:27). The Jews to whom Jesus came had fed upon such passages and were ready to lift up their swords to defeat the hated Romans. They awaited a Messiah who would proclaim rebellion and lead them into battle.

This expectation was strengthened by the fact that some 200 years before Christ there had been a successful revolt by the Maccabees. This had led to the formation of an independent state of sorts, with a tremendous upsurge of patriotism and military courage. The Herods were in some ways the successors of this state, though absolutely subject to the Romans. The story of the Maccabee revolt was ever fresh in Jewish minds and influenced their interpretation of the hopes of the Old Testament. It is still remembered in one of the Jewish feasts, called in the Gospels the Feast of Dedication.

The Hope of Israel

When Jesus began his ministry, the end of the present world order was felt to be imminent; the fortunes of suffering Israel were about to be restored. The temple and its worship was to be revived in its former glory as the centre of worship and praise. The law (or Torah, as the Jews call the main part of it) was to be re-established as the basis of national life. The long night of Israel's misery and suffering would be over. A new day would dawn and Israel's God would reign over all nations. There would be a second exodus from the captivity of centuries; liberation from all kinds of slavery would come to Israel. The enemies would be bludgeoned into submission and Israel vindicated. Wrongs would be put right; justice would be brought to those thirsting for it. The exile would be emphatically over.

Jesus Redefines the Hope of Israel

To people with such expectations Jesus came and proclaimed, 'The time is fulfilled, and the kingdom of God is at hand; repent and believe in the gospel [or good news]' (1 Mark:16–17). He redefined the whole meaning of Old Testament expectations. It must have been bewildering for those reared on a literal expectation of the fulfilment of the Old Testament hopes. Considering Jesus's reinterpretation, the Old Testament forms a significant part of our study of the New Testament.

At the same time, many of the dominant themes of the Old Testament re-emerge newly clothed in the teaching of Jesus. Sin and punishment, forgiveness and election, love and mercy, the sovereignty of God, sacrifice and service are all dealt with in the New Testament. There is considerable reformulation, but the original themes are not discarded. To understand the Christian reshaping we must pay attention to the Old Testament. Change there is, but a totally negative attitude to the Old Testament would rob us of much enlightenment.

And so now we approach the New Testament. As with the Old Testament, my purpose will not be to tell you how to use it. That is your decision. I shall try to provide a guidebook to help you make some sense of it. As I said earlier, you must have your own sense. You must possess your own understanding.

23

Three Connected Gospels
Matthew, Mark and Luke

What is a Gospel?

In the sixteenth century, William Tyndale translated the Bible into English and began to distribute it so that people could read it for themselves. His efforts led to his execution as a heretic by the Church authorities in 1536, because of his Protestant views. Tyndale left us the following definition:

> Gospel is a Greek word and signifies good, merry, glad and joyful tidings, that makes a man's heart glad and makes him sing, dance and leap for joy.

The good news that produces such happiness is about Jesus, how he lived, his teachings, his good deeds, as well as his tragic death, which the writers were convinced was not the end of the story. They continued with the account of his being raised from the dead and coming into their lives with his spirit.

Our bibles present Matthew, Mark, Luke and John as the

authors of these Gospels. Scholars have produced many theories about the way in which the stories were written and assembled. We are not going to examine them here, but shall simply read the Gospels on their own terms and seek the essentials of what they were saying. We can then decide for ourselves if there are any personal actions we should take in response to them. This might involve us in deeper study, but the essence of the message has never had any difficulty in communicating itself and making people – men and women, children and grandparents – 'sing, dance and leap for joy'.

The Synoptics

We shall start by concentrating on the first three Gospels: Matthew, Mark and Luke. These are called the 'Synoptics', because they cover largely the same material and a synopsis or summary of their content can be placed side by side in three columns. This shows that, of the 661 verses in Mark, 606 of them appear in very similar terms in Matthew and over 300 in Luke. In contrast, John's Gospel has a somewhat different character, as we shall see.

It is generally agreed that Mark's Gospel was the earliest to be written and was used by Matthew and Luke as a basis for their own compilations of the story of Jesus. They also have a further 200 virtually identical verses, which are assumed to have come from a common source, an earlier document, usually called 'Q' for '*Quelle*', the German word for 'source'. No one has ever seen 'Q', but it is reasonable to assume it existed. 'Q' and Mark would also have drawn on a number of other writings that circulated among the churches as people tried to preserve the memory of Jesus.

The standard of agreement is high, though, as one might

expect, there are minor variations. The culture of the time and region encouraged people to have good, almost photographic memories. A growing number of scholars believe that the written compilations may well have been completed within about thirty years of the ministry of Jesus (roughly the interval of time since man first landed on the moon, as I write in 1998).

Differences of Emphasis

If so much of the material is common to Matthew, Mark and Luke, why did the early Church feel a need for all three of these Gospels? The answer is that, despite the similarities, each Gospel possesses a special slant and unique material.

Matthew has a Jewish emphasis; he stresses Jesus as the promised Messiah of Israel, though in unexpected ways and with a widening of the definition of Israel. The relationship of the teaching of Jesus to the Jewish law is given plenty of attention and the resulting conflict is described in some detail.

Mark is crisp and action-oriented. Things are always happening 'immediately' or 'straightaway' and the record of teaching is less extended. He places an emphasis on Jesus as the servant king.

Luke has an emphasis on the concern of Jesus for non-Jewish people, the poor, the sick, the despised, the sinful and the so-called dregs of society. He stresses the humble circumstances of the birth of Jesus and introduces the shepherds and the stable into the nativity. He traces the ancestry of Jesus back to Adam, the father of the human race, whereas Matthew traces it back to Abraham, the father of the Jewish race.

Although John's Gospel is the subject of separate treatment, suffice to say now that it contains more of the action going on in Jerusalem. He also emphasises Jesus as the Son and manifestation of God in truly human form. A strong case was made by the late John Robinson, formerly Bishop of Woolwich, for an early dating of John's Gospel. It mentions some of the same events as the Synoptics, but there is significantly less common material.

Putting the Synoptics Together

From this brief summary of the angles of approach adopted by the four Gospel writers it will be apparent that none of them presents a straight biography of Jesus. The accounts have to be collated to arrive at a reasonably clear sequence of events, but even then what is obtained is more like a picture gallery that covers the main happenings but leaves scope for imagination as to what precisely linked them.

There is also possibly some combining of material, such as in the Sermon on the Mount in Matthew 5–7, which does not read like a single speech, and, like any preacher or public speaker, Jesus presumably repeated his ideas with minor variations on different occasions. We don't need a legal document, with everything dated and witnessed by a lawyer or notary, rather than a vivid series of paintings which take us into the presence of Jesus and give us a sense of his overall mission.

We need to come into his presence and allow ourselves to be influenced in a variety of ways. It is not my job to provide rules about this influence. The extent and nature of it will depend on each individual, though there is no doubt that anyone who stays in the presence of Jesus for any period of time and who seriously looks and listens will experience changes in thoughts and perceptions about life.

With Matthew and Luke using so much of Mark and then also drawing on other material from 'Q', we shall not undertake a separate examination of each Gospel. This would be very repetitive, cluttering up these pages in such a way as to obscure the significant differences between the Synoptic Gospels. I will therefore discuss the common material and bring out their key differences and unique aspects. I still think that it is worth reading the Gospels individually to capture their individual emphases. The story is so great that it is worth reading a number of times, and the variations make it easy to do this without getting bored.

24

The Ministry of Jesus in Galilee

Matthew

Chapter 24 will concentrate on Matthew's Gospel, but will from time to time refer to the other two Synoptics to avoid repetition. We shall proceed to the point where Matthew describes Peter's confession that Jesus is the Christ, the Son of the living God, then in Chapter 25 we shall follow Matthew, Mark and Luke to the point where Jesus is about to enter his last days before the crucifixion. In Chapter 26 we shall also highlight any special contributions of Mark and Luke to the whole story, before Chapter 27 goes on to examine all four records of the Last Supper, trial, death and resurrection of Jesus. Before we leave the Gospels, the unique Gospel of John will finally require a chapter or two because of its different coverage and its special content on the humanity and divinity of Jesus.

The Family Tree

A writer usually starts a book by trying to arouse the interest of the reader. Matthew starts with a very unpromising family tree or genealogical table:

Abraham was the father of Isaac, and Isaac the father of Jacob, and Jacob the father of Judah . . . and Judah was the father of Perez . . . Perez . . . Hezron . . . Hezron . . . Ram . . .

And it continues with a total of over forty names. Hardly the way to start a bestseller. But then if we start to look at this list in some detail and check the names against the stories in the Old Testament, we begin to get the point. Jesus is being linked with the Patriarchs of Israel, Abraham, Isaac and Jacob; then he is linked with King David and the dynasty of Kings and Chronicles in the Old Testament. Zerubbabel of fame in the return from exile in Babylon is there, as well as women of mixed repute, such as Tamar who had a child by her father-in-law, Rahab the prostitute who helped the Jewish spies at Jericho, Ruth the foreigner and Bathsheba with whom David committed adultery. Side by side with the emphasis on a royal connection, Matthew is picking out the more dubious connections in the ancestry of Jesus, though any culpability resided with the men involved more than the women.

The Birth of the Saviour from Sin

This list in Matthew leads to 'Joseph, the husband of Mary of whom Jesus was born, who is called Christ'. Since Christ means 'Messiah' or 'anointed', we could almost translate Jesus Christ as King Jesus, as Canon Tom Wright suggests.

Then the circumstances of the birth of Jesus are briefly described. His conception is attributed to the direct power of God, not human activity. Luke has a similar presentation, but nowhere else is the virgin birth or conception mentioned in the New Testament and certainly no theological or doctrinal structure is built upon it. It doesn't seem likely that it was being suggested that the presence of God in Jesus was dependent on biological action or genetic transfer, but the story invests the birth of Jesus with a sense of divine initiative; this particular birth is portrayed as unique and singled out as one upon which much depended.

The name 'Jesus' is explained as indicating that 'he shall save his people from their sins'. Jesus is the Old Testament name Joshua or 'Yahshua' – Yahweh saves.

Jesus Fulfils the Old Testament

Matthew then quotes Isaiah 7 in its Greek version, which speaks of a virgin conceiving (the original Hebrew speaks just of a young woman). This is the first of a number of passages where Matthew quotes from the Old Testament in what at first sight seems a rather forced way, though examination of the original Old Testament reference reveals the idea of a birth of a prince associated with a deliverance in the times of Isaiah. In effect Matthew is saying that the earlier prince was only a half-filment, but Jesus is a full-filment. The earlier prince was a token that God was with Israel, but Jesus is presented as the perfect – complete – 'God with us' (Emmanuel or Immanuel).

'This was to fulfil' or similar words appear elsewhere in Matthew: 2:6,15,18,23; 4:15; 8:17; 12:18–21; 13:35; 21:5; and 17:9. These all create the link between the role of Jesus as the King of the Jews with the expectations in the Old Testament, although fulfilled in a wider way.

Matthew 2:15 uses a passage from Hosea to describe Jesus fleeing into Egypt, whereas the original passage in Hosea talking of Israel as God's son leaving Pharaoh's Egypt. So Matthew is hinting at Jesus being the embodiment of Israel as God's son,

Israel in one person. Matthew 2:5 also quotes Micah to convey the idea of Bethlehem as the lowly place where, as the hymn says, all the hopes and fears of mankind are met. Later on in 21:5 the description in Zechariah's prophecy of the arrival of the king on a donkey is applied to the entry of Jesus into Jerusalem a few days before his death.

Fulfilment at the Deepest Level

Matthew often uses an Old Testament passage as a peg on which to hang a wider fulfilment involving the whole work of Jesus. He is not just quoting proof texts, though many Jews who were used to such artificial procedures would have been impressed at even that level, irrespective of original context. The respected scholar Professor C.F.D. Moule considers that these fulfilment formulae of Matthew use scripture as the vehicle for expressing the conviction of Christians that Jesus Christ was the supreme fulfiller. But he believes it goes beyond that. Matthew and the other writers and apostles had discovered in Jesus the fulfiller of something that is basic in the whole of the Old Testament; in Jesus there was an overall fulfilment at the deepest level of what Old Testament scripture as a whole reflected. 'Jesus in an extraordinary way turned out to be occupying the position that, according to the Scriptures, had always been intended for Israel, and through Israel for all mankind. Jesus was indeed the fulfilment of Scripture because he was the fulfilment of man-in-relation-to-God.'

I have thought it important to alert the reader to this use of the Old Testament in the New by which the writers will continually aim to show Jesus as the comprehensive fulfilment of all that God has been working at throughout history. Matthew is an outstanding exponent of the approach.

The Mission of John the Baptist

Matthew 3 (and the parallel chapters in Mark and Luke) tell of the baptism of Jesus at the hand of John the Baptist. The baptism by John was a token of people repenting – which means 'turning in a different direction' – and as a result their sins were forgiven. All three Synoptics apply Isaiah 40 to John as the 'voice crying in the wilderness' to prepare the way of the Lord. In Isaiah these words are connected with the return from the exile in Babylon, and on John's lips they refer to an imminent return from a long-lasting spiritual exile from God, which God's chosen one would bring about.

John's preaching was quite tough, like his rugged appearance and clothing and his diet of wild locusts and honey. He called the leaders vipers, telling them not to rely on their descent from Abraham and warning of judgement to come on Israel. God could create new children for Abraham (a hint of the Gentiles in the Christian Church later on). Luke also reports John's teaching that people should share their good fortune with the poor; tax collectors should not cheat and soldiers should not bully. John the Baptist also said that the Kingdom of God was near and that he himself was only the forerunner or herald of someone greater than he who would baptise with the Holy Spirit and not just with water.

When Jesus came to be baptised John, according to Matthew, felt it unnecessary. And we can understand that. What sins had Jesus to confess? However Jesus felt it was an essential part of the righteousness he came to bring to the human race. He needed to identify himself totally with the people he had to save. It was a symbol of his mission to carry their sins and blot them out. Then the records tell us of the voice from heaven as he came up out of the water: 'This is my beloved Son, with whom I am well pleased.' This is a combining of two Old Testament passages, from Psalms 2 and Isaiah 42. A dove also is said to have descended upon Jesus as a symbol of the Holy Spirit.

The Temptation in the Wilderness

The next episode recorded by all three of the evangelists is the departure of Jesus into the desert for forty days to be tempted – by the devil, according to Matthew and Luke, by Satan according to Mark. Christians differ about the precise meaning of these terms. Satan means 'adversary' and devil means 'false accuser'. Many believe that they are a personification of the forces of evil with which Jesus, as a member of the human race, had to fight, like the rest of us, rather than a real entity.

For Jesus the testing is very strong. He has to sort out the way in which he will carry out his mission, rejecting the purely human approaches and following the way God had laid down for him. There are three main temptations:

- He can use divine power to feed not only himself but those he could influence by looking after their material needs. He can be a bread king.
- He can work sensational signs that, without any spiritual change in themselves, would force people to accept him as marked out as from God.
- He can use political methods to manipulate people into accepting his kingship.

He rejected all three approaches and was, in effect, thereafter walking on the road to the cross. His period of reflection enabled him to redefine how the kingdom of God would be established in a way quite different from popular military and political expectations.

The Public Mission Begins

His public mission starts in Galilee, in northern Israel. As Matthew says: 'From that time Jesus began to preach, saying "Repent for the kingdom of heaven is at hand."' Matthew tends to follow the Jewish custom of avoiding the use of God's name, speaking of 'heaven' instead. Mark 1:14–15 says: 'Jesus came into Galilee preaching the gospel of God and saying "The time is fulfilled and the Kingdom of God is at hand; repent and believe in the gospel."' He is proclaiming that the prophets' words are now about to happen and Israel's hopes are to be fulfilled. Little did most of his listeners realise how different in action this would be from their expectations (see Chapter 22 of this book).

Around the same time Jesus calls Peter, James and John to join him as 'fishers of men' (or of 'people' in some translations) and he accompanies his preaching by healing the sick, thus fulfilling some of the Old Testament prophecies, such as Isaiah 35. He begins to display God's power.

The Sermon on the Mount

Although the Sermon on the Mount may be a compilation of many teaching sessions by Jesus, it is presented as one discourse and we shall treat it that way. He would no doubt, like any teacher, say similar things a number of times. The intended audience was his disciples, but the end of Chapter 7 tells us that the crowds were also there, being amazed at what he said.

The Sermon on the Mount is specifically rooted in the Jewish context and in particular in that time of living under the Roman occupation. It is not a generalised spiritual sermon about being nice to everyone, and in many ways it contradicts the expectations of the Jews of the time about the Kingdom of God. Of course its specific situation allows us to draw general principles that apply in any age.

The blessings or beatitudes with which he begins are themselves a description of the qualities of the sort of people who would be attracted by the Kingdom of God, and are the opposite of the features that would produce militant rebels against Rome. Blessed are the poor in spirit, the sorrowful, the gentle, those who hunger to see right prevail, the merciful, the pure in heart, the peacemakers, those who are persecuted for their loyalty to God. The disciples of Christ are to be what Israel should have been; the salt that prevents corruption; the light that banishes darkness. Jesus is going to gather the threads of the law of Moses and the teaching of the prophets of the Old Testament and, as Professor C.H. Dodd puts it, 'weave them into the new design. He undertook the task of liberating the treasure of Israel's faith for humanity.' And this meant interpreting the law at a higher level than the norms of the time and going beyond the outward show to the inner attitude.

Jesus moves from forbidding the outward action of killing to condemning the inward mood of anger; also, don't insist on your rights, but seek agreement with your enemy. He has much to say about how we should conduct ourselves in society today, and similarly he shows how sexual immorality starts in the mind well before any actions. Firm self-discipline is required. Divorce is not the ideal of God's intention for men and women. There is also a strong hint that men were not to treat women as their chattels. Absolute standards of truth are required. Yes should mean yes and no should mean no. There should be no revenge but an acceptance of the insults and demands of the Roman occupiers. In fact, love your enemies and seek to do them good. This was all very different teaching from that expected of a Jewish Messiah who was going to lead his people to victory over their enemies. A very different kind of victory!

He goes on to recommend the quiet fellowship with God in prayer, not public displays to secure the praise of the people around. In this connection he offers the Lord's prayer, as it has come to be known, with its emphasis on praying for the will of God to prevail everywhere and for forgiveness to be the very texture of human relationships.

Much of the spirit of rebellion is focused on material improvement. Jesus counsels the holding of material things with a light touch: not laying up treasure on earth, not being the slave of God and money (Mammon), not being anxious about how you will manage your practical affairs, but trusting in God who cares about you. 'Set your mind on the kingdom of God and his righteousness and all the rest will come to you as well.' Avoidance of criticism of others is emphasised, because we each have enough faults of our own. This rule alone would transform the world. Then he describes the spirit of asking God for your needs, but defining those needs in his terms. Do to others as you would want others to do to you, not as they do, but as you wish they did, thus creating a virtuous cycle of good. Warning is given not to be misled by false teachers who would deny the principles of his teaching and lead into the way of revolt and destruction.

The three chapters end with a call to build your house on a rock and not on the shifting sands of human expediency. The idea of a house on a rock is linked with the temple where God was believed to dwell. Jesus and his followers are the new temple of the new age of the Kingdom of God, now being established by his activity. Permanent principles are laid down by Jesus, and the power and the ability to apply them is greatly enhanced when we see how everything he said had an application in a kingdom based on love and trust in God, not on force and political rebellion against enemies.

Miracles of Healing and Challenges to Tradition

Matthew 8 and 9 (as well as parallel sections in Mark and Luke) give emphasis to the healing work of Jesus, displaying the love of God for suffering humanity. A leper is healed. Jesus touches him and would have been unclean, according to the law, but how could anyone say that when the touch cured the leper? Then a Roman centurion asks Jesus to heal his servant with a word, because he recognises his authority. In conveying the cure at a distance Jesus sees the centurion's faith as a foretaste of the entry of the Gentiles into the Kingdom of God, which would not be an exclusively Jewish affair.

Jesus heals Peter's mother-in-law of a fever. No convalescence is needed and she gets straight up and prepares a meal for them. Next he discourages superficial discipleship based on the enthusiasm of the moment without readiness for the hardship that can accompany devotion. Then there is the stilling of the storm, which can be quite rough on Galilee. He reproaches the disciples for their lack of faith. Arriving on the other side of a lake he cures two men possessed by demons, as certain kinds of insanity were described in those days. The madness is said to be transferred to some pigs. This threat to their livelihood caused the local people to ask Jesus to leave.

The next healing is of a paralysed man brought in on a stretcher. Instead of just curing him Jesus opens a challenge to some of the Jewish religious leaders by saying to the man: 'Your sins are forgiven.' This was a serious blasphemy in their eyes. Only God could forgive sins. Who does this man think he is? Then Jesus demonstrates that he has authority to forgive sins by telling the man to pick up his bed and walk – which he does!

Jesus wasn't a tactful person. He calls Matthew or Levi to join the disciples and Matthew leaves his tax collecting and sets up a feast for Jesus. All sorts of unsavoury people attend the party and the Pharisees object. Jesus witheringly points out that it is the sick who require a doctor, not the people, like them, who proclaim themselves as healthy. In this context Jesus points out that the 'wine' of the new covenant with which he was inaugurating the Kingdom of God needed new wineskins (people) to hold it. The old wineskins couldn't manage it – another knock at the Pharisees, many of whom were good people unable to overcome their prejudices.

We then have the resuscitation of the synagogue ruler's daughter, who had died, and the healing of the woman with a perpetual haemorrhage. In both cases Jesus's contact should have made him unclean according to the law. But no one could argue with the fact that with the touch of Jesus the uncleanness disappeared. Two blind men were given their sight in response to their faith in Jesus as the Messiah, the son of David.

The crowds responded to all this healing activity: 'Nothing like this has ever been seen in Israel!'

Scepticism About Miracles

A significant feature of the past 200 years has been scepticism about miracles. Obviously we need to be cautious and not accept every claim made by religious enthusiasts, but there is a tendency nowadays for people to be less ready to rule out miracles as impossible. As scientific knowledge has grown many people are less inclined to say that nature runs according to inviolable laws or that there are no higher principles that we don't yet understand. And if we believe in a God then it cannot be held impossible that he will from time to time step outside the norm as we see it. The power of the mind is recognised as considerable, and we are probably only beginning to understand it. The interest in alternative medicine and its acceptance by many conventional practitioners may also be relevant. It is not my job to tell people what to believe, but perhaps I can suggest that an open mind on the subject of miracles cannot be a bad thing.

The Commission of the Twelve Disciples

The end of Matthew 9 shows the spirit of the ministry of Jesus: 'The sight of the crowds moved him to pity; they were like sheep without a shepherd, harassed and helpless.' He invites his disciples to pray to God for reinforcements and then proceeds to choose twelve of them to be his apostles.

He sends them out with instructions for their ministry. Their message is that the Kingdom of Heaven is at hand and they are to support it with deeds of healing and even by raising the dead, concentrating on Israel and relying on the generosity of the local people for their accommodation and daily food. He also predicts that their ministry will bring them disapproval and suffering, but the Holy Spirit will help them with their defence, giving words to them in their need. Some of these troubles would arise in the future, when the apostles would proclaim the death and resurrection of Jesus. The current mission is part of their training for that day.

Jesus encourages them to stand firm because they are highly

valued by his Father in heaven. He also makes clear that in spite of what he has said about a blessing on the peacemakers, the effect of his teaching and theirs would be such that conflict would surround them, even within families. In this connection Jesus declares: 'He who does not take up his cross and follow me is not worthy of me.'

Reassurance for John the Baptist

About this time a message comes from John the Baptist, who wants to know whether Jesus is really the Messiah. Either John does this for the sake of his disciples, to help them understand that Jesus must supersede him, or as he languishes in prison he is going through a bout of depression. To help convince John and his disciples Jesus tells the messengers to report to John all the healing work he is doing and to describe the preaching of the gospel to the poor.

Jesus then positions John the Baptist for the benefit of his own disciples as the messenger of the last book of the Old Testament: Malachi. In a sense he is the Elijah who will return to prepare people's hearts to receive the Messiah. The positioning is summarised in the words: 'He that is least in the Kingdom of Heaven is greater than John.' John was the last of the Old Testament prophets. He saw only the beginning of the Kingdom of God that Jesus was establishing. The privilege of the disciples of Jesus was greater than that of John at that time. They were part of the new age, whereas John died before its inception.

Debates With the Leaders

Chapter 12 describes further encounters with the Jewish leaders, who complain about the disciples plucking grains of corn and eating them as they pass through the corn fields. They hold that this is work, and as such it breaches the sabbath. Jesus claims to be the Lord of the sabbath, and can provide the true interpretation of the sabbath.

Then they try to catch him out doing deeds of healing on the sabbath. Jesus points out that they would pull an animal to safety on the sabbath, so it was lawful to do good on the sabbath, particularly for humans, who were more valuable than animals. Such petty interpretations of God's will may amaze us, but there are still many people who treat their religion in this narrow way.

Jesus brilliantly supports his words with action. He simply says to the man with the withered hand who was the cause of the discussion: 'Stretch out your hand.' Surely it is not work to tell someone to stretch out his hand. The man did what previously he could not do. As Jesus did no work that could be checked, he defeated their scheme. You can imagine that the Jewish leaders were not exactly pleased.

From this point on, Matthew records the growing antagonism between Jewish religious leaders and Jesus, who replies in an increasingly outspoken manner, saying that the Kingdom of God is not going to come through these leaders and their unloving interpretation of the law. Jesus begins to do much of his work in less public places so that he can quietly fan the little flame of faith in those who followed him. Matthew quotes from Isaiah 42, which describes the servant of God as carrying out this patient unsensational work and bringing hope to Gentiles as well as Jews.

The Pharisees attribute his works of healing to the malign influence of the legendary prince of evil spirits, Beelzebul, but Jesus exposes the lack of logic in the idea of good works being carried out by an evil spirit and goes on to make one of his sharpest attacks. In making Beelzebul responsible for his exorcisms, they are blaspheming the Holy Spirit, an unforgiveable sin. The Father and the Son are in a sense external to the individual; the Holy Spirit is God at work within. To deny the Holy Spirit is to deny the inward self being created by God within. Spiritual abortion will follow.

He calls these leaders a brood of vipers, whose mouths express even in casual ways an inner evil treasured up in their hearts. The call for a sign was answered by the story of Jonah, the man who came back from virtual death and converted the Gentiles of Nineveh, who put the Pharisees to shame. The Pharisees had swept Israel of ritual and legal uncleanness, but left a vacuum in which worse sins could take root.

Speaking in Parables

At this period Jesus does much of his teaching in parables (Chapter 13). They are a kind of mental sieve to sort out people, those who are superficial from those who are ready to probe the spiritual depths. As he says, many listen and listen, but never understand, look and look, but never see.

The parables can be heard at several levels. Take the parable of the sower, with the varying harvests from the same sowing (Matthew 13:1–8). You can hear it at the personal level. The gospel of the Kingdom may be received superficially and not yield fruit, particularly when problems arise or when material things take over. Or it can be seen as the history of Israel since the time of the Babylonian exile, showing the limited response to the will of God. In both cases some people do respond and that is what Jesus and his disciples are working for. In the parable of the wheat and the weeds or darnel, Israel is a field of wheat and the weeds growing alongside will be rooted up in a day of judgement (such as the Romans brought in AD 70).

These parables also teach the disciples that they must not expect great and immediate results. From small beginnings the mighty Kingdom of God that he was establishing would grow, as illustrated by the parable of the grain of mustard seed and the woman putting leaven or yeast into a mixture to make a cake. Hidden treasure in a field, a pearl of great value, a net gathering different kinds of fish: all are symbols for different aspects of the Kingdom of God. And the disciples, as they come to understand, will become a new class of 'scribes', teaching people a new law and a New Covenant without disregarding the old, as the new age dawned.

The people of his own home region admit the superiority of the wisdom of Jesus, but resent it, and feel he is getting above himself, causing Jesus to say that 'a prophet is not without honour save in his own country'.

More Galilean Episodes

After the sad story of the beheading by Herod of John the Baptist as reward for Salome's dancing, we have the feeding of the 5,000 with a few loaves and fishes. Some commentators have thought that the generosity of the little boy caused everyone to share food they had hidden away in their bags. Others see it as a miracle where the processes of nature were speeded up by the Creator's Son. The story of Jesus walking on the water and Peter's brave but faltering attempt to walk to Jesus is placed next. Perhaps there is a suggestion that disciples have to climb out of the boat of human security and place their trust in the one who has called them to his Kingdom.

There are more arguments with the Pharisees because Jesus and his disciples do not observe the ceremonial washings and rituals and because the Jewish food laws are not considered important by Jesus. It's not what someone puts into the mouth that affects character, but what comes out from the heart. What you eat doesn't affect your relationship with God; neither does it hurt other people. Your inner self and its outflow do affect relationships with God and people.

All the time Jesus is healing people and people are glimpsing the Kingdom of God that he is preparing. There is another major feeding, this time of 4,000.

Peter's Confession

The opposition to Jesus is intensifying. The writing is on the wall that he will come to what would be humanly regarded as a bad end. So he steps out of the limelight and travels north into the area of Caesarea Phillipi, to spend time with his disciples quietly. There he asks them, 'Who do people say that the Son of Man is?' (He uses the description of himself based on the prophet Daniel's vision of the faithful minority in Israel as a larger than life human figure. Jesus thought of himself as embodying or focusing that minority in himself.)

The disciples give the various answers to the question. People think of him as John the Baptist raised from the dead, as Elijah, as Jeremiah, or one of the other prophets. Then comes the key question. 'And you, who do you say that I am?'

Back comes the unhesitating answer from Peter, 'You are the Messiah, the Son of the living God.' The answer delights Jesus, who sees it as a revelation from his heavenly Father, not as the result of human reason. He commends Peter – a name meaning 'the rock' – and says, 'On this rock I will build my church and the powers of death shall never conquer it.' There is a play on words here. Peter is given the keys of the Kingdom of Heaven, shared with the other disciples, according to Matthew 18:18.

In particular Peter used the keys, as recorded in the Book of

Acts, first to open the door to faith for the Jews on the day of Pentecost and then to open it to non-Jews when he went to visit the centurion Cornelius. Such preaching had the effect of loosing people from their sins or, if they rejected the gospel, of binding them in their unrepentant ways. This may explain the saying that Peter, and the disciples, would have the power of binding and loosing.

Nothing in the text insists that the promise is to anyone else other than Peter himself (and the other disciples). The Roman Catholic Church, of course, interprets the passage as referring to the Bishops of Rome, or Popes, whom they see as the successors of Peter. I am not trying to tell people what to believe; you must make up your own mind. But in the original story the point is that this was the first and crucial recognition by the disciples of the identity of Jesus, according to what became the Christian faith. It is a key moment.

It was therefore with great excitement that I stood, in 1975, in Banias in Israel, as I came down from the Golan Heights. Listening to the tinkling of a small waterfall nearby, I heard in my imagination the voice of Peter echoing down the centuries, for this is where it happened. And for me, at least, faith was strengthened. 'You are the Messiah, the Son of the Living God!'

This is the turning point in the record of all three of the Synoptic Gospel writers. 'From that time Jesus began to make it clear to his disciples that he had to go to Jerusalem, and endure great suffering at the hands of the elders, chief priests and scribes, and be put to death and to be raised again on the third day.' Peter opposes the idea that such a fate could come to Jesus and, so soon after receiving the praise of Jesus, he is called by Jesus a Satan or adversary.

The episode ends with a new call to discipleship. 'Anyone

who wishes to be a follower of mine must renounce self; he must take up his cross and follow me.' From now on the mood of sombre anticipation of sad events to come casts a shadow over the record, yet some shafts of light appear in the gloom.

25

The Road to the Cross

Matthew

Using mainly the guidance of Matthew we pick up the story just after Peter's confession of Jesus as Messiah and Son of God. Jesus has invited the disciples to take up their cross and follow him, and also indicated that some of those standing there would not taste death till they had seen the Son of Man coming in his Kingdom. This could mean that the death and resurrection of Jesus, which inaugurates the Kingdom, would come in their lifetime, or it could be a reference to the event called the transfiguration, which follows.

Jesus, Peter, James and John go up into a mountain and there Jesus is seen in a transformed condition of brightness and dazzling light. The disciples then see a vision of Moses and Elijah talking with Jesus. Peter wants to retain the vision as reality and provide tents for them all. A cloud blots out the vision; a voice is heard saying, 'This is my beloved Son, in whom I take delight' (the same Old Testament words as used at his baptism). It continues, 'Listen to him.'

The voice terrifies the disciples. Jesus touches and reassures them, and when they look again only Jesus is there. Was the vision saying that Jesus has now replaced or fulfilled both the law and the prophets and that all God's activity is now centred in him?

The experience is followed by more teaching, including more indications of his forthcoming death and resurrection. A childlike spirit is commended as the route to the Kingdom. The shepherd searching for lost sheep is used as analogy for the work of reclaiming the Israelites for God and through them all mankind.

Guidance is given about disputes: don't tell everyone about them, but try to settle them privately, then with help from wise counsellors and only finally with the wider forum of the Church. This was true in principle already, but the Church did not yet exist as any sort of organisation.

Peter's famous question about forgiving his brother seven times follows. Jesus says forgiveness should be given seventy times seven, implying that there is no count involved; it's infinite. And Peter thought seven was generous. This is illustrated by the story of the steward who was forgiven a large debt and did not forgive his colleague a much smaller debt. 'Forgive us our sins as we forgive those who sin against us.'

The Road to Jerusalem

Jesus and the disciples now leave Galilee and take the road to Jerusalem, via the Jordan Valley.

He debates with Pharisees about divorce, refusing to give a precise law and rather directing them to the divine ideal that marriage should be a permanent institution, a perfect unity. He puts a rich young man to the test, challenging him to give up his wealth and follow Jesus, but he goes away sorrowful, for he is very rich. Jesus points out that wealth can be an impediment to entering the Kingdom of God. Those who give up everything to follow Jesus will be more than recompensed, now and in eternity. There is also a hint that the Gentiles and the dregs of Jewish society are being called into the Church in the story of the labourers who only work one hour but receive the same pay as those who worked all day.

As they journey towards Jerusalem, Jesus again describes the expectation of suffering that lies ahead, even saying that he will be handed over to the Romans and be flogged and crucified. And while his mind is preoccupied with such sadness he has to arbitrate among disciples who are thinking in terms of a high place in his Kingdom, which they still see in political terms. He asks whether the disciples can share his suffering. That is where their focus should be.

He uses the occasion to present the essence of his mission: 'Whoever wants to be first must be the slave of all – just as the Son of Man did not come to be served, but to serve and give his life as a ransom for many.'

Triumphal Entry into Jerusalem

Jesus finally enters Jerusalem riding upon a donkey, as the prophet Zechariah had predicted: 'Behold your king is coming to you; gentle and mounted upon a donkey.' In this instance it looks likely that Jesus deliberately arranged to fulfil the words of the prophet. Yet again the emphasis is upon a different kind of king and kingdom from the one the Jews had been expecting.

The crowds welcome his arrival, strewing his path with palm leaves and garments and crying in the words of Psalm 118: 'Hosanna! Blessed is he who comes in the name of the Lord!'

Cleaning Up the Temple

Jesus moves on into the temple. It is expected that the temple will be restored in its full glory by the Messiah. What does he do? He chases out of the temple court all the commercialists trading in the sacrificial animals needed by the worshippers. Profiteering, they have turned the temple into a den of robbers, as Jesus puts it. This activity takes place in the court allocated for Gentiles, the only part they could enter, and now they are being kept out by the traders, the very opposite of the inclusive teaching of Jesus. There is also a hint he is going to replace the temple, redefining it in terms of himself. The old temple would be destroyed.

All this and more might be implied in Jesus telling his disciples that if they have faith they would be able to cast a mountain into the sea. Perhaps he is talking about the very mountain on which the temple stands; the work of Jesus and the disciples is to cast out the system represented by the temple and the mountain on which it stood. (The Romans would eventually remove the edifice, in AD 70).

Direct Challenges

Parables and challenges issue from the lips of Jesus throughout this period. When the chief priests and elders ask where he earned his authority he places them on the horns of a dilemma by saying that it comes in effect from the same source as John the Baptist's. They do not want to deny that John spoke for God for fear of popular anger, but they do not want to admit it either, because Jesus can then ask why had they not believed him. So they feign ignorance.

He tells the story of the two brothers, one who agrees to carry out his father's instructions but doesn't; the other who says he won't, but does. The leaders are in the first category;

the ordinary people and even sinners are in the second. Prostitutes and tax collectors will enter the Kingdom of God before the elders. No wonder they are fuming with anger at his words, wondering how they could get rid of him.

But Jesus makes no attempt to placate them. Rather he increases the power of his attack. He tells the parable of the owner who lets his vineyard to tenants who refuse to send the rent and abuse the messengers who come to collect it and finally kill his son. Punishment will be inevitable and the vineyard will be let to those who would pay their dues in fruit. Based on Isaiah 5, the meaning of the parable is obvious, presenting the history of Israel as a frequent rejection of God's messengers. But now the moment of crisis has arrived. The son of the vineyard owner has come to see if they have produced fruit in the shape of loyal service to God, and they will kill him and sign their own death warrant in doing so. The Kingdom of God will be passed to a new Israel, centred on King Jesus.

Jesus retells the Israel story and undermines their existing understanding of their identity, which relies on seeing themselves as the elite race. He redefines Israel. He summons all his hearers to opt out of the parable's threats while there is time.

A similar parable follows. This time it forms an invitation to a wedding feast. Those who were invited rejected the invitation, so guests were called in from the streets and odd corners of the city. This referred both to the fact that Jesus spends so much time with the lower levels of Jewish society that he understands their needs, and to the call of the Gentiles – the non-Jews – into the new Israel he was creating.

Question Time

The religious leaders are not going to let Jesus get away with all this, so they think up a series of catch questions, all of which he deals with astutely.

There is the question of paying taxes to Caesar, which he passes back to them with the words: 'Render to Caesar the things which belong to Caesar and to God the things which belong to God.' It was up to them to decide which were which.

Then the Sadducees, who didn't believe in the resurrection, poke fun at the idea with the story of the woman who had seven successive husbands. Which one will she have in the resurrection day? You can imagine the crude comments from the crowd, but Jesus quietly clarifies the nature of the resurrection life and reaffirms the fact of the resurrection in a way they could not dispute.

Then a lawyer wants to know which was the most important command in the law. Jesus gives the well-known summary of the whole of the law: 'Love the Lord your God with all your heart, with all your soul and with all your mind . . . That is the greatest, the first, commandment; the second is like it: "Love your neighbour as yourself." Everything in the law and the prophets hangs on those two commandments.'

Finally, on this day of questions, he asks them one of his own. Why does David address as 'Lord' his descendant, who should reign upon his throne? They see the implication: Jesus is claiming to be the heir to David's throne *and* David's Lord. And the record tells us: 'From that day no one dared to put any more questions to him.'

Fierce Denunciation

The love that Jesus teaches is not a weak and insipid approach to life. Jesus can be outspoken when the situation warrants it.

Matthew 23 illustrates this with a catalogue of the ways in which the scribes and Pharisees have perverted the law and their loyalty to God. It is a series of woes that will come upon them. 'Woe to you, scribes, Pharisees, hypocrites! . . . Woe to you blind guides.'

Jesus acknowledges the religious leaders' authority to define the law, so he says people should do what they *tell you*, but do not do what they *do*. They preach, but they don't practise what they preach. They make life difficult with all their minute interpretations, but they are not interested in lightening the burdens of the poor and unfortunate. They love to be seen doing their good deeds. They love the respect that people give them; they make it difficult for ordinary people to enter their version of the Kingdom of God; they invent ingenious ways of shirking their duties, for example to their parents; they are pedantic about tithing small amounts of herbs and vegetables but miss the important things such as justice, mercy and faith; they look good on the outside but inwardly they are greedy and rotten; they are like well-painted graves concealing corruption within. Snakes! Viper's brood! How can they escape being condemned to hell (destruction on the rubbish dump, Gehenna, outside Jerusalem)? Their generation will bear the guilt for all this and doom is staring them in the face.

Yet at the same time the tenderness of Jesus emerges immediately after this diatribe. He weeps over Jerusalem. He would have loved to gather Israel, like a mother hen protecting her helpless chicks under her wings. He can see the temple destroyed and forsaken by God. 'You will not see me till the day when you say "blessed is he who comes in the name of the Lord."'

The Little Apocalypse

We saw in the chapter on the Book of Daniel that a type of

literature in Israel was called 'apocalyptic', from a Greek word for 'revelation'. In the New Testament the Book of Revelation is in this style, using highly imaginative symbols to make predictions of future crises. Dramatic events occur in the sky, lightning and thunder; plagues and disasters respond on earth.

Jesus uses this method to teach his disciples, as described in Matthew 24, Mark 13 and Luke 21. They are impressed by the grandeur of the temple, but Jesus says that not one stone will be left upon another. They will all be thrown down. (It would happen within a generation.)

Jesus is dealing with the end of that age, the period of Israel's spiritual exile. He describes a time of wars, revolts, famines and earthquakes; of false Messiahs and would-be leaders. He tells them that they themselves will suffer persecution because of their faith. Not all the believers will stand the time of testing, but the gospel will be widely preached, thanks to the work of the apostles.

The time will come when Jerusalem will be captured; the Christians, forewarned, are to flee, not stopping to pick up their belongings. This might be a specific meaning to 'lead us not into the time of testing, but deliver us from evil' as one version of the Lord's prayer says. The darkening of sun and moon and the stars is a symbol of the terror of the time. Even Jesus did not know exactly when it would come, but this judgement was certain, and the Jewish Commonwealth would be dissolved until he should come again. Jesus warns them, and the people they will teach, of the need to be alert, to avoid complacency and to maintain a caring attitude to their fellow believers.

In verses 30–32 he speaks of a more distant day when he himself will return 'on the clouds of heaven and in great glory' (based on Daniel 7 and to be read symbolically, as befits apocalyptic literature). So while he is talking of the first century in a specific sense, there is another level which calls upon the believers of all ages to be ready for the final establishment of the Kingdom of God.

The Second Coming

Finally in this section of Matthew, before the events connected with the death and resurrection of Jesus, Chapter 25 features a series of parables that are timeless and speak of the need for believers to maintain readiness to meet their Lord at any time. The exact nature of the final return of Christ and the final establishment of God's sovereignty over the earth is not spelled out unambiguously in the Bible writings, but a final climax to history is mentioned frequently, so in this chapter three parables set out the need for preparedness in mind and character.

First is the story of the five wise and the five foolish bridesmaids. The latter have no oil in their lamps and going out to buy some will make them too late for the wedding. So this is a question of believers making sure that they have kept their light-giving facilities topped up. Perhaps some readers of this guide are using their study to do just this. Understanding the Bible record and applying it to life could be described as keeping one's lamp supplied with oil or as we would say today keeping one's batteries charged – the spiritual ones.

Then there is the story of the businessman who gives money to his employees to trade with. Two of them double its value. One of them feels inadequate and does nothing. The two who doubled their money receive the same reward for their equal effort from their master; they were made his friends. The lazy employee loses all. You are rewarded for effort, not for achievement. In the Luke version the reward is proportionate to the achievement, meaning perhaps that while everyone is equal in terms of receiving the blessing of God, people vary and Jesus did not expect the people in his Kingdom to be boringly uniform.

Finally Jesus in his day of glory judges all nations and categorises people as either sheep or goats. The basis of selection is what they have done to help others. When he was hungry they fed him, when he was thirsty they gave him drink, when he was in prison they visited him. The sheep ask when they did all these things for him. He replies, 'Inasmuch as you did it to one of the least of these my brothers, you did it unto me.' The goats are equally surprised. 'Inasmuch as you did it *not* to one of the least of these my brothers . . .' The sheep, in serving others, did not realise they were serving Jesus. The goats, in failing to serve others, did not realise they were failing to serve Jesus.

So in the last analysis Jesus is saying that people show their loyalty and love for him and for God by the way they treat other people. And he says that this will determine their eternal destiny. It is interesting that he says that this is a judgement of all nations, which seems to take this beyond individual behaviour into a wider social context. Do some nations have a better record of loving their neighbour than others? Whether this is so or not, perhaps its application in our days could lead to voters choosing governments who are inclined to a caring approach rather than a selfish individualism.

26

Unique Contributions

Mark and Luke

One of the difficulties of guiding readers around the first three or Synoptic Gospels is that the level of repetition makes it difficult to devote separate sections to full treatment of each Gospel. It is certainly worth reading each of them, but I would suggest doing so in stages, with intervals in between. This way they each stand on their own merits and their repetitions are seen in a new context, both reinforcing and modifying earlier impressions from other Gospels.

The Mood of Mark

Take for example the shortest Gospel, Mark. Virtually nothing here is not found in Matthew or Luke, yet more than half of the material in those Gospels is not included in Mark. This gives a different flavour and context to the material that Mark does share with the other two, making it starker and more action-led. There is less discussion and interpretation, and Jesus stands out as the servant of his people, ever ministering to their needs with healing and gestures of help. There is a sense of movement, with Jesus and his disciples always travelling from one town or region to another, from one experience to another. There is a sense of drama and surprise.

The following phrases illustrate this: 'They went straight to . . .', 'That evening they . . .', 'Very early the next morning he got up and went out . . .', 'As soon as Jesus had returned . . .', 'From there he went to . . .', 'As soon as they had finished, he made his disciples embark and . . .', 'He moved on from there . . .', 'When they came back . . .', 'As he was starting out on a journey . . .', 'They were on the road going to . . .', 'They were now approaching . . .', 'On the following day . . .', 'Early next morning . . .'.

It is thus well worth reading Mark, not so much for new information, but to develop a sense of the excitement and immediacy of those three years. The writer is reliving what actually happened, remembering what they did on one day and then what happened on the next. He writes as one who was there; his words are those of an eyewitness, even if he is collecting the memories of other observers. The Gospel of Mark has the urgency of a series of quick pencil sketches, rather than of patiently produced oil paintings. You could argue that it should be read first. You would be reading the framework upon which Matthew and Luke build. You would feel as if you had been there, at the scene of these events.

Luke and the Story of Two Mothers-To-Be

Luke has much material that is found in neither Mark nor Matthew, and it is best read in its own entirety instead of just going to the extra bits. It is probably a good idea to do so leaving an interval after reading either of the others.

The variations start at the beginning, where Luke records

some of the events surrounding the birth and infancy of Jesus which Matthew does not, and vice versa. Luke aims to bring together information from various sources. He says he is basically a compiler, who bases his work on a very thorough investigation. He dedicates his work to a Gentile nobleman called Theophilus (which means 'Lover of God').

The story starts with Zechariah, who belongs to one of the twenty-four groups of priests who, month by month, share the temple duties. He is taking his turn on the incense-offering roster, with incense symbolising prayer and people outside praying. An angel appears to him and says that although he and his wife, Elizabeth, are advanced in years she is to bear a child who will be the forerunner of the Messiah. This child will bring a degree of unity to Israel as they await the new age. The priest can hardly believe what he has heard and is struck dumb till the child, John the Baptist, is born.

Then Elizabeth's relative, Mary, receives a visit from the angel Gabriel, who announces that she will be the mother of the Messiah, who shall reign on the throne of David forever. A virgin conception is implied but less clearly stated than in Matthew. Mary accepts this and visits Elizabeth, who recognises Mary's exalted role. Mary breaks into poetry, based on the song of Hannah, the mother of Samuel, seeing in her son the promise of one who will right the wrongs that afflict the poor and fulfil the promises that God made to Abraham. Mary and Elizabeth stay together for three months, which must have been a wonderful time for both of them.

Then Elizabeth's baby is born and the naming day arrives. The relatives and neighbours are amazed at the proposed name: John. Zechariah confirms it and his tongue is loosened and he too bursts into poetry, extolling the future of his son and the Messiah whom he will announce. The poetry presents a lofty view of the promises to Abraham, which are being fulfilled in the work of these two sons. The deliverance the Messiah will bring to Israel will enable them to serve God in holiness. John will prepare the way for the mission of Jesus by teaching knowledge of salvation and the forgiveness of sins.

Luke relates that Mary and Joseph travelled from Nazareth to Bethlehem because of a census. Matthew gives the impression that they lived in Bethlehem, though he doesn't actually say so. If anything, these differences of detailed presentation create confidence in the record. There is no sense of the overall story being contrived, of being tampered with to ensure that it is unambiguous.

The Birth and Childhood of Jesus

The baby is born in an outhouse for the cattle. I don't think this is an unkind gesture on the part of the innkeeper. He has no room in the inn where he could give privacy for the birth of a child, so he does the best he can to make the family comfortable in a stable. I don't imagine they were surrounded by cattle lowing and sheep baaing and I would suppose that the cleanest available bedding was provided. Even so, it was primitive and a very humble entry into the world for the one who later claimed to be the Son of God and the King of Israel.

Luke brings into the picture the shepherds, who come and worship the Prince of peace. He also tells us of the presentation of Jesus in the temple, where the aged Simeon blesses Jesus in words that evoke the Old Testament. He sees Jesus as a light for the Gentiles as well as for Israel, one who will guide the consciences of many. He foresees suffering for both mother and son. Anna, the elderly widow, also gives thanks to God for the babe and tells everybody who will listen what is happening and how it will affect Israel and change their destiny.

Chapter 2 of Luke ends with Jesus missing after the family visits Jerusalem. His parents return and discover him in deep discussion with the wise men of Israel in the temple. Although he is only twelve he seems to think that it is the most natural thing in the world for him to be in his Father's house! He is a spiritual prodigy, but he goes home and then for nearly twenty years is lost to sight. We are just told: 'As Jesus grew he advanced in wisdom and favour with God and men.'

Those first two chapters of Luke provide a remarkable introduction to the story of Jesus. They set the scene with incomparable skill and make it clear that the roots of current events lay in the history of Israel as portrayed in the Old Testament. Now is the time of fulfilment. The best way to read it is to soak up the atmosphere and share its sense of excitement at the prospect of a new beginning.

The other piece of information about the birth of Jesus is the family tree in Luke. It goes back to David by a different route from Matthew, and then back beyond Abraham to Adam. Thus Jesus is firmly fixed in the human race, though even Adam is called Son of God at the end of the genealogy!

Episodes from the Public Ministry

Luke 4 depicts the striking episode of the appearance of Jesus in his home synagogue. He reads the lesson for the day from Isaiah 61. It speaks of a day of release, healing and liberty, when good news will be proclaimed to the poor that the year of the Lord's favour will have arrived. He rolls up the scroll and says to them, 'Today, in your hearing, this text has come true.'

They receive this announcement with astonishment. Jesus then begins to bring their disbelief into the open and to say that it will lead to them being excluded from what he has to offer and he will, like Elijah of old, give the benefits to the Gentiles.

They are outraged and try to capture him and throw him over a cliff, but he walks right through the crowd and goes away. Such was the power of his personality.

The ensuing chapters cover much of the same ground as Matthew, with some slight variations, some of which may result from the fact that Jesus often said the same things with minor changes on different occasions. Luke also gives extra minor details as well as facts omitted in the other Gospels, all adding to the sense of credibility. Chapter 6 gives an example of this with a sermon on a plain that matches many of the words of the Sermon on the Mount, featuring woes to balance the blessings or beatitudes.

Chapter 7 gives the story of the widow's son who has died in Nain, a Galilean village. Jesus stops the funeral, tells the distraught mother not to weep and orders the young man to get up. He does and begins to speak. The statement that everyone was filled with awe is somewhat of an understatement. I used to wonder whether this really happened as recorded; but nowadays I find myself saying – why not? If we believe in a God, and that Jesus represents him, what is so impossible about such acts, especially if we accept the strength of the evidence for the resurrection of Jesus himself? But that's my experience. It may not be yours. We each have to wrestle with our own doubts and hopes. Remember the words of a doubter to Jesus: 'Lord I believe, help thou my unbelief.' The words of the poet, Tennyson, are also relevant to the problems of doubt:

> There lives more faith in honest doubt
> Believe me, than in half the creeds.

Luke 7 shows Jesus going to dinner with a Pharisee. A prostitute from the city comes in, weeps over Jesus' feet, wipes them with her hair, kisses them and anoints them with precious ointment. The Pharisee, Simon, sneeringly thinks that this man can't be a prophet else he would know what sort of woman this one is. Jesus points out that Simon has neglected the feet-washing of Jesus. This woman has washed his feet with her tears. Her sins, which are many, are forgiven. This is a wonderful episode in opening out the meaning of forgiveness. There are no lectures from Jesus about the woman's bad ways; he knows a repentant soul when he sees one. She knows she has encountered someone better than her, through whom the love of God has flowed. He speaks the word of pardon; he gives peace of conscience; he gives hope to the broken. There is no harping on the enormities of her past, there are no denunciations. He lets her know that she is forgiven and the springs of real love are unsealed.

In Luke 9 there is the story of the Samaritans who would not receive Jesus. James and John wanted to call down fire from heaven to destroy them, following Old Testament examples. Many of the early manuscripts give Jesus as replying, 'You don't know what spirit you belong to. The son of man has come to save men's life, not to destroy them.' Other versions simply say that he rebuked them. Either way he was repudiating the old ways of violence as a response to evil.

There is an extra piece of information in Chapter 10. Jesus sends out seventy-two disciples to preach and heal, giving the idea that there was a larger circle of close associates as well as the twelve. On their return he thanks God for revealing himself to ordinary people rather than the intellectuals. He also tells them that they are seeing what prophets and kings in the Old Testament had longed to see: they have a great privilege to see the beginning of the Kingdom of God.

The Good Samaritan

Luke contains a number of parables that do not appear elsewhere. The first is one of the most well known: the story of the Good Samaritan. Its basis comes in response to the question of a lawyer asking how to inherit eternal life. Jesus elicits from him a correct answer: the two great commands, of which the second is love of neighbour. Not wanting to look silly for asking such an obvious question, the lawyer then asks for a definition of 'my neighbour'. One has the feeling that he is really asking who is *not* his neighbour, so that he need *not* do good to him. He wants to restrict the range of his responsibility.

Jesus tells the story of the man who is robbed and left half dead on the road. Priest and Levite hurry by on the other side, no doubt busy about their religious duties – too busy for God to attend to man! A despised Samaritan, hated by the Jews, comes along and offers care for the poor victim, even paying for it out of his own pocket.

Jesus is in effect saying: Don't think that you are the one who is going to have the choice of being a neighbour or otherwise to someone else. Think! You might need a neighbour too. And if you did, would you tell him to go away because he was a Samaritan or anyone else of whom you did not approve? The final blow occurs when Jesus tells the lawyer to take the Samaritan as an example.

The Rich Fool

The parable about the Rich Fool is told to discourage excessive concern with material things. It's a simple story. A rich landowner has been doing very well, so he decides to invest further capital into increasing his market share, as we would say today. He decides to pull down his old barns and build bigger ones and embarks on an expansion programme. He then feels he will be able to settle down, his future secure and his old age sure of prosperity. The only trouble is that he dies that night. He was piling up treasure for himself, but in the eyes of God he was poverty stricken.

There are then several other interesting episodes, such as the story of the president of a synagogue where Jesus cures a crippled woman. Unbelievably he says: 'There are six working days; come and be cured on one of them and not on the Sabbath.' Needless to say Jesus deals with this attitude decisively.

And we have further examples of his lack of tact. When invited to a party Jesus speaks out against the way in which people were trying to grab the best seats near the place of honour, exposing their lack of humility. Doubtless there were some red faces and more enemies made. He also suggests that the poor and unfortunate should be invited to your parties.

The Prodigal Son

Then we return to the parables. Chapter 15 has as its theme the desire of God to find the lost ones. Jesus pictures the joy of a shepherd who finds one lost sheep, even though he has another ninety-nine. The woman who loses a piece of silver and diligently searches for it celebrates when she finds it. Both of these stories emphasise the love of God, who is concerned with everyone, including minorities, and not just with people who think they are good, yet who because of a complacent attitude may in fact be lost.

The most famous of all the parables is the one about the Prodigal Son. A younger son doesn't want to wait for his father to die to have his inheritance, so he collects his father's bequest and then goes off and wastes it all in a life of orgies and excess. He is finally driven to destitution and has to work for a pig farmer, and he wishes he could eat as well as the pigs. He comes to his senses and goes home, ready to ask to be one of his father's slaves. The father doesn't listen; in fact he has been going out every day, searching for his son. (He must have been doing this, because he saw him when he was yet a long way off.)

The father throws a party to celebrate the return of the lost son. The elder brother is in the field, where he was dutifully employed, and hears the merriment. He is angry. The father tries to persuade him to join the festivities. 'But he would not go in.' He tells his father that he has been dutiful all these years: 'You never gave me so much as a kid to make merry with my friends, but as soon as this *your* son [not *my* brother] comes back you kill for him the fatted calf.'

It is a rich pattern of relationships. The father *runs* to meet the returning prodigal, which is not very dignified for a father. Does God really 'run' to meet the sinner who comes back towards him? All the younger son has to do to be accepted is go back home, whereas the older brother thinks only in terms of justice, fairness, rights and duty. 'After all I've done this is all the thanks I get.' He is centred on himself, not on the reclaiming of his lost brother.

Of course forgiveness isn't fair. It goes beyond justice. The Pharisees must have understood this. They were more than ever filled with animosity towards Jesus.

More Parables

Several other parables are unique to Luke. One is the difficult story of the dishonest steward who, faced with dismissal, takes prudent but dishonest steps to protect his future. Jesus is not recommending dishonesty, but is saying that, faced with disaster, you have to behave in an astute manner, like the steward in the story. So you use money and contacts wisely, but you must not worship Mammon.

The parable of the rich man and Lazarus certainly isn't told to give us information about the afterlife, with people going to Abraham's bosom and being able to shout across a gulf to people in Hades or the shades, where fire tortures people without consuming them. Instead, it takes a traditional and legendary picture and uses it to enable the dead to talk to each other. The rich man who used to ignore the beggar Lazarus is now in the bad place, and Lazarus is in the good place. The rich man asks Abraham to send Lazarus to warn his five brothers to behave in such a way that they will not share his fate. Abraham anachronistically replies: 'If they do not listen to Moses and the prophets, neither will they listen if someone should rise from the dead.' The parable presents an attack on the Jewish leaders for their attitude to outcasts, and by implication the Gentiles. There is a suggestion of the dangers of wealth and perhaps a hint of the resurrection of Jesus, which did not persuade the Jewish leaders in general.

In Luke 18 a parable describes a woman who keeps worrying a judge for justice. He does not deal with the matter out of a sense of duty, but as he becomes so tired out by her persistence in the end he gives way. The suggestion is that we need to be persistent in prayer; if godless judges will answer prayers because persistence wears them out, how much more will God answer persistent prayers out of love.

The events with lessons are living parables. One is of the two men in the temple praying. The first, a Pharisee, thanks God for his moral superiority over other people. 'I thank you God that I am not like the rest of mankind . . . or even like this tax collector. I pay tithes on all I get and I fast twice a week.' The tax collector, on the other hand, beats upon his breast and cries, 'God have mercy on me, sinner that I am.' It is the humble man, said Jesus, who goes home acquitted of his sins.

The self-exaltation of the Pharisee is the negation of what God expects from people. Yet how often religious people do think of themselves as superior and look down in superiority on the rest of mankind?

Then there is the story of another tax collector, Zacchaeus, a little man who climbs up a tree to watch Jesus passing by. He is amazed when Jesus stops by the tree and says, 'Zacchaeus be quick and come down, for I must stay at your house today.' The bystanders disapprove of the choice Jesus has made for a dinner companion. He has gone to be the guest of a sinner. Zacchaeus is so overcome at the attitude of Jesus to him that his response is immediate: to undo all the dishonest harm he has caused and to give half of his possessions to charity. Jesus makes people feel that they matter and that their past can be blotted out. As he says: 'The Son of Man has come to seek and to save what is lost.' This is the spirit of the Kingdom of God, rather than the elitism of tradition and the might of military conquest.

Another similar story in praise of the efforts of the humble is the one of the woman who puts two small coins into the temple collection box. Others give what they can spare. She gives all she has. Jesus is always redefining everything by new standards.

Favour to the Outcasts

Most of the rest of Luke, except for the events of the Last Supper, trial, crucifixion and resurrection of Jesus, has been described in previous chapters. This Gospel has a special flavour. It is especially concerned with the poor, the outcasts, the disreputable, the nobodies, the despised and foreigners, Gentile or Samaritan. The poetry of the early chapters is full of reference to the poor being saved and the rich sent away. The stable is a humble birthplace. Shepherds do not belong with the aristocracy; the wise men do not get a mention. Gentile response is highlighted in the early encounter of Jesus in his home town of Nazareth, and many times Luke describes Jesus eating with tax collectors and prostitutes. Gentile cities are compared favourably with Jewish ones from the perspective of repentance. A Samaritan is offered as the model for loving your neighbour. The official classes are constantly criticised and shown up for the heartlessness of their legal pedantry. The rejected are invited to the wedding feast. The prodigal son is welcomed home. The lost sheep and the lost coin represent the divine search to reclaim those who have gone astray. When ten lepers are healed, only one, a Samaritan, comes back to say thank you. Lazarus of the parable is rewarded. The tax collector praying in the temple is forgiven. Luke himself appears to have been a Gentile.

So right through Luke the concept of the Kingdom of God and its citizens is being widened; what constitutes a righteous person is redefined. The compassion of God for sinners is emphasised in numerous episodes. And by contrast any sense of moral superiority is strongly discouraged.

This reaches its climax in the cross.

27

The Death and Resurrection of Jesus

Matthew, Mark, Luke and John

This chapter brings together the story of the death and resurrection of Jesus as perceived by all four Gospels. There are minor variations in the telling, but the versions hold together better than, for example, the usual eyewitness accounts of a serious accident in a court of law. I will tell the story with only occasional references to the specific source where they are pertinent. And I will tell the story; I will not try to interpret it or build up a theology of the cross. Various perspectives on why Jesus Christ died are considered in chapters of this book that look at the epistles of Paul, John and Peter. It will not be possible totally to hide my own convictions.

Preparations

Jesus asks his disciples to fix up a room where they can hold the Passover meal, in commemoration of the exodus from Egypt under Moses, which started the national history of Israel. It sounds as if Jesus has a longstanding arrangement with the man they have to contact, even down to a signal by which to recognise him (a man carrying a jar of water – women usually did this).

At the same time the Jewish rulers are discussing how to get rid of Jesus, because his activities could encourage riots and the loss of their comfortable arrangements with the Roman power. The Pharisees, not normally on good terms with the Sadducee rulers, were in sympathy as they wished to dispose of him for more specifically religious reasons. All agreed that Jesus was a blasphemer in claiming a special relationship with God.

They then experienced what must have seemed a stroke of luck, when Judas Iscariot came and offered to betray Jesus quietly for a sum of money, the famous thirty pieces of silver. The musical play *Jesus Christ Superstar* tends to belittle this crime and see Judas as a victim of circumstances, but the Bible presents it as a heinous crime against the one regarded as the Son of God. Judas was greedy and wanted money; he was a corrupt treasurer of the group and stole from the bag; he was devious, sitting at supper with Jesus while planning treachery; and perhaps, worst of all, when he did realise the enormity of his misdeed he didn't know how to ask forgiveness and committed suicide instead. If he had sincerely asked for forgiveness, he would have been forgiven even this crime.

The Preliminaries of the Last Supper

We need not debate whether this feast was a legally correct observance of the Passover meal. It was certainly intended to be seen as such, and Jesus hints that he himself is the real Passover lamb. John gives an extended report of the things that Jesus said at the Last Supper (see Chapter 29). John also omits the institution of the Eucharist, Holy Communion, breaking of bread, or Mass as it is variously described by different Churches.

What John does provide is the description of Jesus washing the feet of the disciples. The Son of God performs this most menial of tasks to display the 'humility of God', as J. McQuarrie puts it. Peter finds the idea difficult, but once he understands it, with typical impetuosity he wants to be washed all over, which Jesus said isn't necessary. Jesus tells the disciples, 'You do not understand what I am doing, but one day you will.' The key is service to each other, the negation of pride and status.

Then Jesus tells them that they have a betrayer in their midst, which adds to the solemnity of the occasion. They all begin to imagine that perhaps they have in some way unintentionally betrayed him. Judas has the effrontery to ask 'Is it I?' John follows this by describing how Judas gets up to leave and Jesus says, 'Do quickly what you have to do.' The door opens. From the light of the room they see the darkness beyond, and Judas goes out. 'And it was night!' Four dramatic and moving words, full of symbolism and sadness.

Do This in Remembrance of Me

Jesus now takes part in the meal and institutes it as a permanent memorial of his sacrificial death, which is about to occur. We have all no doubt seen the picture in which Leonardo da Vinci imagines the scene, and most Christians know the words well because they are repeated regularly at every communion service.

The Synoptic writers all give the same picture, apart from an extra cup of wine in Luke. The Revised English Bible describes the scene:

> During supper Jesus took the bread, and having said the blessing he broke it and gave it to the disciples with the

words 'Take this and eat; this is my body.' Then he took a cup and having offered thanks to God he gave it to them with the words 'Drink from it, all of you. For this is my blood, the blood of the [new] covenant, shed for many for the forgiveness of sins.'

And for nearly 2,000 years, every week millions of people worldwide have taken that bread and that wine and felt themselves involved in Christ's actions. This fact is probably the strongest evidence that the story of Jesus is true. Christians of all shades of opinion believe it is far too enduring to have been just a piece of deception.

It must have been very puzzling for the disciples, especially when he said he wouldn't do it any more till he drank the wine anew in the Kingdom of his Father. They must have felt disaster was in the air, particularly when Jesus said they would all let him down and that Peter would actually disown him. Yet in the midst of this sombre occasion they start a dispute as to who will be greatest in the Kingdom. And Jesus says, 'I am among you as one who serves.' Whatever you personally believe, the words come ringing down the centuries to ask us whether we are any better, with our career ambitions and status consciousness.

Gethsemane

In the most solemn moment of all, Jesus goes to the Garden of Gethsemane and among the olive trees prays in agony while his three closest disciples struggle to keep awake after all the tension of the evening. 'The spirit was willing but the flesh was weak.'

'My spirit is ready to break with grief' he tells them as he goes a little further on to pray: 'My Father, if it is possible, let this cup [of suffering] pass me by. Nevertheless not my will but yours be done.' Three times, as the minutes tick by towards his arrest, he says the same prayer. God's will must be done; that is he must draw the power of sin and evil by submitting to it, but it is a terrible struggle. This arose not from the fear of pain, but from the sense of isolation from people who should have welcomed him and from the realisation of how much depended on that moment.

One of the most moving moments for me when I visited Israel was standing in the Garden of Gethsemane and looking at a very old and gnarled olive tree and thinking that, maybe, when it was a young olive tree, it stood opposite another old tree, under which Jesus had prayed when it was young. I felt powerfully connected. So did a colleague from my office a few years later. She claimed to be an atheist, yet she had felt the vibrations of more than just history, a sense of the sacred or, as it is called, the numinous.

Arrest and Jewish Trial

The scene is then invaded by a crowd armed with swords and cudgels. Judas betrays Jesus with a kiss. 'This is your man; seize him.' And they do so. Peter slices off the ear of one of the high priest's mob. Jesus rebukes Peter and heals the ear. 'Put up your sword; those who take up the sword shall die by the sword!' The disciples then run away.

Investigation next takes place at the palaces, first that of Annas and then that of his son-in-law, the high priest, Caiaphas. The witnesses cannot agree on what Jesus has actually said about destroying the temple and raising it in three days, so the high priest uses his authority to demand from Jesus a plain answer as to whether or not he is the Son of God. Jesus answers in the words of the prophet Daniel about himself as the Son of

Man, seated at the right hand of the Almighty. In their view this is blasphemy. They now have all the evidence they need to condemn Jesus from a Jewish point of view.

Peter is following at a distance and three times denies that he knows Jesus. Jesus, passing from one trial to another, looks at Peter, who goes out and weeps bitterly.

The priests have to convince the Roman representative, Pontius Pilate, but he is not interested in their religious debates, so they have to take a political stance. They present Jesus as one who claims to be the King of the Jews, and therefore Caesar's enemy. This worries Pilate, yet he knows this man is no threat to Rome, not in the normal political sense. Jesus says that his task is to bear witness to the truth. Pilate sneeringly asks, 'What is Truth?' Pilate is also unnerved by a message from his wife, who has been convinced in a nightmare that Jesus is a just man and asks Pilate to have nothing to do with the case.

Pilate tries various arguments. He offers to free Jesus under the annual amnesty rule, but the crowd shout for the release of Barabbas, a terrorist. He then gets frightened that Jesus might be some kind of a divine figure, but Jesus won't help out. Pilate says, 'I have power to release you.' Jesus replies, 'You could have no power if God hadn't given it to you.'

By now Jesus has been flogged, dressed in mock imperial clothes and crowned with a crown of thorns. Pilate shows him to the crowd stating: 'Behold the man,' as if asking whether this sorry figure was a king. In the end he calls for water and washes his hands of the whole business, but he lets the Jewish leaders get on with their dirty work.

There They Crucified Him

At Golgotha – 'place of a skull' because its limestone rock looks like a skull – he is laid out on the rough wood cross; nails are hammered through his hands and feet, and then the cross with its bleeding burden is thumped into position. And Jesus is in excruciating pain. He is fully conscious, and every attempt to make himself less uncomfortable only makes things worse. Pilate places a notice above the cross. The Jews want it changed from 'The King of the Jews' to 'He said he was the King of the Jews'. But Pilate, fast losing patience, says: 'What I have written I have written.'

Jesus is not just in physical agony. Sometimes this has been overemphasised. Many people have unjustly suffered great physical pain, but there is something unique about Jesus. He has an acute sense of disappointment at the fact that he has not been able to win people over; though he is not actually surprised, it hurts. This is emphasised by the taunts and mockery that come from the crowd and the criminals crucified on either side of him, though one of them relents. That offers encouragement to Jesus and he promises him a place in paradise, a lovely word to a man with a raging thirst.

Jesus is also conscious that he has been given a role for the saving of mankind. This weighs heavy upon him. And worst of all he feels deserted by God, and this is the most bitter feeling of all. He shares a sense of the human race's alienation from God and is sensitive to it in a way we can little imagine. He actually feels alienated himself, though with his mind he knew better. One of his last cries was, 'My God, my God, why have you forsaken me?', a phrase taken from Psalm 22.

Ever full of love and care, he asks the disciple John to look after his mother, and then finally dies, crying, surprisingly, with a loud voice, 'It is finished.' Presumably this means more than his life. The purpose of God through him has reached its climax, or at least its key moment. The scriptures have been fulfilled so far.

Witnessing the end, a Roman centurion is impressed and says, 'Truly this man was a Son of God.' The evangelists report that there was an unnatural darkness over the whole area. An earth tremor is said to have split the veil of the temple that divided the holy place from the most holy place. There is possibly a symbolism here of God being made more accessible by the sacrifice of his Son.

To dispose of the criminals before the next day, a feast day, the Roman soldiers finish off those in whom life still lingers by breaking their legs. This is not necessary in the case of Jesus. A thrust spear causes blood and water to flow out, suggesting, according to some medical people, a ruptured heart – in other words, a broken heart. That was the measure of his suffering. The fact that his legs are not broken is linked by John with an Old Testament prophecy.

Burial in a New Tomb

Joseph of Arimathaea, one of the members of the Jewish Council, comes forward to arrange burial in a new tomb or cave. Another member, Nicodemus, joins him. They bring the spices and clothes necessary for a decent burial. And there the story should end, if it had been merely an ordinary execution.

One other thing: the Jewish leaders remember that Jesus said something about rising from the dead. So they arrange with the Romans to have the tomb secured and appoint a careful watch so that the disciples cannot steal the body and claim he had been resurrected.

The Empty Tomb

'Who shall roll away the stone?' say the women who go on Sunday morning to take spices to complete the hygienic work Joseph has already done. The stone is rolled away, and the tomb is empty. There are variations in the four Gospels, but with a little detective work they can be brought into reasonable harmony. The main facts stand clear, and that is all we need.

In one case two men are mentioned, in another an angel, in another one young man; but all say 'he is not here, he is risen from the dead'. John has Peter and John racing to the tomb and discovering that the women's report is true. Peter, of course, rushes straight in, true to character. Then Mary Magdalene meets Jesus, whom she at first supposes to be the gardener, because she can't see clearly through her tears. When he says 'Mary' she recognises him and goes back to tell the others. Matthew reports little of what went on in Jerusalem at this time, except that the Jewish leaders bribe the soldiers to say that the disciples stole the body while they slept. It is incredible to believe that a universal religion like Christianity should be built on such lies, when its ethical stance is so high. It seems unlikely that a dead corpse stolen from a sealed tomb could start such a world-shaking process. And if he had not risen from the dead, why did no one produce the body?

Jesus Appears

Luke records how Jesus journeys with two disciples back to their home in Emmaus. They are looking sad, and he asks them why. Not recognising him, they say he must be the only person in Jerusalem who hasn't heard about Jesus, who was sentenced to death. They had hoped he would save Israel; some of their women have been saying that he wasn't in the tomb when they visited it and that a young man or an angel had told them he had been raised from the dead. Other disciples had checked the story out and found the tomb empty.

Jesus then explains the Old Testament, showing how its

whole thrust should have led them to expect these events. The Messiah had to suffer, and then to enter into glory. They urge him to stay to supper. When he blesses the bread and breaks it, they recognise him and he vanishes from their sight. They dash back to Jerusalem to tell the other disciples, reflecting on how their hearts had been on fire as he talked with them.

The disciples confirm that Jesus has appeared to Peter. Then he appears in their midst, shows them the marks of his wounds and eats some fish with them. For fuller information we then have to go to John, which features several occasions when Jesus enters locked rooms, suddenly appearing in their midst. The first time Thomas isn't there and refuses to believe what the others told him. 'Unless I see the print of the nails and put my hand into the wound in his side I will not believe.' But next time Thomas is there; he is so utterly convinced that he cries out, 'My Lord and my God.'

Then up in Galilee the disciples meet Jesus, holding a picnic on the shore of Galilee. From the boat Peter realises it is the Lord and characteristically he jumps into the sea to go to Jesus. Jesus three times asks Peter whether he loves him. Three times Peter answers, but the third time he realises that Jesus is giving him the opportunity to cancel out the threefold denial. Peter receives the commission to 'feed my sheep'.

The final meeting is recorded by Matthew, when Jesus gives all of the disciples a commission:

> Full authority in heaven and earth has been given unto me. Go therefore to all nations and make them my disciples; baptise them in the name of the Father, the Son and the Holy Spirit, and teach them to observe all I have commanded you. I will be with you always to the end of the age.

The Impact of the Story

What do you make of it all? I have not been able to hide my own acceptance of at least the main thread of the story. This does not mean that I expect my readers to agree with me. I found it impossible to be neutral. But I still stick to what I said at the beginning: the aim is to help you make sense of the Bible, but it must be your own sense.

The excitement and the emotion and the spirituality and the moral effect contribute to the story. This is not an engineering drawing, nor a mathematical equation. Neither does it depend on all Christians perfectly living up to their standards. Even if your purpose in reading the Bible and this book is driven by curiosity, you can't ignore the feelings and the impact that these events created for the people who recorded them. That is part of the living story.

28

Divinity and Humanity Blended in Jesus

John

The Human Face of the Living God

We turn now to the most profound of the four Gospels. As this is a guide to help you make sense of the Bible I will try as far as possible to limit interpretation and simply talk about what lies in the record.

This is particularly difficult with a book like the Gospel of John; it demands that you seek to understand the deepest of ideas as you read. It is intensely theological. It emphasises that, in a sense, Jesus is divine, but it also emphasises that he is completely human. We are dealing with categories of thought that are to some extent beyond the capacity of the human mind. That is why I have to use phrases like 'in a sense' he is divine.

Tom Wright expresses the mood well: 'John invites us to be still and know; to look again into the human face of Jesus of Nazareth, until the awesome knowledge comes over us, wave upon terrifying wave, that we are looking into the human face of the living God.'

The Word Made Flesh

The very first chapter challenges the understanding, though the text is familiar to many from its use in Christmas services: 'In the beginning was the Word.' Jewish readers would have immediately recognised the first three words as coming from Genesis 1: 'In the beginning God created the heavens and the earth.' It therefore hints of a new creation.

Material creation was originally set in motion by the Word of God in a drama that unfolded over six days. Each day was introduced with the words 'God said'. God's word is creative power. He communicates himself; his word is his self-expression. He and his word are inseparable. What exists in his 'mind' is a reality and is apparent as such when 'He speaks and it is done', as one Psalm puts it.

We little understand what we mean when we utter the word 'God' or speak of the mind of God. But what exists in the mind of God actually exists; it isn't just a plan that might be brought into existence at a later date. And so, according to John 1:14, '*The Word* became flesh'; this is embodied in a human frame and that is Jesus Christ. In Jesus Christ, God's creative Word lived among human beings and showed the qualities of divinity – grace and truth. These words encapsulate many aspects: undeserved favour, forgiveness, empathy, trustworthiness, honesty, reliability, covenant love (*chesed*). Jesus displayed all of these traits, as we have seen in the other Gospels.

Fully Human

Everything previously revealed in the Old Testament (in the law and the prophets) was incomplete compared with this manifestation of God. As the Revised English Bible translates John 1:18, 'No one has ever seen God; God's only Son, he who is nearest to the Father's heart, has made him known.' This creative Word of God, which existed from eternity, is now being embodied in a human being, who had all the human experiences, including growing up from babyhood to adulthood; the eternal nature of his origin enables John the Baptist to say of Jesus 'he was before me'.

You will wrestle for yourself what this really means. You can't expect a simple answer. But you can bear in mind that Jesus equally is presented as fully human and he developed in understanding as well as physique. In fact Luke 2:52 tells us: 'As Jesus grew, he advanced in wisdom and in favour with God and men.' Just think what that suggests; as Jesus developed so God loved him more and more, as the potential for being the Word made flesh increasingly became realised.

The fact that Jesus had pre-existed in God's mind and Word didn't mean that he had existed in heaven from all eternity as a fully formed human being. It did not mean that when he was playing with his toys as a little child he was remembering at the same time things that had happened myriads of years before, when that same Word and mind of God had been the agent of creation.

Jesus says in his prayer to God in John 17, just before the cross and resurrection: 'And now, Father, glorify me in your own presence with the glory which I had with you before the world began.' Glory in the mind and Word of God before the world began was now embodied in him and was about to be shown at the highest level of human existence in a self-sacrificing death. But this prayer doesn't mean that he had a memory of personal pre-existence.

The Source of His Being
At the human level we are constantly meeting in the Gospel of John references to the Father being greater than Jesus, of God

sending Jesus, of Jesus praying to God as his Father, 'not my will but yours be done'. At the divine level, as the 'Word made flesh', Jesus proclaims: 'I and my Father are one'; 'he who does not honour the Son does not honour the Father who sent him' (though there is 'sending' here as well); ' I came down from heaven to do the will of him who sent me'; 'if God were your Father, you would love me, for God is the source of my being, and from him I come' (Revised English Bible translation) 'before Abraham was I am'.

When we piece such passages together we have a picture of a human being who is a progressive incarnation – manifestation in human nature – of the God who contains within his mind and Word the essence that Jesus revealed. We do not have to imagine however that the world was being run by a baby in a cradle or that God was dead when Jesus was in the tomb. When the embodiment of the Father was dead, that which he had embodied from God continued in God. Then after his resurrection the Gospels portray him as receiving all power in heaven and earth, pictorially presented as sitting at the right hand of God.

The First Disciples

Unrecorded in the other Gospels, John 1 presents John the Baptist as pointing out Jesus as 'the lamb of God who takes away the sin of the world'. He is no doubt saying more than he knows. Two of his disciples, probably John and Andrew, go after Jesus and spend the rest of that day with him. That is enough to make Andrew find his brother Peter and announce that they have found the Messiah.

Philip joins them next and he in turn introduces Nathanael to Jesus, who indicates great knowledge of Nathanael, which is enough to make him say: 'You are the Son of God; you are the

King of Israel.' This extra information about the call of the disciples shows that the nucleus is established among the disciples of John the Baptist. When the call by Jesus to the disciples to be fishers of men occurs in Galilee, he already knows nearly half of them.

Extra Material in John's Gospel

The Gospel of John dovetails well with the other Gospels in spite of what many scholars have said. Bishop John Robinson dated the basic material of the Gospel of John as early as Mark and indeed argued that most of the original material of the New Testament was written before AD 70. Though he has not secured a wide following on this matter, he was an outstanding scholar. He also shows that the focus of John's Gospel on the visits of Jesus to Jerusalem is not to be rejected simply because the others concentrate on Galilee. John is a witness in his own right and his additional information easily fits the flow of the story without unnatural contrivance.

The turning of water into wine at the wedding in Cana of Galilee is the first of a number of miracles referred to as signs, as they had additional symbolic meaning. In this case there is a suggestion of new wine coming after old, a hint of the initiation of the New Covenant.

After staying a few days with his family and disciples in Capernaum in Galilee, Jesus goes to Jerusalem for the Passover feast, and at this time turns the traders out of the temple precincts, saying, 'Don't turn my Father's house into a market.' The other three Gospels place what appears to be the same story at the end of his ministry, just before his trial, causing some to suggest that it has been displaced in John and should really come later. But there is no reason why he should not have done this twice, attracting less attention the first time. He also says on this occasion, 'Destroy this temple and in three days I will raise it up.' And John says, 'But he spoke of the temple of his body.' Jesus was the true temple of God, which was going to replace the temple made with hands, a clear reference to the difference between the kingdom the Jews were expecting and the one he was bringing in.

The Visit of Nicodemus

John 3 tells the story of Nicodemus, a leading Pharisee who comes to see Jesus at night. He acknowledges that Jesus must be a teacher from God, otherwise he would not be able to perform such signs. Jesus cuts across his sincere compliments and tells him: 'No one can see the Kingdom of God unless he is born again.' The Pharisee either takes Jesus very literally and sees this as a physical impossibility, or he is saying that you can't change late in life ('You can't teach an old dog new tricks'). Jesus explains the principle of spiritual rebirth as one that is not outwardly visible. It is like the wind; you see the effects but not the wind itself. Jesus also expresses surprise that Nicodemus had not already found these truths in the Old Testament.

John moves from narrative to teaching. Verse 13 sounds like a post-resurrection comment: 'No one has gone up into heaven, except the one who came down from heaven, the Son of Man who is in heaven.' There is also reference to the Son of Man being lifted up so that people might be saved by their faith in him. But then matters are clarified by a plain statement that must be among the most celebrated words in the Bible. 'God so loved the world that he gave his only Son, that whoever believes in him may not perish but have eternal life.' As he continues to talk of Jesus as the light and of people preferring darkness, John is seen as a commentator on the teaching of Jesus.

From Jerusalem Back to Galilee

From Jerusalem, Jesus and his disciples go into Judea by the River Jordan and we learn what the Synoptics do not tell us, that they actually baptised people there. John the Baptist shows his true spirit by accepting his own fading from the limelight: 'He must grow greater; I must become less.'

From Judea they pass through the land of the Samaritans on their way to Galilee. Jesus is tired. He sits down by a well and asks a woman who comes by for a drink. Jews didn't usually show such friendship to the despised Samaritans and she is puzzled. This leads to him teaching her that he has the living spiritual water; when anyone drinks they will never be thirsty again. She takes him literally, but is impressed by his knowledge of her private life and engages him in debate about the right place of worship, Jerusalem or Gerizim. He says that while God's kingdom has a Jewish basis, in the end location doesn't matter. The true worshippers will worship the Father in Spirit and in Truth. It is inward rather than outward.

The woman runs off to fetch her neighbours and many Samaritans become believers that day. John is all the time revealing the spiritual depth of the newly interpreted kingdom of God.

Reaching Galilee, Jesus performs his second sign miracle of healing an official's son at a distance. However he doesn't seem to stay long in Galilee. Soon he is off to Jerusalem for a religious feast of the Jews.

Back in Jerusalem

At this feast he heals a man on the sabbath: 'Take up your bed and walk.' To the legal mind this is work, and therefore against the law. The religious leaders object, unable to see the overriding grace of God at work. Jesus says in effect that his Father has never rested from works of love; neither will he. They then want to kill him because by calling God his Father in such a personal way he has put himself on a level with God. That, to them, is blasphemy.

Jesus tries to reason with them. God is his role model and he works in close fellowship with his Father. It is the will of God that all men should honour the Son, even as they honour the Father. He goes on to claim he is in charge of judgement and resurrection, but his authority comes from the Father. They read their Bibles (the Old Testament), but cannot recognise that Jesus was the fulfilment of those scriptures. If they read Moses properly, they should be expecting him. They are infuriated by such a blatant attack on them and such exalted claims for himself.

The Bread of Life

The story of feeding the 5,000 people in Galilee follows in John 6, and leads on to the teaching of Jesus based on the episode. Jesus describes himself as the bread of life that comes down from heaven and gives life to the world. This is the equivalent of the manna given to the Israelites in the wilderness under Moses. Christ's role was commissioned by the Father, as he usually describes God. His claims are astounding: 'He who has come from God has seen the Father and he alone.' This could have been seeing in the sense of perception, but it makes Jesus unique amongst the human race in his relationship with God.

Jesus doesn't make things easy. Talk of eating his flesh and drinking his blood would be like rank heresy to Jews. They should, he says, be able to understand that he is speaking spiritually, calling upon them to assimilate within themselves his teaching and his spirit. 'Whoever eats my flesh and drinks my blood dwells in me and I in him. As the living Father sent me and I live because of the Father, so whoever eats me will live because of me.'

These words are expanded right through the New Testament, giving the idea that, through Jesus, God becomes the source of their new life. We are taught that this is what goes on in Christian living, so long as people stay close to Jesus as a living and hourly reality for them, influencing all their thoughts and deeds. Jesus is offering a share in his divine life to those who have faith in him.

He reinforces the idea that God is the source of his being with the enigmatic question: 'What if you see the Son of Man ascending where he was before?', that is, to the existence he had in the mind and love of God from eternity. This is later referred to as the ascension and is symbolised as Jesus sitting at the right hand of God. This talk of eating the flesh and drinking the blood of Jesus echoes again the Eucharist, Holy Communion or Mass, where Christians celebrate the memory of what Jesus achieved and their assimilation of its present power into their lives.

His words are too strong for many of his less committed followers, who desert him. Jesus then asks the twelve: 'Do you also want to leave?' With his customary energy and immediacy, Peter answers. 'Lord, to whom shall we go; your words are the words of eternal life. We believe and know that you are God's Holy One.'

Controversy in Jerusalem

For a time Jesus stays in Galilee. He avoids Judea because the Jewish leaders there want to kill him. His brothers tell him he ought to visit the Feast of Tabernacles and display himself to the crowds, so he goes up privately (Chapter 7). Everywhere the people are looking for him, speculating whether he will come. They have not forgotten the dispute at the previous feast, when Jesus so outspokenly attacked the leaders for their attitude, which he had said had sprung from the fact that they did not have the love of God in them (Chapter 5).

Towards the end of the festival he enters the temple and challenges the leaders, asking whether they are trying to kill him for one good deed done to the paralysed man on his last visit. Circumcision could be performed on the sabbath under the law of Moses, so why shouldn't the opposite be done, making people whole?

He continues to assert his divine roots. 'My teaching is not my own but his who sent me.' All these assertions about his close relationship with God and that God is the source of his being and his teaching lie at the root of the Christian doctrine of the incarnation, which means the 'infleshing' of God. If you want to see what God is like, look at Jesus, who shows him in human form. That's what all these sayings add up to. They also say: 'Through him you too can share the likeness.'

The leaders send the temple police to arrest him. They are so impressed that they cannot do it. They tell their employers: 'No one ever spoke as this man speaks.' Jesus meanwhile, in connection with the sprinkling of people with water that was part of the feast, points to himself as the true quencher of people's thirst. 'Whoever believes in me as scripture says: "Streams of living water shall flow from within him".' John adds the important comment that the meaning of this will be seen later when the Holy Spirit will come into the lives of believers and make the work of Jesus operative through them. But until he is glorified – has died and been raised – the work is not complete and cannot therefore be passed on.

Your Home is in This World; Mine is Not

Still in Jerusalem, Jesus continues his teaching. He begins to speak publicly of his going away, which puzzles people. He tells them that where he is going they cannot come. 'You belong to the world below, I to the world above. Your home is in this world; mine is not.' And he tells them his words report what he has heard from God.

There is a constant balancing of the origin of Jesus in God with his coming under the authority of God. 'He who sent me is present with me, and has not left me on my own; for I always do what is pleasing to him.' Here is divine indwelling and human dependence at work in one individual.

There follows a long discussion where Jesus teaches them that merely being physically descended from Abraham doesn't make them free. The truth that Jesus embodies will liberate them, though. They cannot make up their minds whether he is mad or wicked. They take up rocks to stone him, but he leaves the temple.

Sight to the Blind

Chapter 9 is a lovely story in which Jesus restores a blind man's sight. The Pharisees investigate. Was he blind? Oh yes, say his neighbours. They ask the man and he presents the facts of what Jesus did. 'The man called Jesus made a paste and smeared my eyes and told me to go to Siloam and wash. So I went and washed and found I could see.' The leaders then interrogate the parents of the man. They are alarmed. They say: 'Yes, he is our son and he was blind, but by what means he sees we do not know. He is of age; ask him.'

So they do so again and tell the man that Jesus is a sinner. The man says, 'Whether or not he is a sinner I do not know; all I know is this; I was blind and now I can see.' They keep asking for details. The man gets irritated: 'I have already told you but you took no notice. Why do you want to hear it again? Do you want to become his disciples?'

At that they become abusive. They follow Moses and do not know where this man comes from. Then the man becomes really outspoken: 'How extraordinary! Here is a man who has opened my eyes, yet you don't know where he comes from . . . If this man were not from God he could do nothing!'

'Who are you to lecture us?' they retort. 'You were born and bred in sin.' Then they turn him out. Jesus finds him and he expresses his faith and kneels before Jesus.

It is remarkably real. You can feel all the human interactions nearly 2,000 years later. The once blind man then passes into obscurity, though with a fame that outlasts many of the world's great leaders.

The Good Shepherd

God was always known as the shepherd of Israel. The favourite Psalm of many people is 'The Lord's my shepherd' (Psalm 23). Then Jesus says he is this divine shepherd. He refers to Eastern shepherding practice, where the shepherd leads rather than drives the sheep. He sleeps in the door of the sheepfold at night, so that any wild animal or thief has to climb over him. He is the door. He is prepared to give his life to save the sheep. The sheep know the shepherd's voice and will follow him. They will not follow strangers. He hints that the leaders of Israel are thieves and robbers of the opportunity for people to follow God and now him.

He speaks of his sheep; he knows them and they know him. He is the good shepherd. He also has to include other flocks of sheep, which is a reference to the Gentiles coming in, but it will be at the cost of his life, which he will lay down and then receive back from his Father.

The people are bewildered by his claims. It is all so different from what they are used to in their religious life.

Later in the chapter Jesus attends a winter festival in Jerusalem. He again speaks of his flock of sheep. 'My Father who has given them to me is greater than all, and no one can snatch them out of the Father's care. The Father and I are one.' In one sentence he blends the two aspects of his person. He is subject to the Father, yet he is in perfect union with Him. (And, what is more, he invites believers to share in this union.)

The Jews prepare to stone him. He challenges them, and asks for what good deed they are stoning him. They say for blasphemy: 'You, being a man are claiming to be God.' He points out that in Psalm 82 the leaders of Israel are called gods (*elohim* in Hebrew). How then can they charge him with blasphemy for saying he was the Son of God, he whom God had consecrated and sent into the world? He reaffirms that the Father is in him and he is in the Father.

The picture of Jesus presented in John is so profound. In some way Jesus represents God as no other human has ever done. The source of his being is God. He and the Father are one, yet the Father is also greater than him and it is the Father's will that he does, not his own.

29

Christ's Other Self – The Holy Spirit

John

Listening to John

The first ten chapters of the Gospel of John have been seeking to gain some understanding of who Jesus Christ really was. We have been seeing him presented as the revelation of the living God in human nature. To know him was to know God, yet he was fully human and developed like any human child, even if some of his development was spiritually prodigious. He had a communication with God, his Father, that was close and 'out of this world', beyond the merely human. He was the human face of the living God. The source of his being was in God; in the Word and 'mind' of God he had very real existence from all eternity.

These are profound thoughts about the Father and the Son. We can't pretend that we altogether understand all that we are saying, but at least we have some glimpse of God at work in this unique man.

John shows some of the work of Jesus, particularly in

Jerusalem, not covered by the Synoptics (Matthew, Mark and Luke). We have listened to teachings that John adds to some of the events. We have heard the symbols of Jesus as the bread from heaven, the good shepherd, the light of the world, the provider of living water.

We now move on to see him as the 'resurrection and the life' in the story of the raising of Lazarus. Then we look at four sublime chapters, where he talks with his disciples at the Last Supper and deepens their relationship with him and his Father. He promises that he will not leave them as orphans, but will be ever with them through the Comforter, the Holy Spirit.

I am the Resurrection and the Life

Jesus is only a short time from the cross, spending time out of the danger zone, near the River Jordan. He has friends, a family, in Bethany, not far from Jerusalem: Martha, Mary and Lazarus. He receives a message from the sisters that Lazarus is dangerously ill. Instead of going straightaway, he waits for two more days then proposes to go back to Judea. The disciples think that this is asking for trouble, and even death.

Jesus explains that Lazarus has fallen asleep and that he is going to wake him up. To the disciples this seems foolish. If he is sleeping he will get better. Jesus explains plainly, 'Lazarus is dead.' Thomas says, 'Let us also go and die with him' (with Jesus).

When they reach Bethany, Martha meets him. She expresses her faith in Jesus by saying that if he had been there, Lazarus would not have died, and she makes a half leap of deeper faith by saying that even now God will grant Jesus whatever Jesus asks of him.

Jesus says that Lazarus will rise again. Martha says, 'Yes, in the resurrection at the last day.' At this point Jesus says, 'I am the resurrection and the life . . . whoever has faith in me shall live even though he dies; and no one who lives and has faith in me shall ever die. Do you believe this?' Puzzle though it is, she confirms that she does, and adds, 'I believe you are the Messiah, the Son of God who was to come into the world.' This forms a rich understanding of the whole sweep of God's purpose with Israel and Jesus, who now embodies Israel in himself.

Mary now comes out to meet Jesus and also says that if he had been there her brother would not have died. Jesus becomes 'moved with indignation and greatly distressed', angry with the human situation which involved death, and distressed at the sorrow of the sisters. His empathy runs deep.

He goes to the burial place. The simple words 'Jesus wept' say more about the reality of his humanity than reams of theology. Some bystanders criticise Jesus for not having done something to stop it. This was a warped kind of faith. Over the practical Martha's protests that the body will now stink, the stone is removed from the mouth of the grave.

There is a brief prayer of thanks that God has already heard him, proved no doubt by the fact that there is no smell, then the cry: 'Lazarus, come out.' And he does, with the clothes of the grave still binding him.

The Impact of the Raising of Lazarus

This miracle led to many putting their faith in Jesus. Others reported it to the Pharisees, who along with the rulers see it as a crisis. Everyone will believe in him. Caiaphas, the high priest, says it is in their interest that one man should die for the people, rather than the whole nation be destroyed. So they plot to get rid of him, and Lazarus too. John points out that the words of the high priest predict more than what he knew or intended, and are in fact very relevant to the real purpose of the death of Jesus.

So Jesus remains close near the desert for a few days, then makes his entry into Jerusalem on a donkey. He has a brief encounter with some Gentiles who are attending the feast and have asked Philip if they can see Jesus. He talks of what is about to happen to him in terms of a grain of wheat being cast into the earth, where it dies yet produces a rich harvest. Without this death it is useless.

He also says of those who follow him: 'Where I am there will my servant be.' This does not appear to refer to physical location, but a mutual involvement, independent of space; a feeling of connection with family and other loved ones, even though you may be physically absent from one another, is a human analogy. Even that simile lacks the full strength of the idea of Jesus being present in the lives of the believers even though he is physically absent. This is key to much of what follows.

There was a division among the people about him. Some couldn't accept the idea that the Messiah would die. Not even the signs could convince others. What we do not always realise is that 'even among those in authority many believed in him, but would not acknowledge him on account of the Pharisees, for fear of being banned from the synagogue'. Jesus goes into hiding again.

Now is the Son of Man Glorified

We now move past the scene of the Last Supper, already considered in our Chapter 27, and including the washing of the disciples' feet from John's record. Judas goes out. 'And it was night.' Remember those poignant words.

Jesus now has the attention of the eleven. He trusts them,

even though he knows that they will for a time be overwhelmed by events. The die has been cast and the cross is now inevitable. This causes him to say, 'Now the Son of Man is glorified and *in* him God is glorified.' He is in fact saying that an ugly death on a Roman cross is 'glorification', quite different from the glory Jews usually associated with the coronation of the Messiah to take over David's throne. The crown of thorns is more glorious than a triumphant coronation anthem, such as Handel wrote.

In Hebrew 'glory' means weight, in the sense that a prime minister or preacher might utter 'weighty words' or have what people might call a 'weighty presence or personality'. It brings out the essence of a person's greatness. With that understanding we can begin to understand why the crucifixion is glorious and is glorification for Jesus. As a process it extends to include his resurrection and ascension. (The word is *chabod – kabod –* which we find in 1 Samuel 4:21, where the ark is captured by the Philistines and the dying mother names her newborn child Ichabod, meaning 'the glory is departed'.)

I Go to Prepare a Place For You

The core of John, Chapters 14–17, lies in the announcement by Jesus that his departure is imminent. This mystifies and troubles the disciples. 'I am going where you cannot follow me now, but one day you will.' They think in terms of a journey through physical space to a physical destination. Jesus is thinking on a different level: the destination is death, resurrection and ascension. So he seeks to set their troubled hearts at rest. He tells them that there are many dwelling places in his Father's house and that the purpose of his journey is to prepare one for them. In its context this is nothing to do with preparing a place for them in heaven at death. He adds,

'I shall come again and take you to myself, that where I am you may be also', and says that they know the way or route he is taking.

They still understand this in physical terms; if they don't know where he is going, how can they know the route? His reply puts it on the spiritual level: 'I am the way, the truth and the life; no one comes unto the Father except by me.' He is the route to the Father; his death and resurrection are the way by which his disciples will reach the destination of fellowship with the Father.

In some form Jesus is going to come to them so that even in this life they can enjoy his presence. This is not the 'second coming' but the coming of the 'comforter' or advocate, the Holy Spirit – his other self or alter ego – that, as we shall see, will mediate his presence and the fruits of his victory to them.

Show Us the Father

Philip now says that they will be satisfied if he shows them the Father. He rejoins that this is exactly what he has been doing all the time. 'He that has seen me has seen the Father . . . I am in the Father and the Father in me . . . it is the Father who dwells in me doing his own work.' Jesus continues by referring to the works that God has done through him and tells them that they will do greater works than these, because he is going to the Father.

How could they do greater works than he? Though they might not match the substance of his achievements, they could extend his teachings over a greater area, and as we know they carried his message over the whole of the Mediterranean world. And why should his absence make these greater things possible? Because once he is no longer bounded by the limitations of earth to be in one place at a time, he could send them the Holy Spirit and thus be with them everywhere simultaneously – the meaning of the phrase above 'that you may be with me where I am'.

The Paraclete

Jesus goes on to discuss the sending of the Holy Spirit. 'I will ask the Father and he will give you another to be your *paraclete* [in Greek], who will be with you forever, the Spirit of Truth.' I inserted the Greek word because there is debate about its translation. At least we know it is the Holy Spirit, but the choice of *paraclete* is significant, as it creates the idea of someone who comes alongside to help and give strength. An advocate in a court of law performs this for the person being defended, hence that translation in certain versions.

The King James Version in Britain used the word 'comforter'. 'Com' means coming alongside, being with; 'fort' means strength, as in Latin words with the root 'fort'. So it suggests someone who comes close to give you strength and power. Other translations give 'counsellor', 'helper', 'protector'. The New Jerusalem Bible uses the Greek word *paraclete*; now we know what it means I will sometimes use it, along with the other words. I will particularly use the wider term – the Holy Spirit.

Much of what Jesus now says is about this other presence of himself with the disciples after he is no longer visible. They already know him as comforter and helper, because that is what he has been to them. The *paraclete* will be *in* them. This clarifies his earlier statement: 'If I go away I will come again and take you unto myself'; 'I will not leave you as orphans [or bereft]'; 'I am coming back to you.' He will come back to strengthen them for their mission in the form of the *paraclete* or Holy Spirit, which is sometimes described as God at work within a person or community. Jesus even said that they would in this way 'see' him – perceive him.

The Father and I Will Come to You

Jesus repeats the idea a number of times. He says that he and the Father will *come* to them and make their dwelling in them, and also states that the advocate, the Holy Spirit, will be sent by the Father in his (Jesus') name. His role will be to remind them of all the things that Jesus has said. He tells them they ought to be pleased he is going to the Father, because the Father is greater than he and therefore more resources will be made available to them for the work of preaching and establishing the Church.

In Chapter 14 he indicates that he, Jesus, will come, that he and his Father will come, that the comforter will come, that the Father will send the *paraclete*, and this sending will be in the name of Jesus. So there is a delightful mixing of terms. The Father, Jesus and the Holy Spirit are all said to be involved in doing the same things. There is unity between them, so that what one does may be said to be done by the others. There is the basis of a kind of Trinity here; put this way it doesn't sound too confusing.

Other passages in this section of John, dealing with the coming of the Holy Spirit, express the same ideas:

> When the Advocate has come whom I shall send you from the Father – the Spirit of Truth that issues from the Father – he will bear witness to me' (John 15:26). [The role of the Spirit is to support them in their work of preaching and ministering.]

> It is in your interest that I am leaving you; if I do not go the Advocate will not come, whereas if I go I will send

him to you (John 16:7). [He goes on to describe the content of the witness that would be generated by the advent of the Spirit.]

Making Christ Real in the Disciples' Experience

A particularly significant contribution comes in John 16:13–15.

> When the Spirit of truth comes, he will guide you into all the truth; for he will not speak on his own authority; but will speak only what he hears and he will make known to you what is to come [i.e. the suffering Jesus would undergo and the victory he would achieve, which were still 'to come' when Jesus was speaking]. He will glorify me and will take what is mine and make it known to you [i.e. he will make the suffering and triumph of Jesus part of the personal experience of the disciples, so that they can pass it on to others].

This taking of the experience of Jesus and making it present to the disciples' souls is a deepening of their personal awareness, as well as, or thereby, enhancing their ability to witness for Jesus. The Holy Spirit, through their witness (in the New Testament, in the Church and also operating direct on believers) is promised in numerous places as the heritage of believers of all periods of history since. Part of its work is to make Christ real in human experience, so that people can, as it were, die with him, live with, rise with him.

The New Testament is constantly saying that what happened to Christ happens to his followers. All his sadnesses and triumphs are mirrored in the personal crucifixion and constant rising of believers. The key facts of the biography of Jesus are taken by the Holy Spirit and made part of the autobiography of each believer. That is the wider teaching, which has its roots in these chapters in John.

The True Vine

Chapter 15 of John's Gospel has the same message from Jesus to his disciples about the mutual indwelling of the Father in him, of him in the believers, all held together by the Holy Spirit. He uses the analogy of the vine. He is the vine; they are the branches; through his life-giving energy they bear fruit, but they have to stay connected and the main link is love. 'Dwell in my love,' he tells them. 'Love one another as I have loved you; there is no greater love than this, that someone should lay down his life for his friends.' He keeps reiterating this commandment that they should be rooted in and grow in his love, showing it to one another and to the world.

Part of the work of the Holy Spirit or *paraclete* is to provide answers to their prayers in connection with their witness and the maintenance of their faith in the face of opposition, suffering and great difficulty. 'The Father loves you himself, because you have loved me and believed that I came from God . . . I have told you all this so that in me you may find peace. In the world you will have suffering. But take heart! I have conquered the world!'

Prayer For Believers of All Ages

Finally in this moment of communion with his followers before his arrest, he utters in their presence a prayer, which is largely for them and for those who should believe through their testimony. In other words, if what we read convinces us that Jesus is who he says he is and that he and the Father and the Spirit have done what he says they would, then we are included in the prayer.

His prayer is also a prayer of seeking help for himself for the ordeal that lies ahead. He acknowledges the special role he has from God. Speaking of himself he prays: 'You have made him sovereign over mankind, to give eternal life to all whom you have given him. This is eternal life; to know you the only true God, and Jesus Christ whom you have sent.' This is not intellectual knowledge, but personal knowledge of an intense intimacy; a good marriage is an example of it.

Jesus goes on to recapitulate the work he has done with his disciples in teaching them what he had learned from God. He asks God to protect them in their faith so that they may be one, even as the Father and the Son are one, and recognises the problems they will meet. He asks the Father not to take them out of the world, but to preserve them from the evil in it. He asks that just as he is the 'Word made flesh' so God's word may consecrate them:

> It is not for these alone I pray, but also for those who through their words put their faith in me. May they all be one; as you, Father, are in me, and I in you, so they also may be in us, that the world may believe that you sent me. The glory which you gave me, I have given to them, that they may be one, as we are one. I in them and you in me; may they be perfectly one. Then the world will know that you sent me, and that you loved them as you loved me.

Finally he asks that his followers, God's gift to him, may look upon his glory, 'which you have given me, because you loved me before the world began'.

The prayer will have strengthened him for the immediate ordeal. It will strengthen them as long as they live, to look upon his glory for the rest of their days and be sustained by it. Many Christians have found that the inner power of these four chapters has convinced them and kept them convinced, more effectively than any amount of logic and debate. They feel that this is where they come to really know God, through his Son and through the Holy Spirit.

And so Jesus went forward to be betrayed and arrested.

30

Bringing the Good News From Jerusalem to Rome – Unlocking the Doors

Acts of the Apostles

Waiting in Jerusalem

Luke provides two books of the New Testament as a systematic account of the ministry of Jesus and the establishment of the Christian faith in the Roman empire. Volume 1, the Gospel of Luke, finishes with Jesus bidding his disciples 'to proclaim repentance, bringing forgiveness of sins to all nations, beginning at Jerusalem'. They are to wait at Jerusalem for the gift, promised by the Father, of power from above to enable them to witness. This accords with the promises of the *paraclete* as recorded in John 14–16, which we have just considered.

Volume 2 – the Acts of the Apostles – tells us that over a period of forty days Jesus saw his disciples frequently, giving ample proof that he was alive. He told them to wait, as in a few days they would be baptised with the Holy Spirit. They asked whether he was now going to restore the Kingdom to Israel, meaning the Old Testament version of the Kingdom. They still had not understood the nature of the Kingdom that

Jesus envisaged. This underlies the need for the *paraclete* to instil in their memories all that Jesus has taught them.

Meanwhile Jesus brushes their question aside and points them to the job for which they will be empowered. They will bear witness in Jerusalem, throughout all Judea and Samaria, and even to the farthest corners of the earth. What starts as a small band of Jews in Jerusalem develops by the end of the Book of Acts into a large body of people of every race and colour, throughout the Roman empire.

Acts 1 also deals with the election of an apostle to fill the vacancy left by the suicide of Judas. It is not clear whether this is being presented as a requirement of Jesus or as Peter's idea.

The first part of our study of Acts will take us from Peter's use of the keys of the kingdom to open the door for the Jews, through to his opening the door for the Gentiles, following Paul as far as central and southern Turkey. The next chapter will take us to where the Book of Acts ends, with Paul in Rome.

Pentecost – the Pouring Out of the Spirit

On the Day of Pentecost (a Jewish harvest feast), when the disciples were all together in one place, 'suddenly there came from the sky what sounded like a strong driving wind, a noise that filled the whole house where they were sitting. And there appeared to them flames, like tongues of fire, distributed among them and coming to rest on each one.' This sounds like an attempt to describe the indescribable, though the adjective 'electrifying' would aptly describe the power that entered the house. The outward phenomena are pointers only, but the record continues: 'They were all filled with the Holy Spirit and began to talk in other tongues as the Spirit gave them power of utterance.'

This one-off occasion begins the fulfilment of what Jesus

has promised about the comforter or *paraclete*, though the Holy Spirit later settles down to being a quieter ongoing influence. The truly significant outcomes of the Day of Pentecost are less sensational, enduring, spiritual transformations:

- the newly acquired clarity of understanding, which enables Peter to focus his thoughts and make a speech that shows he now understands the nature of the Kingdom;
- the amazing courage that enables the disciples, who only recently had deserted Jesus and fled, to stand up for him in the most public way;
- 3,000 converts;
- the creation of a community, a new Israel, sharing new understanding, new vision, new fellowship and worship with great joy and love.

It is presented as the dawn of a new age in the dealings of God with the human race.

At the dramatic moment of outpouring of the Spirit, great excitement is caused among the crowds when they hear the good news preached in their local languages, covering many of the areas later traversed by Paul in his journeys. Many are impressed as they listen to the great things that God has done in Jesus. Others are sceptical and put it down to drunkenness.

Peter's Speech on the Day of Pentecost

Peter stands up, shouts for a hearing and in his characteristically practical way debunks the idea of drunkenness. It's only nine in the morning! This is a fulfilment of the prophecy of Joel, where the prophet says that in the last days the pouring out of the Spirit will not be confined to official channels or limited by age, gender or social status. All would prophesy, which is to say they would witness to God's mighty deeds, rather than just predict the future. And here the disciples were giving their confident witness.

The expressed and implied argument of Peter is as follows:

- By many signs and wonders Jesus demonstrates that he has come from God.
- But he dies on a cross.
- However this death was predicted in the Old Testament as part of the Messiah's experience.
- Then he rose from the dead.
- We know – because we saw him with our own eyes.
- No, we can't produce him, because he is at the right hand of God, as he said he would be.
- But he is here in the power of the Holy Spirit that you have witnessed today; you have felt him in your midst; so you may be sure of the message we have shared.

'God has made this Jesus, *whom you crucified*, both Lord and Messiah . . . all that you now see and hear flows from him.'

What Are We To Do?

The accusation rings in the ears of the listeners. They cry out, 'What must we do then?' In their different ways they have contributed to the crime (and Christians today often feel their own sins are mirrored in it – as expressed in the spiritual 'Were you there when they crucified my Lord?').

Peter answers:

- Repent – turn right round, having seen yourself as you really are, now live life facing a different direction;

- be baptised – publicly commit yourself, every one of you, whatever your age, gender or status;
- in the name of Jesus (Joel's 'name of the Lord', Yahweh), who is the Messiah (Christ) spoken of by the prophets;
- and your sins will be forgiven, your guilt will be removed;
- and you will receive the gift of the Holy Spirit, and Christ's death and resurrection will become part of your experience as you die to sin and rise to righteousness;
- the promise is for all generations, to all who accept the call (a hint of universality).

There were 3,000 baptisms that day. 'They met constantly to hear the apostles preach and to share the common life, to break bread and pray.' The disciples also attempt to share their possessions, selling property and passing out the proceeds among those less fortunate.

The Lame Man Walks

A lame man lies at the Beautiful Gate of the temple, carried there daily to beg. Peter and John come that way and stop. The man expects some money. Peter says, 'I have no silver or gold; but what I have I give you; in the name of Jesus Christ of Nazareth, get up and walk.' They help him up and he walks and, indeed, leaps and praises God.

It creates a sensation, because the man is well known. People come running towards Peter, who preaches to them. He ascribes the cure to God's power, and brings into focus the death and resurrection of Jesus showing how the promises made to Abraham are being fulfilled by the blessing of the forgiveness of sins offered to them in Jesus. All the prophets predicted this and, in unexpected ways, the victory they expected is being achieved. If people want to be part of it they must repent and turn to God.

The Apostles Prosecuted

The authorities arrest the apostles, who have continued to preach the word of Jesus, crucified and risen, and want to know their authority for the healing. Peter tells them that it is 'in the name of Jesus Christ of Nazareth, whom you crucified'. They add that salvation is through him and through him alone! The boldness of the apostles impresses the leaders and makes them fearful of where this will lead. They eventually let the apostles off with a caution not to speak in the name of Jesus any more.

But notice the new Peter, so different from the one who denied Jesus: 'Is it right in the eyes of God to obey you rather than him? Judge for yourselves. We cannot possibly give up speaking about what we have seen and heard.' The rulers repeat the caution and discharge the apostles, who then report events to the Church which thanks God and prays that it might be enabled to speak the word with boldness. The room shakes and there is a sense of the renewing of the Holy Spirit.

Later the apostles are again imprisoned, but then they are released 'by an angel'. To the Jewish leaders' amazement, they find the gaol empty and then, next morning, the apostles are teaching in the temple. They are arrested quietly for fear of popular reaction, and are ordered to stop preaching. They reply with a restatement of the gospel and a defiant reply: 'We must obey God rather than men.'

The leaders want to execute them, but Gamaliel, a Pharisee, dissuades them. 'If this is not of God,' he says, 'it will come to nothing.' He wants them to be careful that they should not find themselves fighting against God. So they flog the apostles instead, and then let them go.

Stephen's Defence of the Gospel

Around this time, the Church engages in an effort to share all its possessions. Ananias and Sapphira try to cheat and both die dramatically. We hear little more about the experiment in common ownership, but much about generosity and mutual aid is described. To ensure that the care of the poor proceeds in an orderly way, seven wise men are appointed to supervise the daily distribution of alms to poor believers and to leave the apostles free for teaching.

One of these helpers is Stephen, who, in addition to his new duties, also engages in preaching and skilful debate with the Jewish leaders, who then trump up charges against him and bring him before the courts, accusing him of blasphemy against the law of Moses by saying that Jesus is going to destroy the temple and bring the Mosaic system to an end.

Acts 7 records Stephen's defence speech, his face 'like the face of an angel' supporting the conviction of his words. He recounts the history of Israel. The prosecutors remain quiet, clearly listening with satisfaction to the description of the basis of their national pride. At first it sounds as if it is in harmony with their traditions. They possibly begin to think he is a Jewish patriot after all, until the truth of what he is really saying eventually dawns on them.

What seems like a straightforward review of Jewish history has a particular slant, which gradually unfolds. Stephen is stressing how many of the key moments in Israel's history happened outside their land: the call of Abraham, his long stay in Haran; the moulding into a nation down in Egypt, from the time of Joseph to Moses; the vision to Moses at the burning bush in the wilderness and the proclamation of the name of the Lord; the wandering in the wilderness for forty years. The story of the burning bush and the presence of God in the tabernacle show how the wilderness could be a holy place.

Alongside this Stephen hints at the continual disobedience of the Jewish race to the commandments of God: opposition to Moses when he tries to help them in Egypt; worship of the golden calf; frequent idolatry. He reaches the story of David and Solomon and the building of the temple, quoting Solomon as saying that God does not live in houses built by men, for he is greater than any human creation; the whole universe is his temple.

At this point some of the audience become restive. They realise that Stephen is belittling the importance of the external heritage of Israel in land and temple. Sensing this opposition, he thunders out words of rebuke. He attacks them as stubborn, deaf to truth, killers of the prophets, murderers of the Messiah, who even fail to obey the law they profess.

They degenerate into a raging mob, drag him outside the city and stone him to death. As he is dying, like Jesus he asks God to forgive them. He is the first member of the early Church to make it so clear that the promises of God to Israel are spiritual in their intent and are to be fulfilled in unexpected ways: God will live in human hearts, not buildings of stone.

Unobtrusively Paul is introduced, with his original name Saul, and in an unfavourable light. Those who are stoning Stephen 'laid their coats at the feet of a young man named Saul'. The last verse of the chapter declares: 'Saul was among those who approved of his execution.'

The Church Moves Outward

Following the stoning of Stephen large-scale persecution of the Church comes into operation. The early Christians have to scatter into Samaria and further afield. Saul is prominent in the persecution, arresting Christians in their homes and sending them to prison.

Philip is a former colleague of Stephen, on the distribution committee. He is preaching in Samaria with considerable success and Peter and John come down to assist. They have to deal vigorously with an ex-wizard who wants to buy the powers of the Holy Spirit (the word 'simony' describes those who try to buy Church offices). Philip also preaches to an Ethiopian government official as he rides in his chariot in the south of Palestine. He is reading Isaiah 53 and Philip uses it to preach Jesus as the servant sufferer who fulfils these words of scripture to their fullest extent. The official stops his chariot and is baptised.

The Conversion of Saul (Paul)

Saul continues his persecution and is authorised by the high priest to go as far afield as Damascus in Syria to arrest Christians and bring them back to Jerusalem for trial. While on the road to Damascus, a brilliant light flashes around him, throwing him to the ground. He hears a voice saying, 'Saul, Saul, why are you persecuting me?' (notice 'me', for what was done to the Church was done to Jesus). 'Tell me, Lord, who you are,' responds Saul. 'I am Jesus whom you are persecuting!'

Saul gets up from the ground, finding himself blinded, and the frightened members of his party lead him by the hand into Damascus, to the street called Straight where he lodged (a personal thrill has been to walk down this very street, feeling the reality of Saul's experience). A disciple, Ananias, is told in a vision to go there, and he does so with some trepidation, because he knows of Saul, the great persecutor. The vision tells him Saul is a chosen instrument to bring the gospel before nations and their kings, as well as to Israel.

Ananias goes off to Saul and has the power to cure the blindness. Saul is immediately baptised. He wastes no time. His life has been totally revolutionised, and he must tell everyone. He enters into the synagogues and demonstrates from scripture and experience that Jesus is the Messiah and Son of God. People are flabbergasted at this complete turnaround. Saul the persecutor is soon being persecuted himself and has to be let down from the walls of Damascus in a basket.

He goes to Jerusalem, where everyone is understandably rather suspicious of him. However, Barnabas, who in Acts always appears to have been a large-hearted man, befriends him. Eventually, after further plots against him, Saul, a Roman citizen, returns to Tarsus in Turkey, his birthplace.

Gentile Admission to the Church

In Acts 10 we learn how Peter uses his second key of the Kingdom to admit Gentiles.

A Roman officer, Cornelius, is regular in his prayers and joins with the Jews in the worship of God. He has a vision to send for Peter, who will tell him what he must do. The following day Peter is waiting for his lunch. Hungry, he becomes drowsy. He dreams of a fishing boat sail being lowered from heaven. It contains all kinds of animals, reptiles and birds. A voice tells him to arise and eat. He refuses because, as a Jew, he has never eaten unclean animals that the law forbade. The voice replies, 'What God counts clean you must not call profane.' This happens three times.

While Peter is puzzling over the meaning of this vision, the messengers from Cornelius arrive. Peter, prompted by an inner voice, agrees to go with them to Caesarea, where

Cornelius has gathered all his family and servants. Peter tells them of the vision and how God has taught him that he must not call a member of any race profane or unclean. The Jewish rule not to associate with anyone of another race was not God's will, so he had come without demur.

Peter continues: 'I now understand how true it is that God has no favourites, but that in every nation those who are God-fearing and do what is right are acceptable to him.' This recognition and conversion is just as sensational as the revolution in Saul's life. Barriers are removed and the way is open for the call of the Gentiles into the Church. Peter preaches the essential facts about the ministry, death, resurrection and living presence of Jesus, but before he has finished gifts of the Holy Spirit fall upon the company of Cornelius. Faced with this, Peter says that he cannot withhold the water of baptism from these new believers, so they are all baptised.

Peter subsequently goes to Jerusalem, and meets criticism from Jewish Christians for 'visiting men who are uncircumcised and sitting at table with them'. He tells them the whole story of his vision and visit to Cornelius. Their doubts are silenced and they praise God and say that this means that God has granted life-giving repentance to the Gentiles also.

Paul's Ministry Starts

Persecution continues. Believers are increasingly moved out, many of them going to Antioch in northern Syria, where they are first called Christians. Many conversions occur and Barnabas sets off to find Saul in Tarsus. For a year he and Saul work in the Antioch church. A famine is impending in the whole area, and it hits Jerusalem and Judea particularly hard. Barnabas and Saul take contributions down to Jerusalem.

Meanwhile in Judea, King Herod (a different Herod from

the one at the time of the birth of Jesus) is persecuting the church and beheads James, the brother of John. Peter is imprisoned and is mysteriously released, reputedly by an angel. He has to lie low for a bit. Herod himself comes to a bad end (Chapter 12).

Saul and Barnabas are subsequently commissioned to travel further in the Roman world, preaching the gospel to the Gentiles. Their first call is to go to Cyprus, where Saul encounters opposition from Elymas the Sorcerer. Saul denounces him as a fraud and tells him he will be blinded for a period. And he is! Sergius Paulus, the governor of Cyprus, a learned man, is impressed by Saul's teachings, and becomes a Christian. From that time onwards Saul becomes known as Paul. Does he borrow this Roman name from Sergius Paulus?

Paul and Barnabas sail to Turkey, entering it near the modern resort of Antalya and moving on to various cities within a 300-kilometre radius. Antioch in Pisidia, close to the modern town of Yavalc, was then a major city, at the hub of many trade routes. There Paul is invited to address the synagogue.

We Turn to the Gentiles

Paul starts his address in a similar way to that of Stephen, recounting the history of Israel but arriving quite quickly at the promises that God made to King David. He introduces Jesus as the promised heir to David's throne, and reinterprets the nature of his Kingdom, basing it on the death and resurrection of Jesus. Paul uses Old Testament quotations to show Jesus as the fulfilment of those ancient hopes, and he proclaims forgiveness of sins through Jesus.

Paul also indicates that Jesus brings forgiveness and fellowship with God, which could not come by the law of Moses.

This is the beginning of the challenge that becomes a major part of Paul's work. An invitation is issued for him to preach on the next sabbath. Almost the whole city, Jews and Gentiles, attend.

This upsets many of the Jews, who begin to contradict and abuse Paul and his companions. Paul says, 'Right! It was appropriate that we should come first to the Jews with our message, but as you judge yourself unworthy of eternal life, we now turn to the Gentiles.' He quotes Isaiah 49 as his marching orders: 'I have appointed you to be a light for the Gentiles and means of salvation to earth's furthest bounds.' Words spoken of the servant figure – applied to Israel, to Jesus – are now applied to the mission of the whole Church.

This represents a crucial point in the history of the Church. Henceforward Paul concentrates on the mission to the non-Jews, which reaches Rome and beyond.

31

Bringing the Good News From Jerusalem to Rome – To the Ends of the Earth

Acts of the Apostles

The Gates of Faith Thrown Open
We now follow up Paul's declaration that he will in future concentrate on the Gentiles. What is often called his first missionary journey continues in central Turkey.

Wherever he goes, the Jews oppose him, but many non-Jews – and a few Jews too – become believers. At Iconium (modern Konya), Paul and Barnabas speak boldly, but in the end there is a conspiracy to stone them and they have to escape to Lystra and Derbe. They also perform some miraculous healings. One in particular, at Lystra, involving a lame man who has never walked, creates a sensation. The locals decide that Barnabas is Zeus and Paul Hermes. 'The gods have come down in human form,' they say as they prepare to offer sacrifices to Paul and Barnabas.

The apostles are aghast and cry out that they are only human beings. 'The good news we bring tells you to turn from these follies to the living God who made the earth and seas and everything in them.' They fit their teaching to the situation, illustrating the goodness of God from his provision of food in nature.

The crowds are disappointed and become susceptible to agitation by the Jews. Paul is stoned and dragged out of the city as dead, though fortunately it is only concussion and he is able to get up and move on to Derbe.

Such is their courage that Paul and Barnabas go back over their route, gaining further converts and encouraging the believers, and establishing the beginning of a Church order. They offer the warning that only through much hardship can they enter the Kingdom of God.

They then return to Antioch in Syria, and tell the church there of their adventures, and of how God has 'thrown open the gates of faith to the Gentiles'.

The Jerusalem Conference

The Church is still in an early stage of understanding. Jewish believers come to Antioch and begin to teach that circumcision is essential to salvation. It is a matter of Jesus plus circumcision; Jesus plus the law. Paul and Barnabas fiercely oppose this reduction of the significance of Jesus. It is decided that with some others they should go to Jerusalem to discuss the matters with the apostles and elders there.

They tell the story, but some of the Christian Pharisees insist that Gentile converts must be circumcised and keep the law of Moses. After a long debate Peter stands up and takes the conference back to his experiences over Cornelius. 'God made no difference between them and us, for he purified their hearts by faith.' He goes on, 'Why do you now try God's patience by laying on these converts a yoke which neither we nor our forefathers were able to bear? For our belief is that we are saved in the same way as they are: by the grace of the Lord Jesus.' (Notice: 'We are saved in the same way as they are' – not 'they are saved in the same way as we are'!)

Paul and Barnabas amplify their experiences as well as the way in which the power of the Spirit has gone with them and the miracles that have supported them.

James (the brother of Jesus, who had become president of the church in Jerusalem), quotes from the prophecy of Amos to show how it has always been intended that the rest of mankind should share the hope of Israel. He gives his judgement that no irksome restrictions should be placed on the Gentile believers. Simply, they should show empathy for Jewish sensitivity and avoid blood products, the consumption of strangled animals as food and meat offered to idols (with which Paul deals further in 1 Corinthians); of course, they must have nothing to do with pagan temple prostitution, either. A letter is drafted and Paul and Barnabas and two others take it to Antioch, where it is received with great relief. On that letter depends the future of the Church.

Paul's Second Missionary Journey

These apostles are human. Paul and Barnabas want to visit the converts in Turkey, to take the preaching further. Barnabas wants to take Mark (who later wrote the Gospel). Paul disagrees, as he considers that Mark let them down on the first journey. Their disagreement is acute and they part company. Barnabas takes Mark with him to preach in Cyprus, and Paul chooses to bring Silas. (Years later Paul forgives Mark and from his Roman prison cell asks Timothy to bring Mark: 'He is a great help to me', 2 Timothy 4:11). The episode helps one to feel the reality of the situation.

Paul and Silas go back to Lystra, where Paul was previously

stoned and concussed. There Timothy begins his long association with Paul. As Timothy was half Jewish, Paul, out of consideration for Jewish sensitivity, has him circumcised, something he later refused to do for a full Gentile, Titus. This journey includes Galatia, where the Church later receives a tough letter from Paul.

Over to Europe

Then Paul receives a vision in which a Macedonian appeals to him to come over to help them. I used to find it difficult to accept all these visions and angels in the Book of Acts, but the context in which they appear is so realistic that I personally feel happy to believe that something like this happened. After all, a God who raises Jesus from the dead will be able to deal with minor things such as a few visions at crucial points in the campaign. It is interesting that Paul still has to make the decision. We read: 'As soon as he had seen the vision, we set about getting a passage to Macedonia, convinced that God called us to take the good news there.' (Note Luke was there too. He says 'we'.)

The first stop in Greek Macedonia is at Philippi, where a dye trader, Lydia, is converted and baptised. Soon, however, they are in trouble. Paul cures a possessed young woman who has been a source of income for people exploiting her supposed divination skills. They create trouble and Paul and Silas are imprisoned in the inner prison with their feet in the stocks.

They are singing hymns in the middle of the night when an earthquake occurs and everyone is freed from their fetters. The gaoler wakes up and sees the prison doors open and is about to kill himself. Paul takes charge and assures him that no one has escaped. The gaoler goes on his knees and asks, 'What must I do to be saved?' Whatever he meant, Paul answers him on a spiritual level, explaining the gospel to him. He washes the wounds resulting from the ill treatment and he and his household are all baptised.

The city authorities now want to release them. But Paul wishes to protect the situation and insists they come and free them themselves, as they are Roman citizens and the flogging is illegal. The magistrates come and apologise, giving them an escort out of the city after Paul has said goodbye to the new little church.

Thessalonica

Paul proceeds to what is still a large city, Thessalonica (Thessaloniki in modern Greece). He spends three sabbaths in the synagogue, trying to convince the Jews that Jesus was the Messiah and telling of his death and resurrection. Some are convinced, along with a number of Gentiles.

The authorities discover that Paul is teaching about another king, named Jesus, which flouts the emperor's laws. Jason lands in trouble for harbouring them and by night Paul and Silas escape to Beroea. They have a better reception here; the Beroeans are fair-minded and they search the scriptures to verify things for themselves. Many of the Jews and Gentiles are convinced and become believers. The Jews in Thessalonica hear of this and foment trouble in Beroea too. Some of the Beroeans escort Paul to Athens, with Silas and Timothy to follow.

Athens

While Paul is waiting he joins in debate with the Athenian philosophers and debaters in the open place. The story gets around that his teachings involve two new gods – 'Jesus' and

'Anastasis' (resurrection). They think that Anastasis is a female god and bring him to the Council of the Areopagus for an official enquiry into the new ideas.

Paul quite cleverly mentions an altar he had seen – '*To the Unknown God*' – and says, 'That's the one I'm telling you about.' He shows that mankind is searching for this God in its ignorance and quotes Greek poets to illustrate his point. He stresses that neither idols nor images help the understanding of God. God has overlooked the period of ignorance, but now commands all men and women everywhere to repent. He has fixed a Day of Judgement and has proved his intentions by raising Jesus from the dead.

Some scoff. Others say they would like to hear more. A few join Paul and become believers. He suffers no persecution here, but receives little response either. Athens is a city of tolerance, ever learning but never finding the truth as it is expressed. I once read out loud to a business colleague Paul's 'Unknown God' speech as I sat in the very place where it was originally given. My colleague, like the Athenians, was not very impressed, and thought Paul was rather opinionated. I thought it was Paul at his most accommodating.

Corinth

Paul takes a much more definite line when he reaches Corinth, where they spend eighteen months. Fuller details of his experiences are found in his correspondence with the Corinthians. It is a wild city and the church reflects its environment. In the chapters on the letters to the Corinthians I provide more detail than Luke gives us here.

He starts with the Jews but when they oppose him he eventually turns to the Gentiles, meeting in a house next to the synagogue. The Jews bring him before the Roman authorities, who are not interested, and in due course Paul leaves and goes back to Antioch, calling in at Ephesus on the way.

Ephesus

On his third missionary journey Paul spends three years at Ephesus, starting his work as usual in the synagogue, but then hiring the lecture hall of Tyrannus for their meetings. A number of miracles of healing take place. Some Jews try their hands at exorcism using the name of Jesus, but the mad people give them a rough time and they flee naked! After that many Ephesians who had dabbled in magic arts bring their books and spells to the value of 50,000 pieces of silver to be burned publicly! The letters to the Ephesians and Colossians, whether written direct by Paul or on his behalf, tell us much of the kind of teaching that he will have given during the three years.

Paul finally leaves Ephesus after a riot fomented by the silversmiths who make the shrines of Artemis and find that Paul's preaching is bad for trade as it causes many people to reject idolatry. They also appeal to the reputation of Artemis and the disaster that will result from the worship of her being eroded. The demonstration lasts for several hours with the people yelling, 'Great is Artemis of the Ephesians.' It is quite an ugly scene and friends of Paul persuade him not to go into the theatre to attempt a defence. Most people are there for the fun and do not really know what they are shouting about.

The town clerk does an excellent job of calming the crowd. Everyone knows Ephesus is the keeper of the image of Artemis that fell from heaven and as this is indisputable the people should keep calm, he argues. These men have not been guilty of any breach of the peace or blasphemy, and if the silversmiths have any case they should take it to the proper courts. A bigger issue can be dealt with at the higher court. The clerk says they are in danger of being asked to explain this riot, and no answer will be found, so he asks them to go home. And they do.

But it is obvious that Paul can do little more there. He goes on to Macedonia and Greece, including Corinth, and finally back to Jerusalem. On the way he stops at Troas and prolongs his speech till midnight. One young man falls from the balcony and they think he is dead. Paul, with his experience, is able to reassure them that it is only concussion.

On his way back he arranges to meet the elders of Ephesus at Miletus. His poignant speech is reported in Acts 20. He reaffirms his message of 'repentance before God and faith in our Lord Jesus' and commends them to the word of God's grace. He asks them to watch out for false teachers, to help the poor and weak and to recognise that suffering inevitably accompanies faithfulness, particularly in their times. He foresees trouble for himself. They are particularly upset that they will not see his face again. 'There were loud cries of sorrow from them all, as they folded Paul in their arms and kissed him.' If he arouses strong opposition he obviously also inspires warm affection.

Jerusalem

As he journeys back Paul receives several warnings that it is not safe for him to return to Jerusalem. He responds that he will not be weakened in his resolution. He is willing not only to be imprisoned in Jerusalem, but also to die. Arriving in Jerusalem, he describes to James and the congregation all the work of the past few years and how many people have turned to belief in the good news of Jesus.

The Jerusalem church is supportive, but says that the Jewish believers in Christ are troubled because they have heard that Paul has been teaching that people should turn their backs on

Moses and need not circumcise their children. They therefore suggest that Paul should undertake to support four Jewish believers in a ritual of purification, paying their expenses. When the Jews see this they will know that Paul is still a sound Jew, and trouble will be avoided. There is no question of asking the Gentile Christians to observe the Jewish rules.

Paul Rescued by Roman Troops

So Paul agrees. However it backfires. The Jews see him in the temple, and also elsewhere in the city in the company of a Gentile believer, and they assume he has taken him into the temple. A riot ensues. Paul is dragged out of the temple and about to be killed when the commandant and his troops intervene.

The rescue is difficult even for the soldiers because the mob is howling for Paul's blood. Paul surprises the commandant by speaking Greek and is therefore granted permission to speak to the people. He does so in Hebrew and to start with gets a hearing. He describes his rabbinical background in the Jewish religion and how he has seen Jesus on the road to Damascus and become a Christian. He tells them how he shares responsibility for the death of Stephen, but when he comes to recount his mission to the Gentiles they lose control and howl for the death of such a scoundrel.

The commandant decides to extract the truth out of Paul by torture, but when he realises that Paul is a Roman he dismisses the torturers and is worried that he has shackled a Roman citizen.

On Trial for the Resurrection from the Dead

The Jewish Council are now invited to meet Paul in a legal procedure to identify the charges in a proper way. Both Sadducees, who deny the resurrection, and Pharisees, who believe in it, are present. Paul divides them by proclaiming that he is on trial for belief in the resurrection of the dead. The Pharisees therefore decide that no fault lies with Paul and there follows a great dispute with the Sadducees. Again the commandant has to rescue Paul from the crowds.

Some Jews then swear that they will not eat till they have killed Paul. His nephew hears of this and warns the commandant of the plot, so Paul is sent to Caesarea, to a higher Roman authority, Felix, the provincial governor. So great is the danger that 200 infantrymen accompany Paul, and he is held in custody in the palace.

Representatives of the Jews come down to accuse Paul, who makes a reasoned defence to Felix, describing how he is a Christian but has done nothing worthy of all this fuss. He believes in the law and the prophets, but the divisive issue is the resurrection of the dead. The Jews do not necessarily agree, but for Paul Jesus is alive, and this is the key to everything.

Felix has private sessions with Paul out of curiosity, hoping to be bribed. When Paul talks on morals at the first session 'Felix trembles' and brings the session to a speedy end. Paul remains in custody for two years, though with the freedom to see his friends and to receive comforts.

Festus Reopens the Investigation

Festus is the next governor. He reopens the investigation and asks Paul to go to Jerusalem to be tried. Paul knows the danger of this, so using his Roman citizenship he appeals to Caesar. So plans are made for him to go to Rome, which he had wanted to do anyway, though under different circumstances.

King Agrippa, from another province, visits Festus and they

decide to interview Paul in order to decide what to write to Caesar about the prisoner. Paul tells the story of his conversion on the road to Damascus and he summarises his message as preached by him everywhere. Festus thinks he has gone mad from too much studying.

Paul asks Agrippa whether he believes the prophets. 'I know you do,' he adds. Agrippa sarcastically replies, 'With a little more persuasion you will make a Christian of me.' Paul wishes Agrippa would become what he himself is, except for the chains.

Agrippa and Festus afterwards agree that if Paul had not appealed to Caesar he might have been freed.

The Shipwreck

Chapter 27 describes Paul's journey by sea to Rome, a magnificent story told by a superb storyteller.

Paul's dominant personality shines out. He advises the centurion to winter in Crete, but he will not listen. They run into bad weather and terrible storms rage for days. Paul stands up and tells them that they should have listened to him earlier, but he assures them that they will all escape with their lives. He has been told in a vision that he will appear before Caesar and that God has given him the lives of all on board. 'I trust God; it will turn out as I have been told.'

Again Paul takes charge among the other prisoners and persuades them all to have a proper meal. There are 276 people on board. Eventually they sight land, the island of Malta. They are unable to save the ship, which breaks up as it runs aground, but everyone survives. The centurion stops a slaughter of the prisoners, because he wants Paul to be safe.

The Maltese treat them all well. A poisonous snake attaches itself to Paul, and everyone expects him to swell up and drop dead, but he shakes it harmlessly into the fire. They then decide he is a god! Paul does some healing on the island and is treated with great respect during the three-month stay.

Rome

Paul takes a ship to Sicily and then finds fellow Christians at Puteoli and stays a week. And then on to Rome. The Christians travel out to greet him and his companions. He gives thanks to God and takes courage.

The authorities allow Paul to find private lodgings, with a soldier to guard him. The local Jewish leaders come to meet him and he explains what has happened. 'It is for loyalty to the Hope of Israel that I am bound with this chain,' he says. His interpretation of that hope differs from normal Jewish understanding, but its roots lie in the Old Testament.

The Jews and Christians make numerous visits to Paul's lodgings. Although under house arrest, in the relative comfort of something approaching a home he is able to live an active life. Even there he is the human focus of the Gentile churches. He would have said that Jesus was *the* focus. The story ends: 'He stayed there two full years at his own expense, with a welcome for all who came to him. He proclaimed the kingdom of God and taught the facts about the Lord Jesus Christ quite openly and without hindrance.'

Our curiosity is not satisfied about what happens next. Tradition has it that he was released after his appeal to Caesar, but that finally he was rearrested and executed. We learn much more about his work as we seek to understand his letters to the various churches.

32

Paul Explains the Gospel

Romans

The Challenge of the Epistle

We now tackle the most comprehensive and, in many ways, the most difficult of Paul's writings. I would recommend that this chapter on the epistle to the Romans should be read later in your journey through the Bible. A basic understanding will be rewarding, when linked with the rest of the Bible, as a practical guide to the meaning of life as well as a key to a way of living.

Paul's letter to the Romans provides many puzzles for theological scholars and, even without taking an academic approach, we are obliged to acknowledge that more than one interpretation is often possible. We shall be challenged to think deeply. None of the readings contradict the gospel, but they offer different perspectives, some of which may appear to be more helpful than others.

I have also written this chapter without the repeated use of 'Paul says'. Often, in summarising his words, my own beliefs will be obvious, and it is difficult to write neutrally, but I stress that my aim is to help understanding of the Bible, not to tell you what you ought to believe or do about it.

The Context of the Letter

Chapter 15, linked with 2 Corinthians and the Book of Acts, suggests that Paul wrote the letter from Greece, most likely from Corinth, before setting off for Jerusalem to take the money that had been collected for the relief fund to help the poor in Judea. He was going to visit the Romans on the way to Spain, but instead came to Rome several years later as a prisoner, awaiting his appeal to Caesar.

Paul's experience on the road to Damascus of an encounter with Jesus left him with a clear sense of mission to the non-Jews, or Gentiles (without neglecting the Jews, though). This call to witness to the Gentiles lies at the root of everything he says in this letter. He is trying to resolve the relationship between God and the Jews, the role of the Jewish law in the Church and the affiliations of non-Jewish Christians both to the law and to Jewish ethnicity.

As such, these are not directly today's problems, though issues of racism, equality, nationalism and religious smugness are implicitly covered.

The Gospel

Paul introduces himself as called to be an apostle and set apart for the service of the gospel of Christ Jesus (King Jesus). He then defines the gospel. Four verses (1:2–6) are central. The gospel he preaches:

- was announced in the Old Testament;
- is about God's Son;

- humanly he was a descendant of King David;
- in his resurrection he was publicly authenticated as the Son of God;
- all nations are to be brought to faith in this gospel;
- in the name of Jesus;
- and Paul has been specifically commissioned for this work of bringing people to this obedience of faith, irrespective of their nationality.

Paul continues by greeting the Romans and commending their faith, which is recognised throughout the churches. He longs to see them for mutual benefit, for he feels an obligation to fulfil his mission to Jew and 'Greek' in the capital of the Roman Empire. The gospel is not just a theory, but the power of God, which brings 'salvation'. And it brings this fellowship with God, through *faith*, that is, by people putting their trust in what God has done in revealing himself in Jesus.

Covenant Righteousness and the Response of Faith

In this gospel, God displays his faithfulness in the keeping of his promises and remaining true to the covenant which is proclaimed throughout the Jewish Scriptures (Old Testament). This trustworthiness of God, his covenant faithfulness, is called his righteousness. It is sometimes translated 'justice', which, even with its legal flavour, still conveys the idea that God, as judge, may be depended upon to decide and treat people in accordance with his covenant.

God's covenant righteousness, proclaimed in the death and resurrection of Jesus, calls forth a response from those who believe in it. This is the response of faith. It is called the righteousness of faith; placing the person who displays it in the circle of God's love. He or she is brought into the fellowship of the righteous God on the grounds of this faith, and not on the basis of race or law or any other consideration. God considers such people as righteous in his eyes; they are acceptable because of their faith, because they take God at his word and accept what Jesus has done. They are involved in the covenant.

Paul clinches his point by quoting from Habakkuk 2:14, which has been translated: 'He who through faith is righteous, shall live.'

The Human State

If God has gone to such lengths to bring people to this faith, involving the suffering of his Son, the situation that called forth such a drastic remedy must have been grave indeed. So, in the remainder of Chapter 1 and in Chapter 2 Paul exposes that situation, using the currently unfashionable word 'sin'.

Paul castigates the behaviour of the non-Jewish world's worship of idols and its ignoring of the fact that God has given enough evidence of his power and other attributes to have exposed the futility of idolatry. Paul denounces the sexual misbehaviour associated particularly with paganism, including many aspects of which the twentieth century has become tolerant. He describes pagan society as depraved, and lists many forms of 'wickedness', including greed, malice, envy, murder, rivalry, treachery, gossip, scandal-mongering, lack of respect for one's parents, insolence, boastfulness, arrogance and lack of fidelity. Not only do the pagans do these things, but they idolise those who so behave.

An evening of watching typical television programmes would suggest that the new millennium will find that society has changed little since Paul's days.

Are the Jews Any Better?

In Chapter 2 Paul addresses those who may be feeling superior to such behaviour. Are Jews, for example, so much better? Do they in principle commit many of the same sins? No one escapes the judgement of God and all are equally offered his love. God has no favourites. The whole human race is one in sin and one in hope of salvation.

Paul introduces the belief that the law of Moses and circumcision, central to traditional Judaism, are not the basis of acceptability to God. Gentiles outside the law may, nevertheless, follow its principles. Physically uncircumcised people may yet be circumcised in their hearts. They may be spiritually part of God's covenant, with an inward commitment.

Chapter 3 shows Paul wrestling with the problem of the benefit of being a Jew. He sees their special role as custodianship of God's messages – 'the oracles of God'. We have seen the value of this message in the twenty-one chapters on the Old Testament; in Chapter 22 we considered how this led to the mission of Jesus. Paul quotes various Old Testament texts that emphasise the sinfulness of the Jewish race and its failure to fulfil the purpose of their call, which was to serve as a channel of God's covenant mercy to all mankind.

Faith in God's Righteousness

Hence the whole human race, Jew and non-Jew, is exposed to the judgement of God. Law-keeping won't save them; it only emphasises one's inadequacy. The way forward is twofold:

- *on our side*: faith in Christ, who is the medium of God's covenant righteousness; God calls this faith righteousness, a state of being right with him (in legal terms of being acquitted or vindicated);

- *on God's side*: faithfulness to his covenant, which Paul calls the 'righteousness of God'.

All alike have sinned and are deprived of the divine glory; and all are justified [given a righteous status; in the metaphor of the court room, proclaimed 'not guilty'] by God's free grace alone, through his act of liberation in the person of Christ Jesus.

The word righteousness (or justice) is thus used in two ways:

- *the righteousness of God*: his impartial standing by his covenant with men, whatever happens. It is *his* righteousness; it is not something that can be transferred, like a ledger entry, to us. It is how *he* is and how he treats us as a result, forgiving our sins, if we have faith and trust in his fidelity to his promises.
- *the righteousness of faith*: that trust or faith in God's righteousness, which *we* can express in our lives; the faith that God accounts, reckons or calls righteousness; it is our response to what he has done in Jesus, not a matter of good works or law-keeping to earn us a reward from God.

God's Righteousness Demonstrated

Chapter 3:21–6 links these two perspectives on righteousness and presents the self-sacrifice of Jesus as the public proclamation of the righteousness of God, in which people can put their faith and themselves receive a status as righteous, sins forgiven and fellowship with God.

Before Christ, the actual state of mankind was never radically dealt with; God was patient, overlooking people's sins where there was repentance and faith in the anticipated deliverance. Now, in Christ, the covenanted righteousness is focused in his victory over sin and death. The deliverance has arrived. There exists a means by which those who, on their own merits, would be unacceptable can now be accepted, not merely having their sins overlooked.

The two meanings of righteousness are brought together. God is righteous and, by faith in his righteousness shown in Jesus, men and women are regarded as righteous. There is nothing for them to boast about. Their new status is a gift. It is not their own achievement; it is not a matter of successful observance of the law; only a question of faith in what God has done through Christ. And being a Jew doesn't give any special privilege. Jew and Gentile receive the righteous status in the same way – by faith, trust. And these are practical issues, which affect the whole mission on which Paul is engaged, and which he wants the Romans to understand before he arrives.

Abraham's Faith

In Chapter 4 Paul refers back to Abraham, the father of the Jewish race, with whom God made the covenant (Genesis 15). Abraham believed God's promises; he displayed faith. God accounted that as righteousness; God defined righteousness in a human being in terms of that faith. And if God counted Abraham's faith as righteousness, it wasn't a matter of Abraham earning a reward. It was a matter of a gift from God, not of wages due. Faith itself was not 'work', attracting wages; it was gratitude, which responded to the generosity of the giver.

Paul then points out that God made his covenant with Abraham before Abraham was circumcised, so the righteousness of faith preceded circumcision. Abraham's acceptability with God did not depend on this mark in the flesh.

The promise to Abraham also preceded the giving of the law through Moses by some centuries. Thus law-keeping was not the basis of Abraham's hopes. The promises were 'sheer grace'; the response was faith. Through his faith Abraham and his true descendants were appointed the heirs of the world and Abraham was to be the father of many nations. Here Paul is showing that the whole world is included in the promise, including Gentiles, and not just the Jews. And, as children of Abraham, by faith in the death and resurrection of Jesus, both Gentile and Jewish Christians are 'counted' as righteous (forgiven, or acquitted of guilt), in the eyes of God. Such righteousness consists of accepting God's word and living according to it without reservation.

The Magnitude of Grace

In Chapters 5–7, Paul deepens the understanding of what the death and resurrection of Jesus accomplished. They freed humankind from the dominion of sin, death and law, and will lead to the universal nature of salvation, independent of legal achievement or ethnic purity. We have peace and access to God even now and in the future we can share in the full glory of God – a hope not a fantasy! As Paul marvels at the willingness of Jesus to die for us when we were still sinners, he emphasises that not only have we been given a righteous status now, but also ultimate freedom from any punishment our sins deserve. We have been fully reconciled to God.

Paul continues with the story of Adam as the initiator of human disobedience, the one who may be said to have started it all. But in his sacrifice Jesus is a second Adam, who initiates a counter-movement that introduces grace and forgiveness in place of punishment and death. And the gift of righteousness and acquittal far outweighs the earlier sentence of death. One man sinned, and all suffered because they all shared in his sin subsequently. One man gave a perfect sacrifice, and all may share his victory. Law increased the catalogue of sinning that was available; but grace immeasurably exceeded it and brought eternal life in Jesus.

Dead to Sin

In Chapter 6, Paul repudiates the idea of which he had been accused: if God likes dispensing grace and forgiveness, when we sin we are doing him a favour as it gives him more scope for grace! This notion is opposed vigorously.

Baptism is presented as a kind of symbolic dying alongside Christ, burying our old sinful ways as we are dipped beneath the cleansing waters of baptism. (Such immersion was the norm in those days.) Coming up out of the water symbolises a rising from death to a new life. 'Regard yourselves as dead to sin and alive to God, in union with Christ Jesus.'

Paul is emphasising that though we do not earn eternal life by law-keeping, this gives no excuse for moral anarchy. We were slaves of sin; now we serve another master: righteousness. Our bodies are to be yielded to the service of righteousness (the term is here used as a moral one). The end of slavery to sin is death. We are liberated from that to receive the free gift of life in union with Christ.

Freedom From Law

In Chapter 7, Paul uses the analogy of marriage to suggest the idea that when people become Christians the former 'husband' – law – dies, allowing freedom to marry the new 'husband' – Christ, who has been raised from the dead and has initiated the way of the Spirit, rather than perpetuating the old written code.

Law itself is not sinful, but because it defines sin it stirs up the desires that in a law-free world would not be noticed. The law is holy but by highlighting certain acts as wrong it increases their attraction to people. The good thing, law, therefore produces actions that are on the road to death. Law sets up an unremitting struggle, and Paul vividly describes it, possibly as he had understood it in his pre-Christian days or as Israel as a whole would have experienced it whenever they tried to obey it. Committed people would accept the law as good and want to keep it, but 'the good which I want to do, I fail to do; but what I do is the wrong which is against my will'.

'Wretched creature that I am. Who is there to rescue me from this state of death? . . . Who but God? Thanks be to him through Jesus Christ our Lord!' Quite clearly Paul is speaking of the pre-Christian experience. The law is in many ways good, but its effect when perceived as a route to salvation is self-defeating. Again, the solution is God's free gift in Christ and a life of faith in him, which supersedes law. It also sets Jews and Gentiles on an equal footing.

Life Through the Spirit

Chapter 8 takes a positive turn. If law is superseded and faith is the basis of fellowship with God, 'there is now no condemnation for those who are united with Christ Jesus'.

> The life-giving Spirit has set you free from the law of sin and death. What the law could not do, because human weakness robbed it of all potency, God has done: by sending his own Son in the likeness of our sinful nature and to deal with sin, he has passed judgement against sin within that very nature, so that the commandment of the law [its principles] may find fulfilment in us, whose

conduct is no longer controlled by the old nature, but by the Spirit.

Unsuccessful attempts at law-keeping are now superseded by a life run by God's Spirit, also described as the Spirit of Christ. By the Spirit, not by our own unaided efforts, we put to death the sinful tendencies that try to get us in their grip. We are enabled to live on the level of the Spirit, which brings life and peace; we learn that we are God's children and we do not have to have a spirit of fear in relation to God. All very different from the struggle described in Chapter 7.

Ultimately, liberation from mortality will come by the same Spirit. The whole created universe is waiting, whether it knows it or not, for the deliverance that the Spirit will eventually bring.

Meanwhile, the Spirit helps us in our prayers, when we feel at a loss as to what to say. The Spirit also co-operates in our lives for good, though this does not mean escape from suffering.

The chapter finishes with a wonderful song of praise to God:

> If God be on our side, who is against us? He did not
> spare his own Son, but gave him up for us all; how can
> he fail to lavish every other gift upon us? Who will bring
> any charge against those who God has chosen? Not God
> who acquits!

This lies in sharp contrast to whatever seeking salvation by law-keeping can give us.

> Then what can separate us from the love of Christ?
> Can affliction or hardship? Can persecution, hunger,

nakedness, danger or sword? . . . Throughout it all, overwhelming victory is ours through him who loved us. For I am convinced that there is nothing in death or life . . . in the world as it is or the world as it shall be . . . in heights or depths – nothing in all creation can separate us from the love of God in Christ Jesus our Lord!

Paul has considered the sinfulness of the whole human race, Jews and Gentiles. He has highlighted the death and resurrection of Jesus Christ as the way of being pronounced righteous (not guilty), by having faith in the covenant righteousness of God who gave his Son. He has shown that Abraham's faith existed prior to circumcision and to the giving of the law, so that salvation is by faith and not by law-keeping, by grace and not by race. Paul has considered the richness of the forgiveness and the need to die to sin, and has remembered the agony that trying to keep the law used to bring, before the deliverance in Christ, and he has expressed his joy in a Spirit-filled life in the love of God through Christ Jesus.

Now he wants to think about the role of the Jews in relation to his mission to the Gentiles.

Jew and Gentile in God's Plan

Paul has made it clear that Gentiles as well as Jews are part of the family of God by faith. However he himself is a Jew and is concerned that few Jews have become Christians. In Chapter 9 he describes his grief for them. He would even be ready to sacrifice his own salvation, if it could help them. He recounts the many privileges of Israel in their history, which led to the coming of Christ. God must have some purpose with them.

Paul emphasises that not all descended from Abraham are

true Jews. People of faith in Jesus from any nation are the true descendants of Abraham and heirs of the promises. He reviews the lives of the patriarchs, Abraham, Isaac and Jacob, and notes how the birth of each generation had unique, non-natural features, especially Sarah bearing Isaac at the age of ninety. He deals in rather a complex way with the right of God to choose whoever he wishes, making the point that God's selection of people is not based on their deeds. He calls people by his sovereign decision, and it is always mercy, because no one can claim to deserve anything.

Membership of the Covenant

So Gentiles who were not striving after righteousness, nevertheless came to the righteousness of faith. Romans 9:30 to 10:21 is aptly summarised by Tom Wright, who shows how it:

> sets out the results of what God has done in Israel's history. God has called Israel to be the means of salvation for the world. His intention was always to narrow this vocation down to the Messiah, so that in his death all, Jew and Gentile alike, would find salvation. If however, Israel insists on keeping her status for herself, she will find she is clinging to her own death warrant.
>
> Thus, to follow the train of thought from 9:30 onwards, while Gentiles are discovering covenant membership, characterised by faith, Israel, clinging to the law [Torah] which defined covenant membership, did not attain to the Torah. She was determined to have her covenant membership demarcated by the works of the Torah, that is, by the things that kept membership confined to Jews and Jews only; and, as a result, she did not

submit to God's covenant purposes, his righteousness; for Christ is the end or goal of the law, so that all who believe may receive covenant membership.

Christ has fulfilled the covenant purposes, bringing them to their God ordained climax, which was always to deal with sin and so set in motion the renewal of the whole cosmos. Now that purpose is fulfilled, what remains is mission (10:9 onwards).

So the letter to the Romans goes on its way, not as a detached statement of how people get saved, how they enter a relationship with God as individuals, but as an exposition of the covenant purposes of the Creator God. The letter emphasises above all the mission and unity of the church, as the things most necessary for the Romans to grasp if they are to be the base for the further Westward expansion of Paul's mission.

In establishing the theme summarised above, Paul uses a wide array of Old Testament quotations that show the primacy of faith and he applies each to Jesus as Lord. He also quotes passages applicable to his own mission to Gentiles and Jews. He hopes that his preaching to the Gentiles will stir the Jews to a form of jealousy where they will want a share in the gospel, too.

In Chapter 11 Paul pursues this thought and warns the Gentiles not to get puffed up with a sense of importance as superior to the Jews. He is convinced that eventually the Jews will join the Gentiles in one true Israel. In any case, he stresses that for both classes salvation comes by God's mercy. Jews and Gentiles are united in sin. They will now be united by faith in the ultimate deliverance.

Therefore

For eleven chapters Paul has been leading the Romans through the basic principles of the gospel, Jew and Gentile unified in need and in the meeting of that need, salvation from sin and death by faith and not by achievement in law-keeping.

In modern terms, at this point we might say, 'Yes, that's all very well; we now understand much more about the working of God – but what is the everyday implication? So what?'

And the answer comes with the 'therefore' at the start of Chapter 12. Paul is reminding his leaders that in Christ all the Old Testament promises come to fruition. The Church is the new temple; it is a unity of both Jews and Gentiles, so that being a Jew has been redefined. The emphasis is on the Spirit working in human hearts, rather than as a written code; and the conquest is by love, not by military means. 'Therefore' the action that follows transforms the whole of life into a new kind of worship:

> Therefore, my friends, I implore you by God's mercy to offer your very selves to him: a living sacrifice, dedicated and fit for his service, the worship offered by mind and heart.

This implies a complete break with the former Jewish worship. The sacrifice is of whole human lives, not of animals; the worship is in minds and hearts rather than stones and pillars. They are to be transformed, not according to the pattern of the present world, whether Jewish or Gentile, but by the renewing of their minds.

The Unity of the Church

Paul expands these ideas by stressing the unity of the Church with the analogy of the human body, where all the parts contribute to the whole. This follows from his earlier emphasis on the unity of Jews and Gentiles in the Church, with neither having any superiority. Now he asks them to esteem others higher than themselves and to contribute their gifts for the benefit of all. He describes the ideal Christian Church, its members bonded by love and sharing each other's joys and sorrows and having no class distinctions. In their relations with the world, they are not to follow the revenge motif often found in the Old Testament, but rather the Sermon on the Mount, doing good to enemies and using good to conquer evil.

Similarly, on into Chapter 13, they are not to be revolutionaries, fighting against governments, but obeying them and paying their taxes, for in the normal course of events governments are a protection against anarchy. This was a different approach from that current among the Jews and indeed of many Gentiles.

Love is the Fulfilling of the Law

Beyond civil obedience, the Church is to be motivated by love of one's neighbour. Love is the real fulfilment of the law, and does not require detailed explanation. Moreover, Paul believes that the great crisis of history is approaching and Christians need to be ready for it, wearing 'the armour of light', not the implements of human warfare. Within the Church, too, they are to follow the way of peace. Implicit in a mixed Church of Jews and Gentiles are many residual traditions and cultural differences, which can easily erupt into conflict. Paul counsels tolerance. Different approaches to diet and the keeping of certain days and periods as special can co-exist, but there must be no attempt to flout the consciences of others. People were sensitive about certain foods and days; those who knew that it didn't really matter should still respect the prejudices of others and not hurt their feelings, which might be deep-seated.

If it doesn't matter, then this is a two-way road, and there is no reason for the more liberal-minded to force this liberality on those who are not ready for it. 'The Kingdom of God is not eating and drinking, but righteousness, peace and joy inspired by the Holy Spirit . . . Let us then pursue the things that make for peace and build up the common life.'

Accept One Another

Still following the theme of 'therefore', in Chapter 15 Paul prays:

> And may God, the source of all perseverance and encouragement, grant that you may agree with one another after the manner of Jesus Christ, and so with one mind and one voice may praise the God and Father of our Lord Jesus Christ [united worship of the one Church – united in faith in the one deliverance]. In a word, accept one another as Christ accepted us, to the glory of God.

Jews are to accept Gentiles and Gentiles to accept Jews as their brothers and sisters in Christ, as they both, through the righteousness of faith, have been accepted by God. Paul quotes further Old Testament references to the work of Christ in relation to both Jews and Gentiles. 'And may God, who is the ground of hope, fill you with all joy and peace as you lead the life of faith until, by the power of the Holy Spirit, you overflow with hope.'

Paul's Priestly Mission

Paul then emphasises his ministry to the Gentiles, which he describes as a priestly one, offering Gentiles God as an acceptable sacrifice, consecrated by the Holy Spirit. He also makes clear that he always moved into territory not already being cultivated by others, and is now moving from Jerusalem to Greece; he wants to go to Spain via Rome, using Rome as a base. Hence his concern that the Romans should understand. First he has to take to Jerusalem the funds for the poor that he has gathered in Greece. He requests their prayers that he may be delivered from the enemies whom he knows await him there. Of course, we know that nevertheless those enemies succeeded in stopping him. However, this was not without benefits, since it was the route of suffering that brought him to his long ministry to Rome.

Final Greetings

Chapter 16 consists of personal greetings and good wishes to members of the church. One gets the impression that the church in Rome consists of a number of smaller churches; he greets the church that meets at the house of Prisca and Aquila, the Lord's fellowship in the household of Narcissus, Asyncritus and those who are with him and his colleagues, Philiologus and God's people who are with them.

A warm sense of love flows through the greetings: 'my dear friend', 'who were Christians before me', 'Rufus . . . and his mother, whom I call mother too', 'my comrade in Christ', 'Apelles, well proved in Christ's service', 'dear Persis who has worked hard in the Lord's service for so long', and so on. As you read it for yourself, savour the warmth of Paul, which is not always sufficiently recognised.

Paul gives a final warning against quarrels and asks Romans to be 'expert in goodness and innocent in evil'. His associates in Greece then join the greetings, including Erastus the city treasurer, presumably of Corinth. Tertius, who, as we might say, was operating the word processor or doing the shorthand typing, adds a sentence of his own.

As customary, Paul ends with a blessing and praise of God for 'the proclamation of Jesus Christ, according to the revelation of that divine secret kept hidden for long ages, but now disclosed, and by the eternal God's command made known to all nations through prophetic scriptures, to bring them to faith and obedience'.

Finally, in what musicians might call his coda, Paul reassembles the themes of the truths concealed in the Old Testament, now made plain in the reinterpretation through Jesus (his death and resurrection); this revealed secret is being offered to all nations and the response of faith is the means of receiving this grace of God. In other words God is righteous by being true to his covenant. Jews and Gentiles, sinners all, can be acquitted in God's court and forgiven, receiving this righteous status in God's sight when they put their faith and trust in Jesus. This means that there is total equality between Jews and Gentiles in the Church, with salvation by grace, not race, a free gift, not a human achievement by law-keeping.

Having clarified all these great issues, Paul looks forward to getting to Rome and entering upon the next part of his work, which turns out differently from his expectations but still means the continuation of his mission to the Gentiles. Paul is the principal instrument through whose work the Christian Church blossoms from a small Judaistic sect into a universal (or catholic, which means universal) Church.

33

Troubles in Corinth

1 Corinthians

Formation of the Corinthian Church

We learn from Acts 18 that Paul spent eighteen months founding and settling the church in Corinth. It wasn't the most promising of places for a Christian mission, located on a narrow isthmus with harbours on both sides and therefore a meeting place for trade and transport – a cosmopolitan city. As to be expected, it therefore attracted the worst elements of society and was full of temptation and idolatry of every kind. Some people, however, felt the need for something better and responded to Paul's teaching.

The Jewish synagogue soon rejected his teaching about Jesus as saviour and king, though the president of the synagogue joined him. Paul therefore concentrated on the Gentiles. The Christians met in a house next door to the synagogue, so you can imagine the tensions this created. There was also an attempt to get Paul prosecuted by the Romans, but the local magistrate was not interested.

Eventually Paul went back to Antioch in Syria. An immature church was left to grow on its own; although it had a sound foundation from a profound teacher, he wasn't the most eloquent of men according to contemporary standards. He relied on his message and his love for them, rather normal standards of leadership. This we learn from what appear as two letters to the Corinthians in our Bibles.

Response to Reports and Letters

After visiting Syria, Paul came back into Asia Minor (the western and central part of modern Asiatic Turkey) and settled to teach at Ephesus, where there was considerable response. While there, he had a message from Corinth that problems about sexual morality, not surprising in such a city, had arisen. Paul wrote a letter to them, which we do not have, unless 2 Corinthians 6:14–7:1 is part of it. We know there was such a letter from 1 Corinthians 5:9–13. Parts of what we call the first letter to the Corinthians fill out and clarify the letter that actually came first.

We are now going to look at what we call the first letter, but which is really then the second. Paul has had reports from 'Chloe's people' that divisions were developing in the Church and that immorality is being tolerated. Other letters from the church ask his advice about a number of issues. Our 1 Corinthians is his response to the reports and the letters.

The problem areas are:

- Divisions: preferences for Paul, or Apollos, or Peter (Cephas) and some said: 'Well, I follow Jesus' (Chapters 1–4).
- Sexual immorality: the man who was sleeping with his stepmother (Chapter 5).

- Christians having lawsuits against each other in Gentile courts (Chapter 6).
- Sex, marriage and divorce (Chapter 7).
- Eating food that has been consecrated to idols, as most food was (Chapters 8 and 10).
- Payment of ministers, but his non-exercise of such rights (Chapter 9).
- Compromises with idolatry (Chapter 10).
- Public worship, especially the Eucharist or breaking of bread (Chapters 10 and 11).
- The exercise of spiritual gifts; rivalry about who had the best gifts; but love is the supreme gift and all the others serve it (Chapters 12–14).
- The resurrection from the dead; the fact and the meaning (Chapter 15).
- Collecting for poor believers in Judea (Chapter 16).

Divisions

Paul has heard that the church is divided between those who follow different teachers – Paul, Peter or Apollos – and some, possibly with smugness, who say, 'Well, of course, we follow Jesus.' Paul asks, 'Is Christ divided?' Was Paul crucified for you? Whose name were you baptised into? (Apollos had spent a period teaching in Corinth after Paul left, with Paul's approval.)

Paul tries to move the Corinthians away from being influenced by rhetorical skills and human wisdom. The wisdom of the world is foolishness to God, who saves people by what the world counts as the folly and weakness of the cross. They are nobodies, yet they have wisdom that will destroy the world's wisdom, so there is no room for taking pride in human leaders, judged by human standards. He asks them to be led by the

Spirit, which is God at work within them, enlightening them with God's hidden wisdom.

As long as they put their trust in humans, even good ones, they are in spiritual childhood. Teachers are to be seen as a team who fulfil varying roles in the building of the church into a unity in Christ. The teachers, including himself, are to be regarded as the subordinates of Christ and the stewards of God's revealed secrets.

In the second half of Chapter 4 Paul recognises that some teachers in Corinth are filled with self-importance and when he visits he will confront them with vigour. (We hear much more about this in what we call the second letter to the Corinthians; it in fact gets worse before it gets better.) Meanwhile Paul tenderly points out to the church that he has been their father in Christ, not just a tutor. He is also sending Timothy to help them.

The Immoral Christian

The Corinthian church was tolerating a believer who was living in union with his stepmother. This was regarded as serious incest even by Roman law, which forbade it. Paul, spiritually present though physically absent, says the offender must be removed from the church, cast out of the circle of light and life into the dark pagan world where 'Satan' and death prevail. He points out that a little infection creates sickness in the whole body. Just as at Passover the Jews used to get rid of all leaven (yeast), so they must do the same in the Church.

Paul uses this concern to explain his previous letter. Some had assumed that he meant that you should have no contact at all with immoral persons, but to do this you would have to go out of the world, he explains. He had been referring to the need to keep the church free of such evils. In listing them he doesn't restrict himself to sexual immorality but puts slander, greed in money matters, drunkenness and swindling on the same level. Many business and political practices of our day would come under his condemnation.

Lawsuits

Believers in Corinth were going to the pagan law courts to settle disputes with their fellow Christians. To Paul this shows that they have not understood their relationship to the world. One day, he tells them, they are going, with Christ, to take charge of the world. If this is what they are being trained for in this life, they certainly should be able to settle disputes within the Church.

He also reiterates the teaching of the Sermon on the Mount and asks why they do not just suffer themselves to be defrauded, rather than engage in battle about it.

Sex, Marriage and Divorce

Some had misunderstood the nature of Christian freedom in matters of morality and personal relationships. Paul stresses that what you do with your body does matter; you cannot live in a rarefied spiritual atmosphere. He applies this particularly to sexual sins, which are against your own body, and he stresses that their bodies are temples for the Holy Spirit. 'You do not belong to yourselves; you were bought at a price (the death of Jesus); then honour God in your body.'

In the letter the Corinthians sent him they suggested that it would be better for Christians to have no sexual relationships. Paul is very practical. Husbands and wives should not, he says, deny sex to each other; this will create temptation unless it is part of a limited fasting period by mutual agreement. He gives a ruling against divorce, but later allows divorce where one partner is not a Christian and doesn't want to remain with the Christian partner. The Christian should not initiate such a divorce.

Paul then goes on to recommend the unmarried state as one that leaves more opportunity for total commitment to God and to Christ. But you must learn to accept your present state, married, enslaved or uncircumcised. He believes that the coming of the Lord (*parousia* – second coming) is near and he wants to keep the Corinthians from too many difficulties as the dangers and hardships of the last days descend upon them. 'The world as we know it is passing away,' so he feels it is better to avoid the distractions of marriage, though making it clear that he is only giving advice. People are perfectly free to make their own decisions. He also permits widows to remarry, but says it is better if they do not, in his opinion. Some couples were apparently having permanent unconsummated engagements. If they can manage their passions, there is nothing wrong with that, he says. Equally, getting married is all right.

Much of this chapter is conditioned by the times and we may feel that Paul's teaching here is not as beautiful as those writings where he praises marriage as a symbol of the relationship of the Church and Christ. Perhaps Paul's statement 'It is better to marry than burn with desire' is not the noblest view of marriage, but no doubt he was being practical.

Meat Consecrated unto Idols

The next problem on his list is what to do about buying meat from the butcher. Almost all of it would have been consecrated to the pagan gods before being distributed for sale. The Corinthians have observed that we know these gods are not real, so we don't need to take any notice of these pagan associations; we have to eat after all. Paul agrees in principle, but points out that not everyone, even including some Christians, would think this way. If such people followed this liberated example though feeling it to be wrong, from their perspective they would be doing wrong. Their consciences would be defiled, even when nothing is really wrong about the action. So, says Paul, he would rather never eat meat than allow his knowledge and freedom to be the cause of another Christian's downfall. If you believe something is wrong and still do it, then you have lowered your standards and acted as if it does not matter what you do.

Freedom of the Ministry

Paul turns to the question of receiving financial support from the church. He says he is free to do this, but as he feels that, in Corinth, it might impede his ministry, he will not avail himself of this legitimate right. It is the same spirit of 'some things are right, but if they cause others to stumble spiritually, then we should forgo our rights'. The reward he receives in his heart from their response is his pay.

He goes on to explain his approach to his ministry. In all things he will exercise empathy. To the Jews he will take a Jewish perspective, to the weak he will become weak, to the Gentile as if a Gentile. Without compromising, he is nevertheless ready to 'become all things to all men' (as the King James version puts it) 'that I may save some'.

Compromise With Idolatry

While thinking about idolatry, Paul considers the warnings of the Old Testament about the waywardness of the Israelites during the wilderness journeys to the promised land. These things were recorded, he says, 'as a warning to us upon whom the end of the ages has come'. Obviously there was a sense that they were living at the end of the existing system and the start of its replacement by Christ's rule. Perhaps there is a truth here about the need to hold the world lightly as it is temporary and does not belong to the eternal order, as indeed Paul suggests elsewhere.

He moves on to instruct them that they should not attend feasts held in celebration of pagan gods, because we cannot eat and drink at the table of the Lord (Eucharist) and that of 'demons'. On the other hand, if you are invited to dinner with a non-believer, you should eat whatever is set before you and ask no questions, though if someone says 'this food has been offered to the gods', then you should not eat for the sake of the conscience of the other person, even though it is only meat. This is a matter of showing consideration for sensitive consciences.

Public Worship

Paul now moves on to public worship. Some of his words relate to those times and others are of more permanent concern.

For most Christians nowadays it does not seem to matter whether women wear head covering in church or not. It obviously mattered in those times and suggested looseness of morals for a woman to go uncovered, though not to the same extent as Muslims believe. (Even the British Queen visiting a Muslim country pays respect to her hosts in relation to their customs of dress.) Paul wants them to observe such matters.

But Paul also seems to see head covering as a symbol of the subordination of woman to man, reflecting man's glory. Nowadays we prefer to follow what Paul also said (in Galatians) that there is neither male nor female: 'You are all one in Christ Jesus.' Maybe what he was saying was not providing a mandate for all marriages for all time but reflecting marriage relationships in Corinth at that time. This seems to be supported by the reference to exposing the hair or wearing it short as a sign of loose morals in the city of Corinth. It is therefore again part of Paul's teaching that Christians should take note of how their permissible actions may be perceived and lead to misunderstanding.

Paul moves on to the Lord's supper or Eucharist, and rebukes the Corinthians for using it as a feast where the wealthy ate well and the poor did not have enough. Originally the Eucharist was part of a meal or love feast, and is possible that it became detached as a result of what Paul said here.

The situation with which Paul was dealing led him to the most frequently read of all scriptures, which is included in the Communion or Eucharist prayers in most churches: 'Jesus took bread and after giving thanks broke it and said, "This is my body which is broken for you"; in the same way he took the cup, "this cup is the new covenant in my blood."' Paul also suggests self-examination at the Lord's supper.

This section ends with 'the other matters I will settle when I come', so there were several issues that are not dealt with. There are further hints of other troubles rumbling away in the background throughout this letter, and they become important in our next chapter.

Spiritual Gifts

The New Testament speaks of the Holy Spirit in two aspects. There is the presence of God and of Christ within the believer's inward life, as discussed in Chapter 29 on the Gospel of John. Then in Chapter 30 we saw the Holy Spirit in visible outward signs and activities, in the Book of Acts.

Paul now discusses the latter aspect under the heading of 'gifts of the Spirit'. He describes the varieties of gifts, but emphasises that there is only one Spirit. The gifts include wise speech, expression of deep knowledge in simple words, faith that can make possible the seemingly impossible, healing, miraculous powers, prophecy (not necessarily prediction), speaking in tongues and interpretation of what is said. The same God is active in all of them. It is all a matter of the one Spirit sharing out participation in the work of the Spirit within the one community or body of Christ.

Therefore there ought to be no competition among the Christians to secure a supposedly better gift than others. A sense of superiority or inferiority in such matters is totally foreign to the Spirit of Christ. Paul extends the symbol of the body and with a sense of humour talks about the various organs. Why should the eye complain because it is not the ear, or the foot because it is not the hand? How stupid it would be if the whole body were just a nose. This is Paul the cartoonist! All the parts of the body are needed, and similarly all the gifts are necessary to make the one body of Christ whole. As in the human body so also in the Church; even the humblest contributions or ones normally out of sight are all vital. There must no division in the Church about them.

This particularly regards the 'special' gifts, which charismatic churches, such as the Pentecostal groups, believe are still operative. But the words of Paul are equally applicable to the more 'normal' gifts that people may possess. Some can sing, some can administer, some are good speakers, others are counsellors, preachers, priests, scholars: all have roles and there should be no envy or competition among them. That is the permanent message.

Love – the Better Way

So, declares Paul, there are many gifts – but I can show you an even better way. And there follows the most celebrated of chapters (it was read by the British Prime Minister Tony Blair at the funeral of Princess Diana). 'Though I speak with the tongues of men and of angels and have not love, I am a sounding gong or clanging cymbal.' Paul lists many of the gifts and each time adds: 'But if I have no love I am nothing.' He describes what love means in practice, implying that this is more important than particular gifts:

> Love is patient and kind. Love envies no one, is never boastful, never conceited, never rude; love is never selfish, never quick to take offence. Love keeps no score of wrongs, takes no pleasure in the sins of others, but delights in the truth. There is nothing love cannot face; there is no limit to its faith, its hope, its endurance.

He goes on to say that love is the spiritual gift to end all gifts. All temporary and partial gifts given to believers will be absorbed into the permanence and wholeness of love:

> There are three things that last for ever: faith, hope and love; and the greatest of these is *love*.

Orderly Worship

Paul next speaks particularly of the 'gift of tongues'. This was the ability to speak in foreign languages, as on the Day of Pentecost (Acts 2) or in sounds and words of praise that were emotionally satisfying to the participant, but meant nothing to the listeners unless they were interpreted. This can be a sensational sort of gift, but it does not, on its own, contribute to understanding. So Paul, although he has the gift himself, rates it as less profitable than gifts that teach, helping everyone and involving them in thinking, whereas without interpretation tongues can be of little profit.

Also there is the danger with this and some of the other gifts that several people talk at the same time. This is not profitable and Paul appeals for some orderly approaches to worship. Members should take it in turns to speak and understand that these gifts are under their own control. He also says that women should keep silent in the meetings. 'They should keep their place!' 'It is a shocking thing for a woman to talk at the meeting!' This could have arisen from the traditions and culture of the time in society as a whole, though it is still a matter of controversy in the Christian churches, such as the Anglican disagreements about the ordination of women. Elsewhere Paul speaks of women having the gift of prophecy and of praying in public.

Most likely Paul was here dealing with a particular problem in Corinth. Specific women may have been disturbing the worship, perhaps with the gift of tongues, to which women are said to be more attracted than men are. Essentially it is about disorderly speaking. The reference to asking their husbands at home also seems to be specific to certain women interrupting worship with debate over the gifts. Paul said they should discuss it at home. It would not apply to all women. What about the single ones?

He finishes this section: 'Let everything be done decently and in order.'

The Resurrection From Death

The last teaching chapter is Chapter 15, about the resurrection, often read at funerals.

Apparently some members were denying that there was any physical resurrection in the future. People are spiritually raised at their baptism. Paul responds by reiterating the appearances of Jesus after his resurrection, once to 500 people, which if not true would have been contradicted. He also speaks of his own encounter on the road to Damascus. If there is no resurrection he points out that Christ has not risen, then hope in him is empty. If we have no continuation of life through resurrection, then having learned the present joy of Christian living we then lose it all in death. We are more to be pitied than those who have never known Christian joy in this life and have less to lose.

He continues to explain Jesus as the first fruit of a mighty harvest, and he moves forward through the sequence of Christ's work to the final day when 'God will be all in all'. He stresses that they have in Christ hope, which takes them through this life and then beyond it.

In answer to problems with the mechanics of resurrection, Paul makes it clear that believers will rise to what he calls a spiritual body. An immortal person will not require the physical apparatus of the human frame. The heavenly body, such as that of Jesus, is of a different order; it is imperishable. 'Death is swallowed up in victory.' The new body is not mere 'flesh and blood'. Paul does not presume to know more, and he hints that they need not know more either. But he thanks God for the victory in Christ over the merely earthly condition, with all its imperfections.

He concludes his consideration with a moral implication that they should stand firm in their faith and work hard for the gospel, for in Christ their labour will not be lost. It is implicit from this that reincarnation is incompatible with Christian teaching on resurrection. There is a continuity between the present life and the future one, as well as distinctions. Being reborn as someone or something else depending on achievement in the previous life will not fit this criterion.

Closing Thoughts

The last chapter of 1 Corinthians is mainly practical. Paul urges the Corinthians to get ready the collection he is going to take up for the poor believers in Judea, where as well as persecution there has been famine. He hopes to come and spend a long time with them. Also Timothy may visit.

He urges them to accept the leadership of certain named believers, whom he trusts. There is a hint here, which we shall expand in the next chapter, that there were some leaders in whom he had no faith. The first chapter, with its discussion of the cleverness of merely human wisdom, may also have been aimed at these would-be leaders. In Chapter 4 he mentions certain self-important individuals who are obviously opposed to him and may be behind the divisive spirit he has been dealing with at the opening of the letter.

It is important to notice that in this first letter (which is actually his second) Paul does not go on to the offensive against them. This will suggest that when he says later that he wrote a letter to them with many tears and much distress, the subject of this chapter is not that letter. The one we have considered is written in a calm tone, even though it is firm.

Paul concludes: 'The grace of the Lord Jesus be with you. My love to you all in Christ Jesus.'

34

Paul Shares his Heart

2 Corinthians

The Structure of 2 Corinthians

We now come to the second letter of Paul to the Corinthians. Although that is what it's called, appearing in our Bibles as one document, it may in fact bring together in one volume several separate letters or parts of letters relating to different visits Paul made to Corinth.

We have already examined what is called the first letter of Paul to the Corinthians as an entity in its own right. Now we have to put the two letters into the context of Paul's total dealings with the church at Corinth.

Paul's First Visit

Acts 18:1–6. Paul preached to Jews and Gentiles in the synagogue. The Jews rejected him; one leader was, however, converted.

Acts 18:7–11: Paul stayed eighteen months in Corinth, preaching and teaching.

Acts 18:12–18. The Jews stirred up trouble. The Roman official Gallio ignored it, but Paul went back to Antioch in Syria, calling in at Ephesus on the way.

After the First Visit

Acts 18:23. After his visit to Antioch, Paul again visited the churches in Turkey (Galatia and Phrygia).

Acts 18:27–19:1. Apollos taught in Corinth.

Acts 19. Paul reached Ephesus and stayed there for three years. He made many converts, but also experienced much persecution and affliction.

Paul's First Letter

While in Ephesus Paul received news of problems in the church at Corinth, particularly in connection with sexual immorality. He wrote a first letter, which we do not have and is not to be confused with what we call the first letter to the Corinthians. We know this lost letter was sent, because in 1 Corinthians 5:9–11 Paul said, 'In my letter I wrote that you must have nothing to do with those who are sexually immoral' and explained what he really meant.

Paul's Second Letter

Still from Ephesus, Paul wrote what we know as the first letter to the Corinthians (1 Corinthians), but which is actually the second. He dealt with some of the problems that he had heard about (1 Corinthians 1:11, 5:1) or that they had related to him in writing (for example 1 Corinthians 7:1). We have discussed this letter in Chapter 33.

Paul's Second Visit

Still in Ephesus, Paul hears that his letter (1 Corinthians) has not been well received. There is much strife and opposition, particularly to him, with doubts being cast on his ministry by various Christian leaders claiming to be superior to Paul, representing the true gospel and much more effective than him. Timothy probably brought the bad news as he was to visit Corinth, according to 1 Corinthians 16:10–11.

Paul decided to see for himself what was happening. According to what we read in 2 Corinthians 2:1 it was a very painful meeting. In particular he had a face-to-face encounter with one of the opponents (2:5–6). This is not the man who was sleeping with his stepmother. Someone was challenging Paul's authority, not an issue of morality. He gave warnings in person (13:2). In 2:3 he later comments that the pain was so great that this was a major reason for his not undertaking a proposed long winter visit to them, which had been planned to occur in two stages (1:15–16).

Paul's Third Letter

Paul follows up this painful flying visit with a tough letter attacking his opponents, 'super apostles' who were undermining the mission that Jesus had given him. He refers to this letter in 2:3–4: 'The letter I sent you came out of great distress and anxiety; how many tears I shed as I wrote it!' This cannot be what is called the first letter to the Corinthians (but which I have called his second). He was worried when he wrote that letter, but he wasn't in a state of emotional upset.

It is reasonable to believe that 2 Corinthians 10–13 provides the major part of this, written with many tears. It has somehow been bound up with other correspondence but is quite different in mood from Chapters 1–9, which are warm and conciliatory.

Apostolic Authority

In this letter, Paul's concern is to justify his position as an apostle, commissioned by Christ, against the attacks of those who have come in to undermine his work. Because this strikes at the root of his life's work, his defence is vigorous. Its outspokenness could even be misunderstood as possessing a tinge of boastfulness about it, though he also emphasises that his real boast lies in his weakness, so that he depends on God for everything.

The Super Apostles

The super apostles commend themselves (10:12); Paul comments: 'What fools they are to find in themselves their standard of comparison.' In Chapter 11:3–5, he fears that the Corinthians are being corrupted by these teachers: 'If some newcomer proclaims another Jesus, not the Jesus we proclaimed, or if you receive a spirit, different from the Spirit already given to you, or a gospel different from the gospel you have already accepted, you put up with that well enough. I am not aware of being in any way inferior to those super apostles.' Fighting talk!

In Chapter 11:12–13 he goes on: 'I shall go on doing as I am doing now, to cut the ground from under those who would seize any chance to put their vaunted apostleship on the same level as ours. Such people are sham apostles, confidence tricksters, masquerading as apostles of Christ.' And again (11:20): 'If someone tyrannises over you, exploits you, gets you in his clutches, puts on airs and gives you a slap in the face, you put up with it.'

These opponents are undermining Paul by saying that he can write powerful letters but that his personal presence is unimpressive 'and as a speaker he is beneath contempt'. Of course these teachers are well schooled in rhetoric and make a good impression. He responds by saying that, when he comes, his actions will show he is the same man who writes the letters.

According to Chapter 10:12–16 they seem to have suggested that Paul had no commission in Corinth; he has to point out that he only goes where others have not been, as was the case in Corinth. He is not an interloper. He seems to have been criticised for not taking financial help from the Corinthians, which was interpreted as meaning that he was not worth the support, whereas he intended to maintain his independence, though he accepted help from the churches in Macedonia. He is sarcastic about not receiving help from them: 'Forgive me for being so unfair.'

There seems to be criticism from the super apostles that Paul had a poor record of knowledge and skills, so he has to remind the church of his Jewish background as a rabbi of the highest rank and of the many sufferings by which he demonstrated his commitment to the gospel. These enemies appear to suggest that if he was any good he wouldn't have encountered so much trouble. He points out that suffering for what he believed and preached was a sharing of the sufferings of Christ, not something to be ashamed of.

In fact this leads him to 'boast' of his weaknesses. He speaks of some ailment that he calls his 'thorn in the flesh'. He has asked God to relieve him of it, because it is so debilitating, but he has been told 'my grace is all you need; power is most fully seen in weakness'. He adds: 'When I am weak, then I am strong.'

Paul recognises that in a sense he is 'being a fool' for justifying himself, drawing attention to the special visions he had had, perhaps starting with meeting Christ on the road to Damascus, but going on to being 'caught up into paradise' to the very presence of God. What this actually means we can't be sure, but it left a profound impression on him. He says that when he comes to Corinth, he won't hesitate to exercise the authority given him 'by the Lord to build your faith, not pull it down'. He will 'demolish sophistries and all that rears its proud head against the knowledge of God; we compel every human thought to surrender in obedience to Christ.'

Final Pleading of the Third Letter

He concludes this tearful letter by saying that he has written a tough letter because he wants to avoid quarrelling and unpleasantness when he comes. He fears lest he be humiliated in their presence, and takes up the theme of weakness again. Christ will speak with power through him, but 'truly he died on the cross in weakness, but he lives by the power of God; so you will find that we who share his weakness shall live with him by the power of God'. He will if necessary display sharp exercise of power, but would prefer them to take his appeal to heart and live in peace.

Waiting for Their Response to the Tough Letter

If you have ever written and posted a letter and then had doubts about it, you have some sense of what Paul was feeling. As he left Ephesus, Paul went north to Troas, en route for Macedonia. He had planned to preach at Troas, but was too worried to get on with it very much (2 Corinthians 2:12–13). Titus hadn't arrived to tell him how the Corinthians had taken the third letter, so he set off to Macedonia and there he met all kinds of internal and external problems – and still no Titus. Then at last Titus arrived (2 Corinthians 7:5–7). The news was good: the Corinthians had accepted his tough letter and have fallen into line, accepting Paul's authority and wanting to see him soon. 'They long for him!' Paul had regretted sending it, but was then happy that the pain had led to a change of heart (1 Corinthians 7:5–16).

Paul's Fourth Letter

The fourth letter (2 Corinthians 1–9 minus 6:14–7:1) indicates that they did listen and act. Paul is still justifying his ministry, but more its style than its authority. The approach is gentle and tactful, and he is relieved that they have responded to the third letter.

He begins tenderly, showing how suffering enables Christians to offer consolation to each other and telling them how serious his problems in Ephesus had been. He had thought death was imminent and sees it all as a way of God teaching him not to place reliance on himself. This is a more subtle way of reinforcing what he had said in the third letter. In fact throughout he is quietly contrasting his style with that of the super apostles, though he doesn't enter into open attack again.

He deals with the delay in visiting them a third time and indicates that this is not because he is unreliable or untrustworthy. One of the reasons is that he doesn't want another painful visit. He tells them how relieved he was that they had accepted his tough letter and he forgives the member of their own congregation who had injured him and them. He lovingly tells them that they are the only letter of recommendation he needs. God has used him to deliver them as a letter from Christ written with the Spirit. He describes his journey to them as a triumph with sweet-smelling incense; he has a mild knock at those who might find him a noxious fume. He again stresses his reliance on God and talks of himself as a minister of the New Covenant.

He contrasts the glory of the New Covenant with the system of Moses, whose face shone after he had been speaking to God;

he had to wear a veil to avoid dazzling people. Paul does not need to hide the glory of the New Covenant. Its glory is richer and enables all of them to see the light of Christ in each other's faces. As it is available for all, he cannot be other than open in his ministry, even if this might seem to lack sophistication. He certainly can't proclaim such glory with underhanded and cunning methods. It just won't make sense. He is not confronting anyone, but quietly reaffirming his approach. He admits to holding the treasure he shares with them in an earthenware jar, so that the power may be of God not of man. This weakness is displayed in the suffering he endured, which was a matter of sharing the suffering of Christ and even 'dying with him' so that they may live.

Thus he speaks out so that God's grace may abound. Outwardly decaying, inwardly he and they are growing, so that the outward decay may be arrested when they receive their new body in the eternal world to come, when all the weakness and failure will be a thing of the past. So in all the afflictions he experiences, he is confident of the glorious end. There is a little hint that his opponents took pride in outward show, but he is concerned with inward worth. And this is the essence of the new creation.

The new creation is based on God's presence in Christ, reconciling the world to himself. Paul is an ambassador for Christ with this message of reconciliation. His troubles, far from being proof that he is not a very good apostle, demonstrate that he is a minister of God. 'Dying we still live on.' He finishes Chapter 7: 'How happy I am now to have complete confidence in you.'

The Collection for the Poor Believers in Judea

The fourth letter ends by stirring the Corinthians to be ready with the collection of money for him and his colleagues to take to Jerusalem. He tells them how well the Macedonian churches have done and urges them to continue where they left off in the previous year, so that they who gathered much should not have too much and those who gathered less should not have too little, based on the story of sharing the manna in Exodus 16.

He encourages generosity. God loves a cheerful giver. Giving creates fellowship and thanksgiving to God. He finishes Chapter 9: 'Thanks be to God for his gift which is beyond all praise.'

Paul's Third Visit

Finally Paul follows up his fourth letter by arriving in Greece and spending three months there, no doubt mainly in Corinth as the principal church in the region. This is clear from Acts 20:1–3. He goes through Macedonia and finally arrives in Greece, so in the end they received their third visit from him. In Acts, Luke gives little detail of this visit, but there is no doubt that the administration of the collection for relief in Judea will take place, ready for Paul and his companions to take it.

35

Paul Gets Tough

Galatians

The Background of the Controversy

We are apt to consider the early Christian Church as the pure source of the Church's teaching and life. In fact it was full of debate and disagreement, as its leaders hammered out a clearer understanding of what God had been doing through Jesus Christ and how this affected the believers, individually and collectively.

Of all the books of the New Testament, the letter Paul wrote to the Galatians is the most controversial and the most outspoken, suggesting that Christianity is not a bland, supertolerant way of life, all about everyone being nice to everyone else. Love can be tough and Paul's love was tough, yet Christian.

We remember from the Acts of the Apostles that Paul's whole life had been turned upside down when Jesus appeared to him on the road to Damascus. The one he thought was a deceiver and rightly executed had in fact been raised from the dead and was now commissioning him to preach the Christian gospel, or good news, to the non-Jews or Gentiles.

Paul had thought that Israel was the special chosen nation of God and that it was vital for it to preserve its 'boundary markers', which distinguished it from other nations. Chief among these were circumcising all males, obeying rigorous food laws and observing special days and feasts. On the other hand the Christian gospel, as Paul now preached it, said that faith or trust in God, who had raised Jesus from the dead, was the sole criterion of acceptability with him.

The battle in which Paul is engaged in the letter to the Galatians is pitched against those who said that it was necessary for Jewish Christians to maintain Jewish regulations. You couldn't eat your meals or even the Eucharist or Holy Communion with Gentile Christians. This created two Christian bodies, instead of the single body of Christ. Some Jewish Christians went even further and said that you could not be a Christian at all without observing these key regulations of the law, given through Moses. They perceived them as an essential addition to faith in Christ – or even that faith in Christ was an addition to the keeping of the law.

This may seem rather distant from twentieth-century life, but the issues at stake are as fresh today as they were nearly 2,000 years ago. It was a matter of deciding whether your relationship with God was based on your ethnic origin and its traditions, or on faith in the self-giving of Jesus Christ.

One should not dismiss the 'Judaisers', as they are known, as being totally unreasonable. For over 1,000 years the pattern of Israel's life had been shaped by particular laws. To be told that they no longer mattered must have been devastating. It was unbelievable to learn that non-Jews were on an equal level with themselves, the chosen people of God who were marked off from the rest of humanity.

The Letter's Abrupt Start

Paul usually starts his letters with warm greetings, followed by compliments to his readers for the good work they are doing, calling down God's blessing upon them. His opening sections normally contain very little material about the issues he is going to discuss.

The beginning of this letter to the Galatians is very different. The greeting is very short, and even half of that is hinting at what is to come. In the very first verse he emphasises that his commission as an apostle came direct from Jesus Christ and God who raised Jesus from the dead. Right at the start he is claiming to speak with authority, whatever his opponents might say. There is also some 'doctrine' about the way in which Jesus has rescued people from the 'present wicked age'.

Then, after these brief and purposeful greetings, he omits completely the usual congratulations and blessings and goes straight into sharp, though sorrowful, rebuke: 'I am astonished to find you turning away so quickly from him who called you by grace, and following a different gospel.' He goes on to say that, of course, it isn't a gospel at all. Even if an angel or Paul himself taught anything different from what Jesus Christ had taught them they were not to be heeded.

A Gospel Received by Revelation

Paul had preached to these residents in southern central Turkey, as we would describe it today, on a previous missionary journey. His message was of divine origin; no human being had given it to him. Jesus Christ had plucked him out of his eminence in Judaism and his furious persecution of Christians to receive the task of proclaiming Jesus among the Gentiles.

He emphasises this point and makes it clear that he does not merely continue the work of the apostles in Jerusalem. In fact he has very little contact with them. It was three years before he went to Jerusalem to make the acquaintance of Peter and to meet James, the brother of Jesus. Fourteen years later he went up to Jerusalem and met the apostles, arising out of fierce dispute with certain Jewish believers in Antioch, who were insisting that the Gentile Christians must be circumcised. This was probably the conference described in Acts 15. Paul is not particularly complimentary about the leaders of the Jerusalem church, including the apostles, for their ambiguous attitude towards the Gentile mission. However the Gentile Titus was not compelled to be circumcised and in the end the apostles agreed a division of labour that left the Gentiles to Paul and his associates while they concentrated on the Jews.

Rebuking Peter

Then Paul records how Peter came to Antioch and entered quite freely into fellowship with the Gentile believers as well as the Jewish section. They ate at the same table and disregarded Jewish food laws, until some Jewish Christians came from Jerusalem and stirred up trouble. As a result Peter stopped eating with the Gentile Christians, which meant the holding of two separate Eucharist services, because Holy Communion or Mass was originally part of a meal.

Paul was furious and publicly rebuked Peter (it is not clear where Paul's rebuke ends and where it blends into general exposition). He asserted that being acceptable to God, as part of his people, did not depend on 'works of the law' – food, circumcision. These were not the things which distinguished

Christians. Faith in the Jesus who had given himself and trust in the God who raised him from the dead were what made them acceptable to God. Anyway the nation of Israel had never been able to keep the law and clearly claim membership of the covenant family by its means.

Peter had eaten with the Gentile Christians and presumably Jesus had been present in their worship together. So had Jesus been promoting sin? Had Peter been a sinner along with these Gentiles?

Paul is determined not to rebuild the wall between Jews and Gentiles, which had been broken down in Christ. As far as Paul is concerned the law is dead as a means of being accounted righteous. Becoming a Christian means for Paul that he shares the crucifixion of Christ as the only way of salvation, and is alive by faith in Jesus. If acceptability to God comes by the law, then what necessity was there for Christ to die to bear away our sins?

Whence Came the Spirit?

We now arrive at Chapter 3. Paul's vigour is unabated: 'You stupid Galatians.' He now directs his attention to the fact that the Galatian churches have been taken off the track by Jewish Christians who have convinced them that they should observe the works of the law – in particular circumcision – as the badge of belonging to God's family. He asks them how the Spirit came into their lives. Was it through the law or was it because they had faith in the gospel message?

The Abrahamic Family

Then he takes them back to the Book of Genesis and to Abraham, the father of the Jewish race, the one to whom God's covenant promises were originally made. How did Abraham find acceptance with God? It was his faith that was counted as righteousness, as Genesis declares. And his children would be those who had similar faith. These include those not physically descended from him. The very promises said that in Abraham all nations should find blessing. This means that the Gentiles would be involved on that same basis of faith. Those who have that trust are part of Abraham's family and therefore of God's family.

Israel, according to Deuteronomy, would be blessed if it kept the law and cursed if it did not. In fact they never had, as a nation, observed it and therefore were under its curse. It is in this light that the prophet Habakkuk is to be understood when he said, 'He, through faith, is righteous shall live.' This is the boundary marker for defining who belongs to God's covenant people.

Jesus entered this situation, which was seen as cursed and in the manner of his death was considered cursed, because the law had said anyone hung as a criminal polluted the land. He bore the curse that Israel experienced still in exile from freedom, and which all mankind, as sinners, suffered. But, rising from the dead, he had exhausted its power for those who, by faith, became part of the one Abrahamic family of God.

God Has Only One Family

Still staying with the promises to Abraham, Paul illustrates a will that once validated cannot be altered by others. God made firm promises to Abraham: arrangements coming afterwards could not invalidate them. The law came 430 years later and could not rob the promises of their primacy.

The next argument is very powerful. God had made promises to Abraham and his 'seed', 'issue' or 'offspring'. Paul makes the point that the seed or offspring is singular, and he applies it to Christ, but he is thinking of Christ as incorporating all those who put their faith in him and become part of his body or family. As all Christians are 'in Christ', Christ is multitudinous, as well as individual. And there can only be one Christ, individual or collective. There are not two bodies of Christ, two 'seeds' of Abraham, one Jewish and the other Gentile.

At the end of the chapter he makes clear that God has only one family, those who are in union with Jesus, baptised into him. If you belong to him, you are part of the singular seed or offspring of Abraham, and you are an heir of the promise. It is quite impossible, then, for there to be two families of God. There are no subdivisions of the Church, no boundaries to mark off different groups. 'There is no such thing as Jew and Greek, slave and freeman, male and female; for you are all one person in Christ Jesus.'

Childhood Regulations

In Chapter 4 Paul continues to try to work out the rightful place of the law. He likens it to childhood, where children are taken to school by a slave or custodian, called a pedagogue, whose job is to apply discipline to make sure that the child both learns and behaves himself. This continues into the mid-teens, when the child is regarded as grown up enough to be recognised as a son, responsible to his father for his own discipline.

The child is no freer than a slave. Paul uses this as an analogy. The law is the pedagogue and its regulations restrict the freedom of sonship, which however develops when Jesus buys them back from their slavery and gives them freedom. Whether his readers are Jewish or Gentile Christians, they have been under the 'elemental spirits or forces of the universe', subjected to the elementary forms of religion, whether

Jewish or otherwise, or to superstitions about the fatalistic influence of the stars. Paul places subjection to the law on the same level as pagan worship and superstition!

But now they are released from that by becoming the children of God in Christ; by the Spirit they were able to call God 'Abba', similar in meaning to our 'Daddy'. Why then should they want to step backward into their previous primitive state of servitude? In particular, he mentions the concern for special days and festivals of the Jews to be regarded as obligatory. He is afraid that all his hard work with them has been wasted.

Paul for a few lines breaks off his argument and his tone of rebuke to plead with the Galatians. He reminds them how, when he first met them, he was ill, and they had had such a warmth of love for him that they would have done anything to help his recovery. Why should they now regard him as an enemy because he is being so frank with them? The people who are trying to make them 'Judaise' are being very attentive, but this cannot be compared with the fact that he is their mother, who has given birth to them in Christ. Is he required to go through the labour pains of birth again? He wants to speak in a gentler tone, but he is at his wits' end as to how to handle them.

Freedom Through Christ

Having expressed his emotions he returns to the subject. To people anxious to live under the law he uses a traditional type of exposition to underline his teaching. We might find this style of reasoning – allegory – rather strained, but the early Church would have been accustomed to it.

Paul takes the fact that, in the Genesis story, Sarah, the wife of Abraham, gave him her female slave, Hagar, to bear a child, which would legally belong to Sarah. Ishmael was the result.

However God had other ideas, and when she was well past the age of child-bearing, Sarah bore Isaac, the true heir. So Paul gives a picture: on the one hand, Ishmael and Hagar represent slavery, the law and Mount Sinai, where the law was given through Moses; on the other hand, Sarah and Isaac represent freedom, Christ's deliverance and the new Jerusalem from above.

Paul makes the additional point that just as Ishmael, the natural born son, persecuted Isaac, the spiritual son, so the Jews are persecuting the Christians. Why then should the spiritually born Christians want to go back to the natural born, ethnic slavery? 'For freedom, Christ has set us free.'

He then summarises his theme by saying that insistence on circumcision and use of the law as the boundary marker of their position as Christians invalidates the saving work of Christ. The Jewish law is replacing faith and they are preferring it to the arena of God's free grace. When we are in union with Christ, he declares, circumcision is irrelevant and must be left in that position. 'The only thing that counts is faith expressing itself in love' (5:6).

He rounds off this section with a hope that they will listen to his guidance and with a violent attack on the disturbing teachers, wishing that they would go the whole way with their circumcision and castrate themselves.

Freedom – Not Licence

After Paul's personal history in relation to the controversy, and his rational exposition, he finishes with the moral and spiritual implications.

He wants to make sure that they don't mistake the freedom in Christ for licence. Letting love have its way, without detailed regulations, doesn't mean that you can just do whatever you like. When Augustine once said, 'Love God and do as you please', he meant that if you really love God then what pleases you will be identical with what pleases God.

Paul selects one command as summing up the whole of the spiritual intent of the law. Jesus chose two: 'Love the Lord your God' and 'Love your neighbour as yourself'. Which one did Paul choose? You might expect it to be the first, but he chooses the second, the love of neighbour. He does this because it is more visible. Your neighbour can be seen and, as the apostle John puts it: 'If you don't love your brother whom you can see, how can you love God whom you can't see?' Also, with all this controversy in the air, it was necessary to implore them not to fight each other to mutual destruction.

Flesh vs Spirit

Paul goes on to contrast the Spirit in conflict with the flesh or natural desires and makes the point that the Spirit is more all-embracing than law and makes the latter superfluous. He sets out the 'works of the flesh,' or as a modern translation puts it less powerfully, 'the behaviour that belongs to the unspiritual nature'. It is interesting that sex is involved only in two or three; the rest are the common sins of quarrelling, contentiousness, envy, rage, selfish ambitions, dissensions, party intrigues, jealousy, drinking bouts, orgies, idolatry and sorcery. The Kingdom of God is not for people like that. And some of these 'works of the flesh' were involved in the behaviour of certain of the Galatians.

I carry Paul's description of the opposite fruit or harvest of the Spirit around with me on a card. It is beautiful in fixing our priorities in life. 'But the harvest [or fruit] of the Spirit is love, joy, patience, kindness, goodness, fidelity, gentleness, and self control.' It is all one fruit or harvest, not a list of separate qualities. The Spirit creates them all as an integrated behaviour. For those whose religion is a burden the high profile of joy is worth noting. 'Those who belong to Christ Jesus have crucified the old nature with its passions and desire . . . If the Spirit is the source of our life let it also direct its course.'

Christian Fellowship

The final chapter lies in calmer waters and consolidates the idea of the Spirit as guiding the church in the path of personal harmony. Rivalry and jealousy are ruled out. If someone does something wrong, gentle help is called for, because it could happen to anyone. In this way we carry one another's burdens and thus fulfil the 'law' of Christ (a subtle use of the word 'law').

Still in the same mood, the Galatians are warned against delusions of greatness and engaging in comparison of their achievements. In this sense everyone is responsible for his or her own behaviour and has to bear their own burdens. We must not expect other people to save us from ourselves, though we may be grateful if they do.

Various minor instructions are then provided. Teachers in the Church should be helped in material things by those who are benefiting from spiritual instruction. Then he reminds that if you sow in the field of the flesh (unspiritual nature) then you will reap corruption. If you sow in the field of the Spirit the ultimate harvest will be eternal life. Never tire of doing good, especially to the household of faith. Note that Paul still focuses on faith.

Finally he pens a few sentences in his own rather large letters. These go back to the main issue, appealing to the Galatians not to let the false teachers persuade them to be circumcised. They only want to do it to escape persecution and boast that the Jewish party has won. As for himself he is not going to boast of anything but the cross of Christ.

'Circumcision is nothing and uncircumcision is nothing; the only thing that counts is new creation. All who take this principle for their guide, peace and mercy be upon them – the Israel of God.' There is an echo of the 'one family' concept here. There is one body, one Church, and *it* is the true Israel, the Israel of God.

Paul hopes the Galatians will give him some peace now. He feels wounded, with the marks of Jesus in his body, and feels like Jacob did when he wrestled with an angel and had his name changed to Israel but thereafter walked with a limp. This subtle allusion is making the point that there is a cost in belonging to the new Israel; some of it will be persecution by those who haven't understood the new creation of the Spirit – the way of faith.

36

The Message of Unity

Ephesians

From Whom – To Whom

The letter to the Ephesians is unique among those attributed to Paul. It has no personal greetings, no particular issue that needs urgent attention and its style is different from other letters. Its theology has different emphases, though it is consistent with everything else Paul wrote. If Paul was not its author, it is difficult to know who was. It would have to have been someone very close to him, to whom he had outlined what he wanted to say, leaving them to put it into its final form. For all practical purposes we can take it as a letter from Paul, particularly as it makes reference to his mission and to his sufferings in a familiar way.

The absence of specific greetings and the general nature of its theme have caused many to suggest that this was a circular letter sent to a number of churches in what we today call Turkey. The name would have been inserted in a blank space and the copy that survived was the one sent to Ephesus, which was also the base that Paul had used for several years. Another copy perhaps went to the church at Laodicea and may be the one mentioned in Paul's letter to the church at Colossae. Where Paul's authorship is accepted, it is generally considered that he wrote it when he was under house arrest in Rome.

The letter presents a very exalted view of the place of Christ in the Christian life, both individual and collective. In fact its language is so rich that it could be a little indigestible to read it all in one session. Throughout Paul makes much of the idea of being 'in Christ', of a collective Christ incorporating all the believers. This is reflected in the very first verse, along with the assertion that he is an apostle specifically by the will of God. He never forgets his encounter with Christ on the road to Damascus.

Everything Gathered Into Unity in Christ

Paul opens with what may be regarded as a hymn of praise to God, who from the beginning of creation always intended to have a family of his own, his children filled with love, blessed with every heavenly blessing, released from their failures by his own self giving in Jesus, given wisdom and insight into his secret purpose, which was 'that the universe, everything in heaven and earth, might be brought to a unity in Christ'.

This purpose is sometimes described as predestination and it has to be clear that this refers to a class of people, the family of God, not to the idea that God decides on the eternal destiny of individual people before they are even born.

The idea of everything and everyone ultimately in harmony focused on Christ is an exciting one. Acceptance of it does not mean that we are exempt from trying to contribute to this harmony in the world now, but it will make a difference to whether we despair when we see the disharmony daily displayed on our television screens. Paul encourages belief in this hope in his contemporary readers as he reminds them of the experience they have had of the Holy Spirit of God at work in their lives. They have experienced it as the reality of the influence of Christ in every part of their lives, not just in the more sensational miracles and gifts. The Spirit is the down payment of the glorious future to come.

A Prayer for his Readers

Paul's prayer for his readers, which completes the first chapter, gives a view of the meaning of being a Christian, which is richer than conventional church-going and reasonable acts of kindness. He thanks God for their faith in Jesus and the love they show to all God's people, and asks God to shower upon them the spiritual gifts of wisdom and vision and the knowledge of God. He asks God to open their eyes to the wonderful future that is their inheritance in Christ and to the vast resources of moral and spiritual strength available, now, from Christ.

This empowerment flows from the power let loose in the world when Jesus Christ was raised from the dead and elevated to a share in the throne of God, ultimately sovereign over the whole universe. This does not imply that, in this age, his sovereignty is universally accepted, but that it will be in the end. And meanwhile he is head of the Church that is his body, the fullness of him who is filling the universe in all its parts.

Unearned Grace

Most of Paul's readers are non-Jews and he looks back at their past to emphasise the greatness of the deliverance they have experienced. Previously they were ruled by their physical desires and instincts; they followed the way of the existing world order. They were therefore not sharers in God's fellowship. But

God did not leave them to sink in the sinfulness of the world, but because he is rich in mercy and because of his great love, he saved them by his grace – his favour, which they had in no way earned. And he brought them to life in Christ. The language may sound rather lush if you are not already familiar with it.

Paul continues by stressing that they had not earned this kindness. It is God's gift, not a reward for work done. This is important, because so often religious people spend so much effort 'trying hard to be good', instead of relaxing into the influence of Christ. 'There is nothing for anyone to boast of; we are God's handiwork, created in Christ Jesus for the life of good deeds which God designed for us.' Even Christian behaviour is not based on human effort. It is the gift of God, but it has to be willingly received and prayerfully implemented.

Access for Gentiles

Paul never forgets his mission as the apostle to the Gentiles, commissioned personally by Christ. Even though this is not a controversial letter, he has to make clear the position of equality between Jews and Gentiles in the Church. The Ephesians themselves were Gentiles and were seen by the Jews as beyond salvation, primarily because they were not circumcised and did not observe even the main provisions of the law of Moses. They were outside God's covenant, which had been channelled through Israel. They were without hope and without God, from a Jewish perspective, even apart from the way they behaved.

But now, in Christ, this has been corrected. They have been 'brought near' by Christ's self-giving. Jews and Gentiles have been brought together in one humanity and the barrier between them in the rules and regulations of the law has been broken down. They are a single body and peace prevails between them. They both have equal access to God, as part of his one family, by the Spirit. The Ephesians are no longer aliens, but fellow citizens with the rest of God's people. All of them together, Jew and Gentile, on the foundation stone of Jesus Christ, were being built into a holy temple, a spiritual dwelling place for God.

Paul's Mission

In Chapter 3 Paul speaks of his own role in unveiling this secret purpose of God to bring the whole human race into the orbit of his purpose in Christ. This was not obvious in former times (though there were many hints of it in the Old Testament), but now the gospel made it clear that the Gentiles are fellow heirs with the Jews of the promises of God. And Paul had been given the mission to preach this among the Gentiles and to make them aware of 'the unfathomable riches of Christ', riches so deep that you could never get to the bottom of them. Jew and Gentile now have this freedom of access, for which the only condition is that they should trust God – put their faith in him.

So they are not to worry about Paul's own sufferings. They are all endured for a good cause, not a sign that God's purposes are not succeeding. He prays that they may have inward strength through the Spirit and that 'through faith, Christ may dwell in their hearts in love'.

> With deep roots and firm foundations, may you, in company with all God's people, be strong to grasp what is the breadth and length and height and depth of Christ's love, and to know it, though it is beyond knowledge. So may you be filled with the very fullness of God.

Such words are foreign to the spirit of our age and don't fit our normal patterns of speech and thought. To some they may seem rather overdone and sentimental, lacking solid content, grandiose, overblown, too far removed from everyday life to find a response in ordinary people, who would feel it embarrassing to use such language. Yet millions of ordinary people throughout the past twenty centuries have been stirred by such words and in their hearts have had some idea of what they meant. So were they living in a dream world or are we missing the key to a full life?

Christian Conduct

In Chapter 4 Paul comes down to earth and seeks to suggest what all this high-flown speech might mean for daily living. What a difference it would make on this planet if we could all follow the words:

> Be humble always and gentle, and patient too, putting
> up with one another's failings in the spirit of love.

He asks them to spare no effort to make the unity of the Christian body a reality. They are to use their diverse spiritual gifts to build up the Church, so that it may grow to maturity. He encourages them not to live like the pagans, with hardened hearts and abandoned to all manner of vice. Our own days could well be described in the words 'there is no indecency they do not practise'.

Instructions that follow include: 'be renewed in mind and spirit'; appeals to avoid all falsehood and speak only the truth; not harbouring anger beyond sunset into the next day; no stealing – find an honest job so that you will have something left over with which to help those in need; foul language is to be avoided; speech should be used to help others; spite, bad temper, rage, insults and slander are not to be entertained.

> Be generous to one another, tender-hearted, forgiving one another as God in Christ forgave you. In a word as God's dear children, you must be like him. Live in love as Christ loved you and gave himself up on your behalf.

The mood of these words may gradually capture the hearts of those to whom they represent an unfamiliar way of speaking. And maybe we shall discover also that the restrictions he insists upon are in fact a way to freedom. Is there permanent satisfaction in a way of life characterised by fornication, ruthless greed, coarse, stupid and flippant talk? These, says Paul, belong to the way of darkness and are exposed by the light of Christ for what they really are. Drunkenness is also out, with a touch of humour that one should be filled with the Holy Spirit (rather than the unholy spirit distilled by men).

Make music to God in hymns as part of life and not just in a half-hour on a Sunday. And be always giving thanks to God. Of course Paul is not asking Christians to make public exhibitions of themselves, but that these attitudes quietly become part of the calibre of their lives.

Christian Relationships

The conduct Paul has been talking about is largely individual, but in the second half of Chapter 5 he moves specifically to human relationships. He begins with marriage, where, in spite of the man being expected to take the lead, which was customary as through most of history, he moves beyond this with the idea of mutual submission and a tenderness by the man beyond the norms of those days (and often of our own days).

Love her as part of your very self. He lifts marriage on to a very high level by making it a symbol of the relationship between Christ and his Church. Such a spirit was to guide married life. He hints at the Song of Songs in the Old Testament when he says that Christ wants the Church to be his unblemished bride.

He goes on to deal with the rest of the family. Children, obey your parents. My father often quoted this one to me even into my teens. As I got older I sometimes used to quote back the next verse: 'Fathers, don't provoke your children to resentment.' Neither of us was really reflecting the spirit of Paul's teaching on such occasions, though Paul usually won both of us over.

Next came slavery. The overall spirit of the New Testament rules this institution out and most nations have been sufficiently influenced to recognise this now. But it was the way of life in the first century and so Paul seeks to modify its conditions. The Christian slaves should do a good job, cheerfully, as Christ's free men. Masters were to give up threatening behaviour and to remember that they had a master in heaven. The spirit of Paul's words could be adapted to industrial relations in our day with benefit.

The Christian Armour

The letter finishes, apart from a short salutation at the very end with a description, based on the Old Testament, of the Church as a soldier protected by various kinds of equipment: the whole armour of God; the belt of truth; the breastplate of integrity; as shoes the gospel of peace to give them a sure footing; the shield of faith to repel the darts of the wicked; the helmet of salvation; the sword of the Spirit – the Word of God. Seek God's help in constant prayer and be watchful like any good soldier. And while Paul is on the subject of prayer he asks for their support to him (he was chained to a soldier in his imprisonment). He wants God to give him the right words and the boldness to go on telling the hidden purpose of the gospel for which he was an ambassador.

This letter is very much an insider's epistle; and non-Christians may find it difficult to feel comfortable with it. To them I would suggest that it is enough to be aware of its content and its spirit. Later it may come to speak more powerfully to the needs of the human situation. It is certain that it has a quality that implies that there must be something in Christianity for people to have felt this way about what had happened to them as a result of hearing and accepting the Christian gospel.

37

A Warm-Hearted Thank-You Letter

Philippians

Paul and the Philippians

This is Paul at his warmest, showing a loving relationship with the first church to be formed in Europe. Acts 16 tells the story of the vision in which a Macedonian Greek appeared, appealing to Paul to come over and help them. Paul went, and soon made converts there. However he fell foul of vested interests and was imprisoned. The gaoler was converted, but Paul had to leave, with apologies from the authorities, because they had breached his Roman citizenship.

From then on the Philippian church always had a special place in Paul's heart. The particular cause of his writing was to thank them for the way in which they had looked after his material needs, even when he was preaching in other cities. He tells them that he thanks God for them every time he thinks of them, and he mentions them in his prayers every day. (He did this for a number of churches and must have had a busy prayer schedule.) He feels joyful because of the part they have played in the work of the gospel and he declares his great affection for them. 'I hold you in my heart' is how it is expressed in the more literal translations.

The Fragrant Gift

Paul reassures them about the health of their member Epaphroditus, who had brought the latest contribution to him in prison in Rome at some risk and had fallen dangerously ill. He wants to assure them that he has now recovered and that he had fulfilled the mission to deliver the gift, but the sickness has delayed his return and reporting back. (We believe he was in Rome because of the reference in Chapter 4 to Church members working in the emperor's civil service.)

The last part of Chapter 4 deals specifically with the gift. He is grateful that circumstances have enabled them to revive their tangible marks of care, a concern which they always feel, even when they cannot help. He makes clear that he doesn't depend on material things. In the older translation his words read: 'I have learned in whatsoever state I am therewith to be content' (Philippians 4:11). My stepgrandmother engraved it on my mind when I was about nine years old as she explained to me that complaining was not a helpful procedure! It became a lifelong slogan. It doesn't mean that you should not try to improve poor situations, but you should face them with a sense of peace. Paul goes on to say he can face anything in the strength that comes from Christ.

Then, in case they think he is not thankful for their gift, he adds 'all the same it was kind of you to share the burden of my troubles'. He goes on to make this even clearer; from the early days of his mission to Greece they have been the only church to share with him in giving and receiving. Then he makes it plain that it isn't just the material gifts that have touched his heart, but the spirit in which they have been sent. Interest on their contribution is mounting in heaven!

He adds probably the most gracious words of appreciation that any thank-you letter has ever employed: 'It is a fragrant offering, an acceptable sacrifice, acceptable to God.' He puts it into the language of religious service. And if it is a sacrifice then 'my God will supply all *your* needs out of the magnificence of his riches in Christ Jesus'.

Paul's Prayers and Care for Them

The thank-you parts of the letter lie in a context of prayers and the sharing of news. Paul prays that their 'love may grow ever richer in knowledge and insight of every kind, enabling' them 'to learn by experience what things really matter'. This is not sentimental love, but well-informed and stable love, learned in the school of experience.

It is in this letter that we meet the famous reference to the 'peace of God that passes understanding', along with an invitation not to be anxious but to share their problems with God in prayer. Another gem is his recommendation: 'Whatever is true, whatever is honourable, whatever is just, whatever is pure, whatever is pleasing, whatever is commendable, if there is any excellence and if there is anything worthy of praise, think about these things.' He seems to be making a general statement on how Christians should use their minds. He would take it for granted that they would be paying attention to scripture, but there is a hint that in their relationships to everything around them — art, literature, culture — their minds should be filled with the best. Paul himself, for example, was well read in contemporary literature.

Culture is not to be regarded in a neutral manner. Some

aspects are 'better' than others; some uplift the soul; some are debasing. Sensationalist commercial interests tend to encourage the opposite of Paul's guidance in what they invite us to think about as we read their literature and watch their films. Thus Paul does not fall out of date in his comments on society and the Christian's tastes in relation to it.

Paul Shares his Troubles

Quite early in the letter Paul tells his readers that his imprisonment is not imprisoning the Word of God. The Roman soldiers who guard him are being influenced by the fact that he is no ordinary criminal but locked up for his convictions about Christ. His experiences are also giving added courage to the Christians in Rome to speak up about their faith. There are also some contentious Christians in Rome, who although they preach Christ do so in opposition to Paul, criticising him and causing him distress. Their motives are of self-interest. But he says 'What does it matter? One way or another, sincerely or not; Christ is proclaimed, and for that I rejoice.' Nothing will stop him from speaking boldly.

Paul continues by considering the uncertainty of the verdict on him when it reaches the highest court of Rome. He is unmoved by whether it will be life or death. 'For me to live is Christ, and death is gain.' If he lives, there is much fruitful work to be done. If he is executed he 'will depart and be with Christ'. The latter would be best for him personally, but there is much to be achieved, including helping the Philippians, that he is sure he will live and be able to rejoice in his mortal body at their progress.

In all these words we achieve an insight to the total nature of being a Christian as far as Paul is concerned. It is not a Sunday religion — an hour's service and then back to the everyday concerns of life. For him it is the heart of life and it affects everything he does, not least his love and care for fellow believers and for those who are not yet believers.

In the early part of Chapter 2 he also encourages the church at Philippi to hold fast, united in their struggle against opponents who are a constant source of danger. They should meet the danger without so much as a tremor. They are sharing with him the privilege not only of believing in Jesus but also of suffering for him. He is not suggesting that they should court martyrdom, but says that if it comes they should approach it positively. Any who have seen the classic films *Ben Hur* and *Quo Vadis* will have in their memories a vivid representation of what 'suffering for the gospel' could mean.

But the enemies of the gospel are within the churches as well as outside them. Paul interrupts his letter to deal with these. He is telling them to rejoice in the Lord at the beginning of Chapter 3 as a prelude to his final comments, when some news must have arrived, causing him to break off into stormy waters of controversy.

The Threat From False Teachers

'Be on your guard against dogs' Paul warns. He is talking about Christians, so this is tough language indeed. He is referring to the party we have met in the letter to the Galatians, who wanted to impose circumcision on the Gentile Christians. Paul is so angry that he uses the word 'mutilation' to describe circumcision, because insistence on it mutilates the gospel, which is based on faith, not on ethnic boundary markers.

He says that the Christians are the true adherents to the meaning of circumcision, namely the repudiation of the merely physical symbols of religion as having no bearing on salvation.

'We worship by the Spirit of God, whose pride is in Christ, and who put no confidence in the physical.'

He describes his former eminence in the Jewish religion and how he gave it all up for the gain of knowing Jesus Christ as his Lord. He has given up the so-called righteousness of law, which said you have an acceptable status before God by observing these boundary-marking laws. Instead he has moved to the true mark of acceptability before God, which is faith in the once dead but risen Christ. He is prepared to share Christ's suffering so that he can share his resurrection.

He describes his Christian struggle and theirs in terms of the Olympic Games of his day, ' pressing towards the finishing line, to win the heavenly prize' to which God has called him. Even here he doesn't earn it. It is the gift of God.

Paul warns against these enemies of the cross of Christ and their way of life, which is concerned with acceptability with other humans rather than with God. Stick to the Jewish ways of distinguishing oneself from other human beings and avoid trouble from the Jews, although this is not how Jesus delivers people from sin and death. Paul tells them to stand firm, whatever persecution it brings, because the day will come when Jesus will transfigure their lowly human bodies and give them a form like his own.

Then he returns to more encouraging words. In the older translations: 'Rejoice in the Lord; and again I say Rejoice!'

The Humility of Christ

I have left till last the most beautiful and challenging part of the whole epistle, from the first half of Chapter 2.

Paul begins this section by urging the Philippians to have a shared attitude of mind and the same love for each other, thinking and feeling alike. This will fill his cup of happiness. They are to reckon others better than themselves, and leave no room for selfish ambition and vanity, looking after each other's interests and not merely their own.

Then he turns to the example of Jesus. It may be something he wrote himself or he may be using a hymn that had early entered the Christian repertoire. However you interpret his origin in the mind, purpose and Word of God, it remains that the stamp of divinity, of 'godness', was upon Jesus. But he did not try to snatch personal advantage from this closeness to God, the Father. He did not seek equality with the Father. For him divinity consisted, as Professor Moule has expressed it, not in privilege, but in self-giving. God has always been giving himself and Jesus reflects this characteristic of the Father.

He therefore empties himself of all self-assertion, accepting the role of servant. Bearing human likeness, sharing the human predicament, he humbles himself and is obedient, even to the point of death, even death on a cross.

And therefore 'God raised him to the heights, and bestowed on him the name above all names, that at the name of Jesus every knee should bow – in heaven, on earth and in the depths, and every tongue acclaim, "Jesus Christ is Lord", to the glory of God the Father.' Paul applies the words of Isaiah 45 about Yahweh, the God of Israel, to Jesus, so that, in some sense, Jesus Christ is Yahweh, represents him, displays him and shares the worship due to God alone.

This passage is sometimes thought to mean that Jesus pre-existed as a specific person, involved in God and emptying out his divinity so that he could be born as a baby in the human race, truly human. Professor Moule points out that there can be no question of divine self-emptying in order to become human, for self-emptying is what God has always been doing. It is the essence of divinity as seen now through the lens of

Jesus, so to be rid of it would be for God, manifested in Jesus, to empty himself of his self-emptying quality, which would negate the whole point Paul is making.

Paul wants the Philippians to empty themselves of all pride and self-seeking and to follow the path of Jesus. Professor John McQuarrie wrote a book called *Humility of God*, which showed that eternally and from the beginning of Earth's creation God has always been pouring himself out in love for the benefit of everything there is, and, in particular, for the human race. Jesus demonstrated this divine humility in all his actions, as he shared human existence. He is therefore the prototype for all Christians. What Jesus did was, of course, the opposite of what Adam is portrayed as doing in the Eden story, trying to snatch a form of equality with God to gain the knowledge of good and evil for himself. Jesus emptied himself of Adam's search for glory.

Jesus is an example for humans, for in spite of his link with the eternal God, he was truly human, bearing in a finite nature the impress of the divine nature. He showed what humans were and are meant to be, even though there is still a long way to go.

The late Bishop John Robinson expressed these ideas:

> One who was totally and utterly man, and had never been anything other or more than a man, so completely embodied what was the meaning and purpose of God's self expression, that it had to be said of that man, 'he was God's man.' God was in Christ. He was God for us . . . He was a man who by total surrender of his own gain or glory was able to reveal or unveil the glory of God as utterly gracious self giving.

There is a hint at the relationship between God and Jesus in

Chapter 2. Paul tells the Philippians that they have to work out their own salvation with 'fear and trembling'; yet 'it is God who works in them to inspire the will and the deed'. They do it, yet God does it! So in Jesus. As a man he did what he did, but God was at work in him.

We are trying to understand what as humans is bound to lie somewhat beyond our comprehension and we cannot pretend to have all the answers. However it seemed appropriate at this point of examining a key passage that we should go for a brief swim in the squally waters of deep theology. After all, this book is aiming to help people to find their way around the Bible.

38

Rescued From the Power of Darkness

Colossians

The Colossian Error

The town of Colosse was in what we today call Turkey, about 100 miles inland from the Aegean Sea and the city of Ephesus. Paul had never visited it, but was in close touch with Epaphras, who had founded the church and was currently in Rome, where Paul was under house arrest or in prison. Doing a little detective work we get the feeling that Epaphras was worried about unsound views that were beginning to influence the young church at Colosse and that would have a bad effect on Christian behaviour.

These views are referred to by scholars as the 'Colossian heresy' or the 'Colossian error'. But we don't need to be scholars to work out for ourselves a broad idea of what was worrying Paul when he said that he was writing 'so that none would deceive them with plausible arguments' (2:4).

It doesn't appear that these views had as yet taken over the church and so Paul is able to begin his letter in a very complimentary manner. He praises the Colossians for their 'faith in Christ Jesus', 'their love for all God's people', all arising from their strong 'hope' that the heavenly promises of God will be fulfilled. As the letter proceeds it becomes obvious that this hope of a bright future, along with a sense of the living Christ present in their lives, reduces the sense of unease or even of terror with which the ancient world was obsessed.

Appeasing the Powers

To the ancient pagan world, the universe and their own particular part of it was full of forces or powers fighting among themselves to control affairs on Earth. It was difficult for the ordinary mortal to know which ones they ought to please, because these gods, goddesses, angels, demons and devils had different concerns, which often conflicted with each other. You had a worrying time working out how to appease them and keep them on your side.

Tom Wright, then Dean of Lichfield, helps the understanding of these 'powers' in his book *Following Jesus*. He points out that in those days if you were in love you had better get Venus on your side; if you were going on a sea journey, you had better get the sea god Neptune on your side; if you were engaged in war you had better get Mars, the god of war, on your side. Then there were all sorts of minor gods or demons waiting everywhere to harm you if you displeased them. As Tom Wright puts it, there were so many of these powers about 'that life became extremely complicated , and not a little threatening. A lot of ordinary folk went about their daily business in a climate of fear and uncertainty. They did their best to stay out of trouble; but often their best wasn't good enough, and the demons that lurked behind every bush would get you anyway.'

These heavenly powers were the inner dimension of what appeared to be the ordinary events on the earth. They were 'what was really going on'. These 'principalities and powers', as the King James version and the New American Bible translate the key phrase, were never far away. 'They were the inner dimension of exterior events.'

Gnostic Philosophies

At the deeper level the popular views and fears reflected philosophies that are lumped together under the label 'dualism', associated with some forms of what is known as 'gnosticism'. The last word describes the superior 'knowledge' (gnosis) that an intellectual elite supposed it had reached by climbing a ladder of ever higher understanding. It supposed matter to be basically evil, impeding the development of good and intangible 'spirit'. For these people the spiritual quest was to get out of the material realm into the esoteric, world-denying, celestial arena. For them Jesus may have been just one of the superior powers. They ascended their ladder of superiority with the aid of various matter-denying disciplines, including dietary and ascetic practices. They also followed angel cults, with different angels involved in different spheres. They graded all the mystical influences that affected the soul's ascent and speculated on the angelic and demonic powers, which either helped or hindered.

We know of these beliefs from various other sources and we recognise them at work in the Colossian situation by reading between the lines. Particularly we find out about the dangers assailing the Colossian church by the counter-emphasis that Paul places on the supremacy of Jesus, who delivers us from the anxieties of a life peopled by 'the powers' – these invisible demons and angels who stop us getting on with a rational life.

Christ's Power

Paul prays that they may be 'made strong with the strength that comes from his [Christ's] glorious *power* . . . to share in the heritage of God's people in the realm of light . . . He has rescued us from the power of darkness and transferred us into the kingdom of his beloved Son.'

He goes on to elevate Jesus in such a way as to nullify the power of all these other supposed powers and the terror they inspired. 'He is the image of the invisible God, the firstborn of all creation; for in him all things in heaven and in earth were created, things visible and invisible, whether thrones or dominions or rulers or powers – all things have been created through him and for him.' Jesus is presented as the embodiment of the creative Word of God. 'In him all the fullness of God was pleased to dwell, and through him God was pleased to reconcile to himself all things, whether on earth or in heaven, by making peace through the blood of his cross.' Thus former pagans are finding peace in place of the previous demon-populated terror.

Rulers and Authorities

'Powers' are to be reduced to their proper place as intended by God – as rulers and governments, who should provide discipline and good order and avoid anarchy on Earth. However they too have become the servants of sin and superstition and this has created the atmosphere in which the Colossians have in their former days been 'estranged and hostile in mind, doing evil deeds'. Christ has delivered them by his 'fleshly body, through death to present them to God holy and blameless'. Note how this opposes by implication the dualistic theories. It is in the flesh that Christ really offers himself to put things right. Paul describes it as a 'mystery', not in the gnostic sense of something esoteric, known only to the privileged few, but as a mystery in the sense of a secret long hidden but now made known to the believers (1:26–7). There is still a sense of stripping away the pagan mystery and terror to enjoy the freedom of Christ's deliverance.

As for the powers in the sense of governments and rulers, Jesus through his death has 'disarmed the rulers and authorities and made a public example of them, triumphing over them in it'. The rulers thought they had prevailed over him, but he had exposed their weakness and gained the real victory. This triumph makes Christ ultimately 'the head of every ruler and authority', a headship which will be fully realised 'when Christ who is your life is revealed' (3:4), a reference to the final establishment of the Kingdom of God.

Elemental Spirits of the Universe

The powers in the broadest sense are referred to in the letter by terms such as 'elemental spirits of the universe'. So Paul warns them: 'See to it that no one takes you captive through philosophy and empty deceit, according to human tradition, according to the elemental spirits of the universe, and not according to Christ.'

Fear of these elemental spirits is banished when it is realised that 'in him the whole fullness of deity dwells bodily . . . when you were buried with him in baptism, you were also raised with him, through faith in the power of God,' putting to flight faith in or fear of these pagan powers (2:8–12).

Then, as to the superior wisdom that the gnostics claim, it is in Christ himself that 'all the treasures of wisdom and knowledge [gnosis] are hidden' (2:3). No doubt Paul has the false wisdom of the gnostics in mind when by contrast in his opening words he says 'we have not ceased praying for you that you may be filled with the knowledge of God's will in all spiritual wisdom and understanding' (1:9).

Self-Mortification

The gnostic approaches and, indeed, the general fear of the powers, or elemental spirits, were associated with external acts of self-mortification. There was great concern to observe external rituals, special days, food laws and the worship of angels from a visionary extrasensory world, as well as being 'puffed up with a human way of thinking'. A mixture of paganism and Judaism is hinted at. Paul tells the Colossians not to submit to regulations about what they should touch, handle and eat. 'These things indeed have an appearance of wisdom in promoting self-imposed piety, humility and severe treatment of the body, but they are of no value in checking self-indulgence' (2:20–23).

In other words he is suggesting that the gnostic approach was not producing sound Christian behaviour. From the beginning of Chapter 3 he addresses the question of how Christians should behave, the true way of life as distinct from the conduct influenced by the supposedly clever wisdom of the elite and the superstitions of the common people.

Christian Behaviour

'So if you have been raised with Christ, seek the things that are above, where Christ is, seated at the right hand of God. Set your minds on the things above, not on the things that are on the earth, for you have died and your life is hidden with Christ in God.' Gnostics tried to direct people from the things of the earth, by which they meant that matter was evil. Here Paul is using similar words, but for an opposite purpose, as his continuation in Chapter 3 makes clear. He is very concerned to encourage them to live their earthly life in a new way as disciples of the new heavenly Christ. He also gives specific guidance on daily Christian living.

There is nothing 'highfalutin' about being guided away from sexual irregularities, evil desires and greed, or being told to avoid anger, malice, slander, abusiveness, foul language and lying. When you are renewed by the knowledge of Christ these things lose their attraction, if the knowledge is knowing in the sense of intimacy and not merely factual or esoteric.

Positive qualities are recommended to be developed by the Word of Christ dwelling richly in them, such as compassion, kindness, humility, gentleness and patience. Forgiveness is to be practised. Love is to bind everything in perfect harmony. The peace of Christ is to rule in their hearts. 'Whatever you do, in word or deed, do everything in the name of the Lord Jesus, giving thanks to God the Father through him.'

Detailed teaching on family relationships is then given. If some of these instructions seem not to meet the full sense of the equality between the sexes and generations acceptable today, it must be remembered that they were advanced for their time. Also it is possible that the asserting of rights, rather than the recognition of mutual responsibilities, is not necessarily the best route to Christian harmony in the family circle. Slavery is not forbidden, but regulated in such a way as to take much of the sting out of it, with masters being told to treat slaves justly and fairly.

The letter finishes with greetings to a number of individuals in the Colossian church and greetings to certain of his associates by name. They are encouraged to share the letter with the nearby churches in Laodicea and Hierapolis (modern Pammukele, where I have swum in the famous hot springs).

The Powers Today

Tom Wright has a challenging approach to the application of these 'powers' to the life of the twentieth and twenty-first centuries. He is not thinking of the current preoccupation with astrology, which possesses this same sense of fate and interference from higher, mysterious powers. He speaks of the forces we are always being told run this world. If there is a recession that politicians cannot control, it is the fault of economic forces. If we can't sort things out in the Balkans, it's a matter of political forces. If we can't organise the world to feed everyone, it is because of forces beyond our control, such as globalism or currencies or the inevitable push and pull of market forces.

Today there are forces, powers, bigger than the sum total of the human beings involved. They are the equivalent of the invisible forces that used to terrorise the lives of the ancient pagans, and those old-style powers still seem very real in many parts of the developing world. Ancient or modern in style, they create a sense of helplessness, whereas once we know the power of Christ and his supremacy over all other forces, then, says Paul, the peace of Christ drives out the power of these forces to imprison us, even though we have to endure their effects with the rest of the human race for the time being.

The Runaway Slave

The references to slavery and the mention of Onesimus, one of the Christians, carrying the letter, come alive in the Book of Philemon, which ties in very effectively with the letter to the Colossians.

This letter is written to one of the members of the Colossian church, whose home held a house church, as we would call it today. (It seems that although there was a sense of unity in the whole church in a city, it would also function through smaller groups who met in homes. We have examples in Romans 16.) His name is Philemon and greetings are also sent to Apphia, who may have been Philemon's wife, and Archippus, who may have been his son or another relative living with Philemon.

It is a masterpiece of a personal letter and contradicts any views which do not see Paul as a man of tact and sensitivity. Onesimus, one of the bearers of the letter to the Colossians, had been a slave to Philemon and had run away: he had apparently stolen from Philemon, but had been converted to Christianity by Paul and had become a valuable assistant to Paul. His return to Colosse was therefore a serious test for the Christian love of Philemon and Paul writes to help him accept the situation graciously and positively.

Paul's Persuasiveness

After the warm personal greetings to Philemon, 'our dear friend and fellow worker', Paul goes on to speak of Philemon's love and Christian service in glowing terms. He prays that this love may grow even deeper, as he commends the way in which Philemon has been generous in his hospitality to the believers.

Having thus encouraged Philemon into a mood of joy at receiving such praise, Paul moves to the point of his letter by saying, in effect: 'I am going to ask you to do something; I could order you to do your duty, but I would rather appeal to you on the basis of love.' He reminds Philemon that he is an old man and that he is a prisoner, thus touching Philemon's heart. 'I am appealing to you for a child of mine, whose father I became, while wearing these chains.'

Onesimus the Useful

He goes on to make a play on the name of Onesimus, which means 'useful'; though he had proved useless to Philemon as a slave, he was now very useful to Paul in the service of the gospel. This light-heartedness in Paul is not what we would expect, but shows another side of his character. He could have his little joke, but was using it for the serious purpose of making a point to Philemon.

Then follows a deeply felt appeal and a recognition of how changed was Onesimus. 'In sending him back to you I am sending my heart.' Paul says he would like to have kept Onesimus to look after him in his imprisonment, on Philemon's behalf of course, but he wants Philemon's free consent rather than to work on a basis of compulsion.

The appeal deepens still further: 'Perhaps this is why you lost him for a time, to receive him back for good – no longer as a slave, but as more than slave; as a dear brother, very dear to me and dearer still to you, both as a man and as a Christian. So if you consider me your partner, welcome him as you would welcome me.' How could Philemon resist such an affectionate appeal, even though under Roman law Onesimus could have been executed? Doesn't it show that although Paul accepted the fact of slavery – he could do no other – he believed that logically Christ had struck its death knell?

A Living Situation

In verse 18 there is a hint that Onesimus had stolen from Philemon; either this was the cause of his running away or it was to finance his escape. Paul writes an I.O.U. for any money missing and puts his signature to it formally. Then softly he reminds Philemon that he owes his very self to Paul, who had obviously been the cause of his conversion. 'Yes, brother, I am asking this favour [or benefit – another play on the word Onesimus] of you as a fellow Christian; set my mind at rest!' He expresses his confidence that Philemon will even do more than he has been asked and as one last thought asks Philemon to have a room for him as he is sure he will be freed soon and hopes to come and see the church at Colosse.

This short letter takes us into the emotional life of Paul and ties in beautifully with the spirit of the letter to the Colossians. As you read the two letters you get a sense of reality. These events really happened and with this recognition there is a sense of the truth of Jesus Christ, as risen from the dead and seen as living head of the Church. The Church is complete in him, in whom God's fullness is manifested.

39

Letters to an Infant Church

1 Thessalonians, 2 Thessalonians

The Story Behind the Letters

In the north-east of Greece, on the Aegean Sea, stands the modern city of Thessaloniki, in the region of Greek Macedonia. Previously known as Thessalonica, this city was equally important in the days of the apostle Paul and of great significance at an early stage of his mission to the Gentiles of Europe.

Acts 16 records how Paul had a vision in which a Macedonian appeals to him to leave Turkey and come over and help them in Macedonia. He was convinced that God was calling him to take the good news there and immediately set about getting a ship sailing in that direction. He and his companions quickly reached Neapolis, now known as Kavala, and he travelled ten miles inland to the Roman city of Philippi, where he preached until opposition drove him out after a brief imprisonment ended in the conversion of the jailer.

His next stopping place was Thessalonica, where he

preached in the synagogues and increasingly to a wider audience, which upset some of the more rigid Jews. They stirred up trouble, saying that Paul was preaching another king, one Jesus. There was a riot; the magistrates were alarmed and relieved when Paul moved on to Beroea (nowadays called Veria), further inland. A number of Jews and Gentiles accepted the gospel, after careful search of the scriptures, but trouble followed and Paul moved south to Athens, where he worried about what was happening to his Macedonian converts and whether they would stand firm.

Timothy and Silas had stayed behind for a while and when they joined him (probably in Corinth) he sent a letter to encourage the Thessalonians and give them some further guidance on the implications of accepting the gospel. This is the first letter to the Thessalonians.

Opening Praise

Paul praises them for their faith, hope and love and the way in which they had accepted his message, even though it meant suffering for them from the many opponents. He regards them as a model for all believers in Macedonia and the rest of Greece (Achaia). Everyone is hearing the story of how they 'turned from idols to serve the living God' and to await the return of Jesus from heaven. At this early stage the second coming received more prominence than later; it was seen as imminent.

He reminds them of how he worked to support himself financially so as to be no burden to them. This suggests that some had doubts about Paul's motives and, for the sake of the work, he is concerned to clear himself. He describes himself as their nurse and their father as he had urged them to 'live lives worthy of the God who calls you into his kingdom and glory'.

He alludes to the suffering that the anti-Christian party of Jews had caused them and links this with the history of the Jews, with their killing of the prophets and their part in the crucifixion of Christ.

His Anxiety About Them

Paul then moves on to tell the Thessalonians that when he had to leave them so urgently they were out of sight but not out of mind and he had been trying to find a way of coming back to them. When this proved impossible, he stayed in Athens and sent Timothy to find out how they were bearing up under all the testing circumstances and hardships. He was afraid they might give in under the pressure.

However Timothy has now returned and has reassured him. 'It is the breath of life to us to know that you stand firm in the Lord.' He still hopes to come and see them and prays that the Lord may make their 'love increase to one another and to everyone, as our love does to you'.

Standing Firm in an Evil Environment

Paul then moves on to spiritual guidance. He knows the evil that surrounds them in their environment and he counsels them on a range of matters. Sexual 'freedom' is rife in the local society, but they are to 'gain mastery over their bodies, to hallow and honour them, not giving way to lust like the pagans who know nothing of God'. He hints that the intimacy of their Christian fellowship might lead to temptation in this area, but true love would keep them from such temptations. They are 'called to holiness not impurity'.

They should be diligent in their daily work, so that outsiders might be impressed and also so that they might be able to keep all the members of their church from poverty.

Death for the Christian

Apparently there had been some uncertainty among them about the death of Christians. He tells them not to grieve over bereavement with the intensity of those who do not share their hope. Jesus was raised from the dead, and believers would be too. Those who might be alive at the second coming of Christ have no advantage over those who have died. All would be caught up to Christ and ever be with him. The details are somewhat ambiguous and contain apocalyptic symbolism, but the certainty that death is not the end was clear and they are to be consoled by this conviction.

When Will Christ Come?

He proceeds by making it clear to them that the actual timing of the second coming is quite unknown and it could occur quite suddenly and unexpectedly. (Nearly 2,000 years later it still has not happened and in later writings of the apostles it receives less emphasis than the immediate presence of Jesus by the Holy Spirit.) It is important to be always ready to rendezvous with Jesus, whenever he might appear or whenever they might die, in other words whether they are 'awake or asleep'. If they are awake and alive they must be sure that they do not fall asleep spiritually. Their destiny is to live in the company of Jesus.

Wise Guidance

The letter finishes with some wise sayings to help them:

- Give their leaders support.
- Live at peace with each other.
- Don't encourage people to be idle and not work for their living.

- Avoid the desire for revenge if you feel you have been wronged.
- Be joyful and prayerful, whatever happens.
- Encourage utterances from members who offer spiritual teaching, but test that they are truly from God.

He ends with a prayer that God will make them holy, not meaning spiritual superiority in their attitude, but separation from the evils that surround them, keeping them sound in body, soul and spirit so as to be pronounced ultimately faultless in the presence of Jesus Christ. He greets them all, requests their prayers for himself and asks that everybody should have access to his letter.

The Second Letter

The second letter seems to be a quick follow-up to the first, because it seeks to clarify some of its issues. Silas or Silvanus and Timothy are with him, having returned from delivering the first letter. They are obviously experiencing trouble and persecution, but their love for each other is growing under this pressure. He comforts them by pointing to the return of Jesus, who will punish their enemies (not the highest approach). He prays that they may be among those who are acceptable to Jesus and who will share his glory and dwell in the presence of his majesty.

Premature Expectations

He then goes on to warn them against premature expectation of the coming again of Jesus in visible form. In apocalyptic language he tells them that wickedness has to grow before the final work of establishing the Kingdom of God can be initiated. He describes the secret forces of wickedness and idolatry that are already at work and points out that some of them may have a degree of plausibility, deceiving certain believers. In this connection there are several difficult statements, such as the idea that God deliberately gives some people delusions to make them believe a lie. Yet he also speaks of human choice. Other New Testament writings are clearer on the principles of human responsibility, side by side with divine control, but to be clear in one's mind on free will and predestination has never been easy and we have to accept what we can understand and leave some things for later clarification. It would be foolish to reject what we can understand because of what we cannot.

High Hopes

But for them he has high hopes that they will 'possess the splendour of our Lord Jesus Christ'. He prays: 'May our Lord Jesus Christ and God our Father, who has shown us such love, and in his grace has given us such unfailing encouragement and so sure a hope, still encourage and strengthen you in every good deed and word.' Such words may sound lush and embarrassing to the modern mind, but perhaps we should give them a chance to convey the living power that these early Christians experienced.

After further prayers at the beginning of Chapter 3, Paul comes back to the idle habits of certain Christians who are not working for their living, perhaps because they think the second coming is so imminent. They are not to be supported in their laziness; if they would not work they couldn't expect to be kept alive by the generous gifts of the other believers. The hard-working believers are in fact asked not to encourage them by such generosity. They should protest against their idling their time away in 'minding everybody's business but their own' and instruct them in the right behaviour. They are not to co-operate with the idle ones, though neither are they to count them as enemies; such an attitude would ultimately make them ashamed of themselves.

Paul concludes with a prayer that they may be granted peace from the Lord of Peace. He signs the letter with his own hand and ends in the usual way 'the grace of our Lord Jesus Christ be with you all'. Just because it is a usual ending it should not be seen as of no significance. It actually sums up his view of the Christian life in a sentence, suggesting that every minute of every day should in some way be touched by the awareness of Christ.

Comparing Paul's Early and Later Letters

These two letters have a sense of reality and credibility. They are dealing with the sort of problems you could expect in an infant church. And the style of Paul is much less profound than that of his later letters, for example to the nearby Philippians, when they were no longer newly converted Macedonian Christians. Similarly they lack the theological concern found, because of new situations, in the letter to the Galatians or the consolidation of his teaching of the gospel in the letter to the Romans. This development of thought and teaching is what one would expect in a growing movement. Nevertheless the fundamental place of Jesus Christ and the meaning of love for all these communities and their sense of the grace of God in Jesus Christ is present in all of them, early or late.

40

Pastoral Epistles

1 Timothy, 2 Timothy and Titus

The First Letter

After the great riot in Ephesus over the goddess Artemis and the trade of the silversmiths, Paul left for Macedonia and Greece (Acts 20), asking Timothy to remain behind to look after things in the church. Timothy was a relatively young man, but Paul had confidence in him and regarded him as 'his true born son in the faith'. Paul had nurtured the church in Ephesus for three years, but it was still immature and in need of guidance. Timothy may well have felt inadequate to be such a shepherd, pastor or minister, so Paul wrote to give him some guidelines and encouragement.

Opposing the Speculators

His opening concern is to remind Timothy that his last instruction to the young minister was to be very firm in opposing certain teachers in the church who were involved in false ideas based on myths and genealogical tables from which they drew speculative ideas. They sound as if they were following the elitist approach of the gnostics, who had a fondness for special secrets known only to the initiated. In contrast Paul points out that the gospel works through faith, trust in God, not clever so-called wisdom.

The aim of true Christian knowledge is the creation of love, springing from a pure heart, a heart that is true and straightforward and not devious. The route taken by the false teachers led into just 'a wilderness of words'. These teachers were also emphasising the law in ways which we considered when examining Romans and Galatians. Paul says they don't understand either the words they use or the subjects they are talking about, and anyway where you really understand the gospel of Christ you will do the right thing from the heart. Law is for the control of people who want to do the wrong things, and he lists some of these.

The Gospel of Forgiveness

Paul continues by showing humility to his protégé. He refers to his own former sinfulness when he had persecuted the Church of God and was forgiven because he did so ignorantly, out of unbelief. He still remembers himself as among the chief of sinners, but God's mercy to him should encourage others to accept the forgiveness of God. All sin can be forgiven if there is repentance, such is the character of God and Jesus. They display inexhaustible patience and to none more than to Paul.

Emboldened by this knowledge, Timothy is to fight the good fight of faith, including resistance to those who would make a shipwreck of faith. Two of them are mentioned, whom Paul had placed under severe discipline because of their blasphemy. He calls this exclusion 'consigning to Satan', but even then the aim is their repentance and restoration.

Procedures for Worship

Paul then continues with guidance about the content and procedures of worship. They are not to be antagonistic to governments and rulers, but to pray for them, so that the Christians will be left in peace to get on with their lives of service to Christ, free to worship. They should also pray for the conversion of their neighbours, because God wishes everyone to share in the salvation he offers.

Men are to do the praying. Women are to keep quiet and not teach in church. 'Their role is to learn, listening quietly and with due submission.' Elsewhere Paul said that there was neither male nor female in Christ Jesus; they were all one in him, so perhaps there was a special localised situation, where the women were taking over. However the argument he uses is of a general nature, as he says that they should keep quiet because it was Eve who was deceived and then tempted Adam into sin in the Garden of Eden. If Adam was so weak you could argue that this was a good reason why men should not be trusted to teach! In any case Paul is stereotyping gender on the basis of a specific story and we would find this argument unconvincing. Even apostles were children of their times in the methods of expression they used.

Paul also worked closely with women himself and gave them great respect. Priscilla and Phoebe are two that come to mind from other letters. He was writing in a time when women were regarded as inferior, which he did not accept, but he did limit their role in Church activities. However in Chapter 3 of this letter he gives instructions about the qualities required from women deacons in the Church, so that they should be dignified and avoid scandal-mongering. He also suggests that all women in the Church should avoid elaborate dress and jewellery and be clothed modestly and be known for their good deeds rather than for their display of the latest fashions. There is a topical message in this. The fashion shows reported on television news could hardly be recommended as providing a basis for Christian women to follow.

The Administration of the Church

In Chapter 3 Paul prescribes the characteristics of a bishop, who is simply a local pastor or minister. He uses words like sober, temperate, courteous, hospitable. They should be good teachers, not be new converts, have a good reputation in the outside world and manage their families well. He promises that he will give further guidance when he comes, though it is unlikely that he ever visited Ephesus again (Acts 20). Meanwhile he stresses the importance of Timothy's work, for the 'church is the pillar and bulwark of the truth', and he sums up that truth in an early creed: 'God was manifested in the flesh, vindicated in spirit, seen by angels, he [Jesus – the manifestation of God] was proclaimed among the nations, believed in throughout the world, raised to heavenly glory.'

Timothy's Task

In Chapter 4 he returns to warning of the dangers of unsound teaching and plausible theories that can cause a forsaking of the faith. Celibacy would be insisted upon, abstinence from certain foods would be demanded by these teachers, although God has given the food to be accepted with thanksgiving. Timothy is to avoid superstitions and old wives' tales and to keep in training for his spiritual functions. Bodily exercise is useful but spiritual exercise produces health of an eternal nature.

Timothy is then encouraged not to be put off by his relative youth. He must not lose confidence and let people underrate him, but be an example in speech, behaviour, love, fidelity and purity. He is to concentrate on the public reading of scripture and on teaching and exhorting on that basis, making such activities his absorbing interest. He is to persevere and to keep close watch on his duties in the Church, especially his teaching, whereby he might save himself and those who heard him.

I remember being stirred by these words at the age of twenty. In the King James Version they read: 'Give attention to reading, to exhortation, to doctrine; meditate upon these things; give thyself wholly to them.' My then new wife (long since deceased) and I made them our motto and they have stayed with me ever since, though in a way we were misinterpreting them as referring to personal growth rather than to the work of public ministry. However it was a misinterpretation that did no harm.

The Church as a Family

Church administration follows. Treat the Church as a family: the old men as fathers, the young women as sisters. Advice is given about showing care in admitting widows on to the roll for material support. The widows' families have the first responsibility and where they can stand on their own feet they should. Widows over sixty might be a different matter. Paul seems to be in two minds about young widows; he seems both to disapprove of their remarriage and yet a few verses later he advises it.

Elders who work hard for the Church in teaching and preaching should be supported. 'The labourer is worthy of his hire.' Elders should not be appointed without due thought and disputes should be handled with fairness and careful attention to the evidence, not with prejudice. Slaves are not to take advantage of their masters if they are Christians, but give them all the better service as their brothers.

There was a significant development of structure in the Church, which has led some scholars to date this letter as later and by another author. Personally it seems so tied up with Paul's experience that I can't imagine someone else writing it and dressing it up to look like a letter from Paul.

Concluding Guidance

The letter concludes with general advice and warnings about those who look to religion for material advantage. Contentment with simple standards, unlike our age of consumerism, is recommended and the rich are not to trust in their wealth, but to use it generously and store the real treasure for the eternal future. Interjected into the advice are words of praise to God; some of these are the basis of the favourite hymn 'Immortal, invisible, God only wise'.

An endearing touch is some practical advice: 'Stop drinking only water; in view of your frequent ailments take a little wine to help your digestion.' This shows another side of Paul.

The letter concludes with a final warning against the false knowledge proclaimed by the gnostics as implied by the reference to knowledge (gnosis). (Note that gnostics should not be confused with agnostics, who are people who don't know whether there is a God or what the truth is about a matter.)

The Second Letter

Whatever debates the scholars may undertake about the author of this Second Letter to Timothy, the Church for eighteen centuries took it to be Paul's letter and I will stay with them. It makes sense, even though its style is different from other letters of Paul.

I see it as his death cell letter, written towards the end of an imprisonment late in his life, although we are not sure whether it was his last one. He certainly had fears that any day now the executioner would come along and chop off that noble head, which had contained so many profound thoughts. It therefore is an excellent example of a Christian attitude to death, untroubled by it because he could see beyond to the promises of an eternal future, in which he had unwavering faith.

From His Prison Cell

Paul begins the letter by reference to his personal relationship with Timothy and alludes to the sound upbringing Timothy received from his mother and grandmother. These are touches that convince me that Paul is the author, even if the style owes something to the person to whom he dictated its substance.

From his prison cell, Paul exhorts Timothy to courage and to keep the flame of the Spirit alive in his life. His attitude to his own impending death is illustrated as he speaks of the fact that Jesus Christ has 'broken the power of death and brought life and immortality to light through the gospel'. Paul is confident that Christ will not allow his life's work to be to no avail.

He goes on to say how many of his Christian brethren had deserted him, though he mentions how Onesiphorus had visited him in prison in Rome after searching for him. This is obviously a later imprisonment than the earlier house arrest mentioned in Acts 28.

Paul encourages Timothy to be a good soldier of Christ and proceed on his Christian path like an athlete running a race, who abides by the rules. He speaks of his criminal fetters, but says that the Word of God is not chained. He sums up the Christian hope in a hymn: 'If we died with him we shall live with him; if we endure we shall reign with him; if we disown him he will disown us; if we are faithless he remains faithful. For he cannot disown himself.' Then he gives more advice to oppose the false teachers, such as those who said that the resurrection had already taken place and was presumably only spiritual. Paul in his prison cell hoped for something permanent beyond this life on the basis of living in Christ during this life.

As he sits chained, Paul is somewhat frustrated and alone in his cell. He longs to be in action to preserve the truth of the gospel in the Church in a time when the evils of the world are in danger of penetrating the Christian brotherhood. He talks further of the need for fortitude under hardship and exhorts Timothy to stand firm. He looks back at Timothy's life: 'From early childhood you have been familiar with the sacred writings [the Old Testament of course] which have power to make you wise and lead you to salvation, through faith in Christ Jesus.' This is an important statement. The Old Testament has to be read in the light of Christ. Then it has a saving influence. This is why the Old Testament has been covered in this book, and the New Testament chapters have much to say about how to interpret the earlier writings (see especially Chapter 22).

So Timothy is not to surrender, but to keep spreading the gospel and not to allow the false teachers to divert him from this course.

Faith in the Face of Impending Execution

The letter concludes with greetings to various believers by name. Paul also reports on the progress of his case. No one has come into court to support him, but he feels the strength of Christ supporting him. He is not therefore thrown to the lions in the arena. This might be because as a Roman citizen he can opt for beheading as a more instant death. His faith shines out as he sees beyond the present: 'The Lord will rescue me from every attempt to do me harm, and bring me into his heavenly kingdom.'

The most moving expression of this faith comes just before the greetings:

> As for me, my life is already being poured on the altar, and the hour for my departure is upon me. I have run the great race, I have finished the course, I have kept the faith. And now there awaits me the garland of righteousness (the spiritual athlete's prize) which the Lord, the righteous judge will award me on the great day, and not to me alone, but to all who have set their heart on his coming appearance.

If you are a Christian you will be stirred by those words. If you are not, you cannot fail to be impressed by the confidence and hope that Paul's faith engendered. You might even wish you could believe it. But that is your decision. My task is to make the text a little clearer, though I cannot hide my hope that understanding the text may have significant results in the lives of readers.

Titus and the Happy-Go-Lucky Islanders

The third of the so-called pastoral epistles is written to Titus, whom we have also previously met in the Book of Acts.

All three pastoral epistles tend to wander somewhat; they do not have one set theme. As Paul thinks of things, so he writes them down. However in the case of Titus we can see a thread. It is a letter written to Titus in his capacity as the pastor or minister in Crete, where Paul had left him to set up the administration of the local church and to continue the teaching mission.

The Spiritual Condition of Crete

Crete is an island with a number of ports that were much more significant in the first century. Where you get ports you get sailors, who land looking for a good time with wine, women and song. The tendency is towards a riotous seeking of pleasure. Some of them were partly converted to Christ, but had difficulty in following the Christian way of life. The sailors also influenced the locals, who would get caught up in the mood and provide some of the facilities for drink, sex and entertainment. Hints of this are scattered throughout the letter.

The elders are to be free of involvement in the undesirable side of Cretan life. They are not to be overbearing or short-tempered, or given to drink, or brawlers, or money-grubbers. Brawls and drunken riots must have been daily occurrences in the ports on the island. The elders must be models of the opposite sort of behaviour. The elders also had to be sound in their teaching and ready to correct the Jewish party, who wanted to invoke the law that Jesus had superseded.

Paul quotes a Cretan poet who described the inhabitants as liars, vicious brutes and lazy gluttons, not the most favourable ground for sowing the seed of the gospel. Advice similar to that to Timothy is given, with special emphasis on the need to educate the church members away from scandals, gossip, excessive drink, malice and envy, which belonged to their former way of life. Slaves are to be trustworthy and not go in for pilfering. The government is to be respected and they are not to involve themselves in protest movements. They are to 'renounce godless ways and worldly desires and to live a life of temperance, honesty and godliness in this present age, looking forward to the happy fulfilment of our hope'.

Christ the Cure

He emphasises that it is the self-sacrifice of Jesus Christ that has set them free from all wickedness and turned them into a people eager to do good. Titus: 'These are your themes; urge them and argue them with an authority which no one can disregard.' The main theme by which Titus is to draw the Cretans away from their happy-go-lucky, self-pleasing ways is summed up towards the end of the letter: 'Our days were passed in malice and envy; hateful ourselves we loathed one another, but when the kindness and generosity of God our saviour dawned upon the world, then, not for any good deeds of our own, but because he was merciful, he saved us through the water of rebirth and the renewing power of the Holy Spirit, which he lavished on us through Jesus Christ our saviour, so that justified by grace, we might in hope become heirs to eternal life.'

Consolidating the Churches

When you consider the nature of the population it is incredible that such changes should have taken place at least among the minority who formed the church for which Titus was responsible. The letter finishes with advice to maintain order, to resist the contentious members; if they persist Titus is to have nothing to do with them. The positive approach, devoting themselves to good works, reduces the dangers to the Church.

Paul makes some final arrangements, hoping to be in Greece at Nicopolis for the winter. It is obviously therefore an earlier letter than 2 Timothy, as he is still free.

All in all, these three letters, the pastoral epistles, give an idea of the needs and difficulties of infant churches as they began to develop and create structures. Full of practical advice and less occupied with the major doctrinal controversies, they are concerned to secure sound behaviour among the members and give a valuable window into the early Church in its second stage of consolidation.

41

A New Way

Hebrews

This chapter is about a letter probably written before the destruction of the temple and the Jewish system by the Romans in AD 70. It was attributed to the apostle Paul, but it is now generally accepted that it was not written by him. Its style and approach are very different. Some have suggested it was written by Apollo, whom we met in Acts and the Corinthian letters, but this is speculation. It doesn't make any difference to the letter's contribution to our understanding.

The key thought behind this letter is that the Jewish (or Hebrew) Christians, particularly those living in and around Jerusalem, should separate completely from the Jewish religion and cease to try to merge it with the Christian religion. The two could not be seen as one. The law of Moses had come to the end of its run; the Old Covenant was now superseded by the New Covenant of which Jeremiah had spoken. Salvation was solely through Jesus Christ. The laws, rituals and temple observances codified by Moses were superseded as the result of the life, death and resurrection of Jesus.

Many of the arguments the author employs are not of a kind that would appeal to the modern mind, but they are of a type familiar to his readers, who would have found them convincing. If we approach them sympathetically they are not irrelevant to us, though the territory is less familiar.

There is nothing in the New Testament that depends more on understanding the Old Testament writings than this letter. Quotations and analogies abound, which is not surprising as it is being addressed to Jewish Christians.

God Speaks by His Son

The letter begins with the fundamental statement that God has in times past spoken in a variety of ways through the prophets, as recorded in the Old Testament, but now he has spoken through a Son. This Son, Jesus Christ, is described as reflecting the glory of God and as he sits (symbolically) at the right hand of God he sustains the whole universe. Bearing the divine stamp, he is superior to angels, who were traditionally associated with the institution of the law of Moses. Jesus is God's final word.

The author quotes from various Old Testament passages that he sees as demonstrating this superiority. He quotes from the promises made to David, which were the basis of Israel's hopes for the future. The king and the dynasty were also to be regarded as God's Son and this would especially apply to the ultimate king or Messiah. Jesus was foreshadowed in the Psalms as having a permanent kingship and as sharing in the eternity of God, in contrast with the Jewish system, which was temporary and ministered by angels, who are just God's messengers.

The writer brings out the seriousness of his message by pointing out that the old law, spoken by angels on behalf of God, brought punishment for disobedience (Chapter 2). How much more serious then it would be to disregard the salvation that came through the Son. For a little while man, and Jesus as the representative man, have been subordinate to angels, but according to Psalm 8, the human race was to have control of the earth and everything upon it. Jesus had already obtained this position on the basis of his suffering of death, which he 'had tasted for all mankind'.

Jesus – the Great High Priest

As the pioneer of salvation, Jesus was perfect through his suffering. Sharing the common human experience, in the same human nature, Jesus delivered the human race from the bondage of sin and the ever present fear of death. He shared fully the human experience and, having done so, was able to show sympathy to people in all their problems and testing times. This was the task of a high priest under the Mosaic law. Jesus was supremely qualified to be a high priest of a superior kind. This is a continuing theme of the letter.

Jesus in this capacity was also superior to Moses, the giver of the law (Chapter 3). Moses was a servant in God's house; Jesus is the ruler of God's house. And the house in question is in fact a house of people – the Church, if it is faithful to its calling.

The Danger of Rebellion

But just as Israel was not faithful to its calling as God's house in the time of Moses, the same danger exists for the new Israel. The writer is hinting that if it goes back to the Old Covenant and seeks to incorporate the Mosaic system into the Christian gospel, they would be as guilty of unbelief as the Israelites in their own day. There is always a 'today' in which people can be obedient or rebellious. If they stay with the Old Covenant, they would never reach the promised land, any more than old Israel did.

Chapter 4 continues this theme of transferring the experience of the Israelites, as they followed Moses through the wilderness, to the experience of contemporary Christians. Joshua was then supposed to bring the first Israel into a 'rest' from their wanderings, but Psalm 95 implies that the 'rest' still lay in the future, suggesting that there was no finality in the system established by Moses.

God's word to the Christians is far more incisive than the knife used to dismember the animal sacrifices of the old law. It is not concerned with flesh and bones, but cuts right through to the very thoughts and intentions of the heart.

The Merciful High Priest

Yet the Hebrews are not to despair of ever pleasing God, for Jesus is their high priest. He can sympathise with human weakness, for he himself was tempted, though he never gave in to sin. To him, as their priest in heaven, they should go to find help and mercy, which the ancient priesthood could never have provided.

Chapter 5 continues this theme. The former high priests were chosen by God, though, unlike Jesus, they were not without sin. Jesus was chosen by God and did not belong to the old order of priests that descended from Aaron. Jesus symbolically belonged to the high priestly order of Melchisedek, referred to in the story of Abraham. This priest had no human genealogy, which suggested, according to Psalm 110, a superior order of priesthood to the Aaronic or Levitical one.

The superiority of Jesus is expressed in beautiful words describing his suffering, by which he was made perfect. The loud cries and tears of Jesus in the Garden of Gethsemane as he approached his death are mentioned to emphasise the greatness of his priesthood. He did not offer animals in sacrifice, but himself, and so became the source of salvation for Christians.

Watchwords of Warning

Chapter 6 goes on to say that these interesting examples from the Old Testament are being used to teach vital truths, which go beyond the repetition of basic principles of the law. Now they have come to the New Covenant they must not go back to the Old one. To do so is to commit apostasy, to fall away from Christ. It would be like joining the Jews and Romans in crucifying Christ all over again.

But Paul is sure that they will do better than that. They have already endured much suffering and persecution and God will not forget that. They are on the right path. Surely they will stay on it.

More About Melchisedek

The author now goes back to Abraham, who preceded the law and Moses. The promises made to Abraham did not depend on the law of Moses for their fulfilment. They were unconditional. God's word to Abraham was not invalidated by a later word through Moses. It had the priority and Jesus was the one through whom the promise to Abraham was to be fulfilled.

Moreover, Abraham paid tithes to Melchisedek. This meant he was recognising the authority of Melchisedek. The as yet unborn Levi, the father of the Aaronic priesthood was, in a manner of speaking, in Abraham's loins at the time. The Melchisedek priesthood was therefore superior because this priest blessed Abraham. This argument, in Chapter 7, is not of a kind we would find very helpful today, but it was familiar in its day.

Melchisedek had no genealogy; there is no record of his

birth or death, there is no record of his appointment. He is wrapped in the mystery of eternity as far as the record goes and thus makes a suitable basis for illustrating the special kind of priesthood exercised by Jesus who, as he belonged to the tribe of Judah, would not have been a priest under the law of Moses.

The writer builds his argument further using Psalm 110. If a new order of priesthood was foreshadowed in the Psalm then a new law would accompany the change. The words in the Psalm are: 'You are a priest for ever after the order of Melchisedek.' Christ's priesthood is for ever. The hope he brings is better than anything the Old Covenant can offer. The offered communication between God and man is superior to the temporary nature of the law, with its repeated sacrifices. Jesus is able for all time to save those who approach God through him. His sacrifice occurred once only, not daily like those under the Old Covenant. The former priests were sinners like the rest of us. Jesus was perfect.

The New Covenant

The author continues in Chapter 8 to describe Jesus as operating in the heavenly tabernacle in contrast to the tent of former centuries, which later became the temple. His ministry is of the New Covenant. There follows a full quotation from Jeremiah 31. In the closing days of the kingdom of Judah, at a time when the temple was about to be destroyed and the nation to go into exile, Jeremiah envisaged a New Covenant that did not depend on external ritual but was a matter of God writing his law on people's hearts and in their minds. Their obedience sprang from within and God's forgiveness would be permanently available.

The fact that it was a New Covenant, says our author, makes

the Old one obsolete. It is now ready to vanish finally away and they should cling to the better hope of the New Covenant.

The Heavenly Tabernacle

Chapter 9 begins by describing the tabernacle that we read about in the Book of Exodus. It has two sections: the inner one or Holy of Holies, containing the ark of the covenant, the incense altar, the golden cherubim; and the outer one, containing a table for bread and the seven-branched lampstand. These represented various aspects of God's potential fellowship with the people.

Into the inner shrine the priest went once a year on the Day of Atonement (Yom Kippur) to obtain forgiveness for the people with the blood of animal sacrifices. It was only temporary forgiveness, for it all had to be repeated the following year. The sacrifices offered did not create perfect consciences or establish a religion of the heart.

To go into the inner tent, the Holy of Holies, the priest first had to pass through the inferior tent, which was used every day. The writer makes an analogy of this. Jesus doesn't operate in the outer tent, but in the inner one. And not literally. The inner tent represents heaven, where he ministers perpetually for the believers. He didn't go there with the blood of bulls and of goats, but with his own blood, the offering of himself. Such an offering could procure change of heart and not just the removal of external defilement. It 'could purify the conscience from dead works to serve the living God'.

The New Covenant was ratified with the blood of Jesus shed on Calvary, that is, at the cost of his own life given up in the pursuit of righteousness. He passed the death sentence on sin and death. He did so once and Christians are to wait for him to complete the establishment of the Kingdom of God when he appears the second time.

The Final Sacrifice

Chapter 10 places the accent on the superiority of the sacrifice of Jesus himself over the old animal sacrifices. The old sacrifices were only a shadow, not moral realities. You had to keep offering them to remind yourself of your sin. They did not transform your way of life. They could not take away sin.

Psalm 40 is quoted as implying that sacrifices and offerings of animals are not what God permanently desires. He is interested in the offering of people's wills, freely given to him. And this is what Jesus did superlatively. The New Covenant chapter from Jeremiah is again quoted with emphasis on the permanent forgiveness of sins. If sins are forgiven permanently through the one offering of Jesus, then there is no purpose in continuing to offer the animals. In fact the practice placed a question mark over the one sacrifice of Jesus and was therefore a repudiation of the truth found in Jesus.

So they are to end all association with the Jewish ritual and law and concentrate their spiritual energy on the new and living way in Jesus. They are to stay together in the new worship and to show the works of Jesus in their relationship with one another, in love and good works.

To go back to the Old Covenant is to treat the sacrifice of Jesus as of no consequence. They would be rejecting the only sacrifice that was worth anything in favour of those that are useless. Using language from the Old Covenant, perhaps because it is the kind they would understand, he warns them that this going backwards would incur God's anger and judgement.

So they must stand firm and maintain their faith, whatever the cost in suffering and persecution.

The Honour Roll of Faith

Chapter 11 goes through many of the heroes of the Old Testament as encouragement to the Christians, showing courage in face of Jewish persecution. It is quite a subtle idea to take these Old Covenant heroes and to say in effect: Yes, these men and women did not have the truth as you now know it in Jesus, but, with their lesser light, how brave they were. In view of this, how much more should you, with Jesus before you, show similar courage in your day and situation.

Old Testament characters such as Abel, Noah, Abraham, Isaac, Jacob and Moses are paraded before them, each introduced with the words 'By faith'. They had less substance in their religion yet what examples they gave. A number of them are listed together at the end; their ill treatment is mentioned and it is said that the world was not worthy of such people.

When you read the Old Testament history of some of them, such as Samson, you have to admit that they were not all consistently admirable characters, but for all their faults they had this one characteristic – faith – and they stood firm. If they with their lesser light did this then the privileged Christians should do no less.

Looking Unto Jesus

Chapter 12 picks up the roll of the faithful with a 'therefore'.

> Therefore since we are surrounded by so great a cloud of witnesses, let us lay aside every weight and the sin which clings so closely, and let us run with patience the race that is set before us, *Looking unto Jesus*, the pioneer and perfecter of our faith, who for the joy set before him endured the cross, despising the shame and is seated at the right hand of the throne of God.

Jesus is the highest in the honour roll and the one on whom they are invited to pin their hopes and their faith.

The writer continues to encourage them to persist in faith in spite of the trouble that would come their way for rejecting the Old Covenant. They are to remember what Jesus went through and to recognise that suffering, taken in the right way, can have a purifying effect. It loosens earthly concerns and strengthens heavenly aspirations. He contrasts the grace associated with Mount Zion, the New Jerusalem, with Mount Sinai, where the law was promulgated. The latter was terrifying. The former speaks of more permanent and hope-giving prospects. But remember that God is still God and rejection of his offers is a serious matter.

Jesus Christ: The Same Yesterday, Today and Forever

The last chapter gives advice of a practical nature on how faithful people should behave. They are to be hospitable, pure in sexual matters and not afflicted with the love of money. Contentment is possible when you realise that God is your helper in all the problems of life, as even the Old Testament characters realised.

They are to esteem their faithful leaders and to remember that Jesus is unchanging, unlike the Mosaic arrangements, which have been superseded. They are not to be worried about what kinds of food they should eat; they do not affect their characters. They are to realise that Christ was their altar and that he had suffered outside the city walls of Old Covenant Jerusalem. They must join him in spirit there, for in the Jewish system they have no permanent citizenship.

The sacrifices they are to offer are those of praise to God, of doing good and of sharing their belongings. They are to make the labours of their leaders a joy and to offer prayer continually.

The letter finishes with a prayer which has echoes of all that has been said about the New Covenant, the true and permanent sacrifice of Jesus and its impact on their way of life:

> Now may the God of peace, who brought again from the dead our Lord Jesus, the great shepherd of the sheep, by the blood of the eternal covenant, equip you with everything good that you may do his will, working in you that which is pleasing in his sight, through Jesus Christ; to whom be glory for ever and ever.

42

The One God

James

Who Wrote the Letter? And to Whom?

James was a common name (Jacob in its Hebrew origin). The author cannot be the James of Peter, James and John, the special three disciples, as he was executed very early in the history of the Church (see Acts 12:2). Church tradition has assigned the text to James, the brother of Jesus, who was prominent in the church of Jerusalem and presided over the Council of Jerusalem (Acts 15). His background was Jewish and the letter is addressed to the twelve tribes scattered abroad, suggesting that it was addressed to the Jewish Christians who lived in various parts of the Roman Empire. He may also have been aiming to correct some misunderstanding of Paul, where some thought that in emphasising faith he was teaching that works did not matter.

This is more like a general guideline than a personal letter. Its theme is Jewish with its emphasis on the oneness – the unity – of God, though it was of equal value to Gentile

Christians, who were encouraged to understand the Jewish Scriptures.

The Theme of the Letter

The most important creed of Israel is found in Deuteronomy 6.

> Hear O Israel: the Lord our God is one Lord; and you shall love the Lord your God with all your heart, and with all your soul and with all your might.

This provides the key to this letter of James. It brings together with a common theme what might otherwise look like a New Testament Book of Proverbs, all separate and unrelated. However it is not just talking about God, but of the need for believers to be *one* as well. We speak of the desirability of an integrated personality, but we often seem to have a divided personality, even if we are perfectly sane. For example, we might say one thing but then do another. We are not consistent; if it is too noticeable, people call us hypocrites.

James takes the Shema, as Deuteronomy 6:4 is called, and gives at least six categories for illustrating the oneness of God in action.

God is One

1. God is one! His words and his actions match. So to be like him our belief and our action should be one; our faith should not be contradicted by our actions.

2. God is one! There are not different gods for different activities and different purposes. Therefore all our loyalty belongs to one God only. Our life should hold together in a unified way in service to the one God.

3. God is one! So there are not different gods with different characteristics; and Christians should not be emphasising some aspects of good behaviour above others; our lives should be aiming to express all the good qualities, not just some that we might feel are our particular strengths.

4. God is one! One God made all creatures; there are not different gods for different places, races, classes and nations; he is not partial in his attitude to them. So we should not be partial in our judgement of people, races and nations. We should treat them all equally and fairly. We should love them all, as their one creator does.

5. God is one! He is not fickle; he does not act in one way at one time and in a different way in the same circumstances at another time.

6. God is one! He is complete. There is nothing missing from his perfection. 'Be ye perfect', that is, in each aspect of life we should seek in the strength of God to be 'whole' and let him complete his work in us.

As we move through the epistle we will indicate by their numbers from this list which categories of God's oneness are involved, as well as making any necessary explanatory comments.

A Testing Time

At the beginning of the letter it is obvious that the Jewish believers to whom James was writing were enduring difficult times. The quality of their faith was being tested. Such trials were to develop patience or perseverance in them. 'And let perseverance have its full effect, so that you may be mature and complete, lacking in nothing.' They are invited to share God's completeness, his wholeness, and where any such lack appears they are to pray to have the deficiency made up. Here is our sixth category (no. 6).

Such prayers must be wholehearted; the person praying should not be 'in two minds'; there should be conviction and total loyalty to God (no. 2). The failure to show this attitude is described as double-minded (also no. 2).

Rich and Poor in the Church

James moves on to speak of the class distinctions likely to arise in the Church between rich and poor (no. 4). The brother who is poor or lowly should rejoice because he is lifted up to a high status in Christ. The rich should be pleased because in Christ they share the Lord's lowly life when on earth. Thus there is equality, oneness of class, in the Church where this attribute of God to be without partiality is followed.

Throughout the letter James shows a distinct lack of sympathy for the rich. Like the grass upon which the burning heat of the sun pours down they will fade away (1:11). 'Come now, you rich! Weep and wail over your impending miseries'; goes on to describe their end in reward for all their oppression of the poor (5:1–6).

Don't Blame God

Category no. 5 is illustrated by Chapter 1:13–16, where they are not to blame God for their inner temptations. God's nature could not be so fickle as to influence people to evil behaviour while commanding them good actions. He is one. He can't move in two contradictory directions at once. James stresses that people are tempted by their own desires. When they yield, sin is born and sins breeds death.

In this kind of teaching James is not contradicting Paul, who emphasises the fact that we depend on God to overcome sin through Jesus Christ and the Spirit dwelling within us, but he is putting an emphasis on our own responsibility, lest we should think that faith is enough without it also being reflected in our actions.

The epistle is not as Christ-centred as those of Paul, but neither does it assume that we can find righteousness in our own strength. In fact he goes on to say that 'every good and generous action and every perfect gift come from above, from the Father'. The source of right action is in God not in humans. God brings us to birth by his word of truth.

Luther the reformer thought James emphasised works at the expense of grace and so called the letter 'an epistle of straw'. Notice God's gifts are perfect or complete, reflecting category no. 6 in our list. With God, says James, there is no variation or play of passing shadows. You get the real thing from God, and you know where you are. This supports category no. 5 in our points derived from the fact that God is *one* in so many ways.

Doers of the Word

In 1:22 he reaches his key message that they must be doers of the word and not hearers only, later expressed as 'faith without works is dead' (no. 1). He describes God's 'law' as the perfect (complete) law, which actually gives us liberty, freeing us from the tyranny which disobeying God causes (no. 6).

He goes on to say you might seem to be very 'religious' but if your actions contradict your religion by the way you use your tongue or by your neglect of compassion for the unfortunate your religion is empty (no. 1).

God Has No Favourites

In Chapter 2 we return to the need to reflect God's impartiality. The one God made everyone; he has no favourites (no. 4). And so in the Church there should be no special consideration for the wealthy, while the poor are treated as inferior. 'God has chosen the poor of the world who are rich in faith.' Loving your neighbour as yourself, James asserts, means having no 'respect of persons'.

All Good Qualities Blended in God

Category no. 3 is illustrated in Chapter 2:10–13. God is the one God with all the good qualities. His requirements from us are not that we should specialise in just some of them, but follow all his commands. Unity of person is required. God is the perfect blender of all the ingredients that make up the complete person, even balancing mercy and judgement.

Theory and Practice

Then back to category no. 1. If your fellow believer is without food or clothes and you do nothing about it, your actions and words are not matching. If anyone says, 'You have faith and I have works' he is talking nonsense. You can only show faith *by* your works. You might as a matter of theory believe there is one God, he continues, but if you don't act on it, it is valueless (2:19). The only value of any doctrine of religion is what it does in us, how it affects our conduct.

The rest of Chapter 2 supports this with the example of Abraham, who is extolled by Paul as the supreme example of faith. James points out that Abraham demonstrated his faith by his works.

Taming the Tongue

Chapter 3 is devoted largely to the misuse of the tongue, of speech. The tongue is only a small organ of the body, but consider how much trouble it causes. It seems incapable of being tamed, he says. And he relates this source of confusion, where instead there should be fusion between the Church and the theme of the oneness of God, by saying that the one tongue should reflect the unity of God, who has all the qualities in perfect balance (no. 3). Speech cannot be used both to bless God and to curse people; this is like poisonous and pure water coming out of the same fountain.

War as the Negation of God

God's wisdom is without partiality (no. 4) and makes for peace (the word *eirene*, which means unity, not just the absence of war).

But it leads him into Chapter 4, discussing internal conflicts in the Church, perhaps over the faith and works, law and grace arguments. War is the absolute negation of unity. God is never at war with himself in the power of his oneness and they must reflect this. This is implicit in most of our categories based on the oneness of God. He calls the warring factions adulterers and adulteresses, because they have left the unity with the one God in Christ and have become united with the world.

They have rejected the symbolic meaning of marriage which is supposed to reflect the unity ('one flesh', the two, man and wife, become one). Disloyalty destroys this unity in marriage; it does no less for human relationship with God. But there is help available: 'God gives grace to the humble.'

There is more about double-mindedness being shown in what they might say about each other (often behind their backs, while being pleasant to their faces). Also it is often the case that people judge others for the very sins of which they are guilty.

Doctrine and Action

Then there is the inconsistency between believing that we are mortal and that death can come at any day and the making of plans as if we were immortal. James says they ought to say and mean that they will do this or that if God permit.

Chapter 5, as we have seen, reflects category no. 4 in dealing with the presence of rich and poor in the Church. James particularly attacks the selfishness of those rich people who seem oblivious of the way in which their riches were often gained by exploiting the poor. He also seems to be talking of the rich in the outside world, who are on the side of power in persecuting the Christians.

Concluding Fragments

James comes back to the testing time being experienced and pleads for perseverance of the kind that the prophets and Job evinced.

He finishes with a few helpful guidelines. He says they should not take oaths; their word should suffice – oneness again; there is one standard of truth. If you swear an oath it implies that your normal speech is not necessarily truthful and needs an oath to make it clear that this time you are definitely speaking the truth. As Jesus said, for Christians, yes should mean yes and no should mean no. (The only thing I don't understand is why James introduced this piece of guidance with the word 'Above all things', as if it was the most important thing in his letter.)

Oneness with God is then shown to be the outcome of prayer and can lead even to the healing of sickness and certainly the forgiveness of sins. Openness among the believers, where they can confess their faults to each other, can be helpful.

Finally they should all be at unity with the one God in his desire to see sinners converted from the error of their ways. Elijah is given as an example of effective prayer and a desire to convert sinners.

The Underlying Unity of the Tract

This is not an easy letter to grapple with, because it doesn't seem to flow. It jumps from point to point, often without a connecting link. But overall the theme of the one God, in all the aspects of his oneness, gives some sense of unity to the diverse aspects of the tract, for that is what it is, rather than a normal letter.

43

The General Epistles

1 Peter, 2 Peter, 1 John, 2 John, 3 John and Jude

The six letters attributed to Peter (two), John (three) and Jude (one) are known as 'the General' or 'Catholic' epistles because they are not addressed to any specific churches or situations. There are varying views as to whether they are written by the apostles whose name is linked with them, but this makes no difference to our appreciation of their message.

Peter's First Letter

The First Letter of Peter keeps the idea of the second coming of Jesus prominent in its flow of thought, but it is thoroughly pastoral in its intention and has considerable beauty as it deals with the impact of Jesus on the lives of the believers. It links with the kind of theology that was the basis of the early preaching in the Book of Acts, which Peter himself led. The death and resurrection of Jesus lay at the root of all the teaching along with his ascension to the right hand of God, to be present by the Spirit in the lives of the believers.

The letter was sent to the 'strangers' or 'exiles' in what we would now call Turkey – strangers and exiles because Christians were not at home in a wicked world. The text of the letter suggests that they were mainly Gentile Christians. They were in the midst of much suffering, increasingly persecuted because of their faith. Their separateness from worldly aspirations and their engaging in private worship made them suspect and disliked. They seemed to threaten the established order.

Born Again to a Living Hope

The letter begins on a note of thankfulness for all the blessing that accompanies being a Christian. They have been born again to a living hope through the resurrection of Jesus Christ from the dead, and God has an imperishable future in store for them. This should give them joy, in spite of the persecution they are facing. These trials are to test the quality of their faith, just as gold is purified in a furnace. They will be rewarded for standing firm when Jesus appears. They haven't seen him, but they love him with exalted joy.

The grace they have received through the sufferings of Christ was predicted in the Old Testament by the prophets, often in ways that the prophets could not themselves understand. They were in fact really writing for the benefit of the Christians, who can draw comfort from the glory of Christ that was being foretold.

Separate From the World's Futile Ways

In order to ensure participation in the ultimate glory they are to resist the ways of the world and be holy or separate from the evil in the world. Christ's sacrificial love (described as 'the blood' of Christ) has brought them back from the futile ways of that world and given them confidence in God and a sense of permanence, which contrasts with the temporary nature of human existence.

Their new relationship is demonstrated by their love for the brethren, as their fellow Christians are described. Malice, slander, envy, hypocrisy and deceit: all are to be avoided for they are being built into a spiritual house for Christ to dwell in. They are called to be the new Israel, a royal priesthood, a people chosen to offer themselves as sacrifices to God.

They are to turn from bodily passions, which 'warred against the soul', and to be known by their non-Christian neighbours for their good deeds, thus giving them little excuse for persecuting them. They are to be respectful to the Roman authorities and feel free within themselves as the servants of God. They are to give due honour to everyone.

Christians in the Extended Family

Peter then gives advice to the groups in an extended family of the times. Servants are to submit to their masters, even unpleasant ones, thus reflecting the spirit of Jesus who endured unjust treatment patiently and did not meet abuse with abuse. This teaching reflects the Sermon on the Mount and Isaiah 53 is applied to Jesus 'by whose wounds you are healed'. He carried our sins to the tree, they are told, so that we might finish with sin and live for righteousness.

Wives are commended for a gentle and quiet spirit, which would adorn them rather than flashy clothes and showy jewels, They are to be jewels to their husbands, who, in turn, are to show them consideration and respect, and even a measure of equality 'as sharers of the grace of life'.

Unity in the Church

The Church is to be characterised by a spirit of unity, sympathy, tenderness, humility and love. They are not to repay wrong with wrong, but rather meet evil with blessing. They are to be ready to defend their faith and hope to those who challenge it and to do so with courtesy and respect.

Christ's death is again invoked as the means by which they have been brought to God. They have sealed the relationship in baptism, which was an appeal for a good conscience and the entrance to the path of salvation, through the resurrection of Jesus, who is now at the right hand of God, with authority over all.

Christ as Their Example

Christ's course of action, which led to his death, was to give them an example. Whoever has suffered in the flesh has finished with sin and this is to be evident by their non-participation in the profligate activities of most people, who think it strange when people become Christians and cease to join in revelling, sexual misbehaviour and drunken orgies.

They are to keep sober and prayerful and their church life is to be dominated by love, 'which covers a multitude of sins'. A picture of a unified, hospitable church follows, where everyone employs their gifts for the benefit of all and serves the others in a way which will glorify God. Thus they would receive strength to endure the trials that are upon them, knowing that they are sharing the sufferings of Christ. Suffering for being Christian is a matter for rejoicing, but let no one suffer for bad behaviour.

Encouragement in Persecution

Peter encourages the elders among them to be good shepherds of the flock, with whom the Chief Shepherd would be pleased when he appears. The members are to listen to the elders and indeed to each other, being clothed with humility. They are to cast out all their anxieties on God, 'for he cares about you'. The enemies who are persecuting them are described as the devil and as a roaring lion. They are not to be frightened but to stand firm in their faith, knowing that God will see them through and share his eternal glory with them.

Altogether it is a letter that encourages them not to be defeated by persecution, but to keep Christ ever before them so that would feel that as they are sharing his sufferings, so he is sharing theirs. And standing firm means many practical actions and attitudes which the apostle details to help them hold on. And in the end there will be a sharing of the glory. The suffering was temporary. The letter may seem fairly simple to us, but it must have meant much to them.

Peter's Second Letter

The Second Letter of Peter is different in style from the first, though it speaks of the author having been present at the transfiguration of Jesus, which suggests that Peter had some involvement in the letter, even if he did not write it all. It is in other respects very different from the first one and the tone lacks its beauty. It is largely concerned with resisting the activities of those who are preaching false doctrine and predicting a bad end for these false prophets and the fiery end of the world in general. The epistle of Jude is very similar and uses many of the same words, so does not require separate treatment.

If I had to choose a book in the Bible that I could do without, this would probably be it. But then I would miss the early reference to the righteousness of our great God and saviour Jesus Christ, one of the few places where Jesus is referred to as God, in any sense. I would miss the way in which the divine power has given us everything that makes for life and true religion and the reference to the priceless promises of God, through which they could escape the corruption with which lust had infected the world and come to share the very being of God.

Verse 5 of Chapter 1 gives what some have called Peter's addition sum, a list of virtues that, added together, will make people effective in their Christian life. The list is: faith, virtue, knowledge, self-control, fortitude, piety, brotherly affection and, at the pinnacle, *love*. With these they would be sure of an entry into the Kingdom of God. Peter affirms that they have not been duped by fables but are following the beloved Son of God, whom Peter had seen in glory at the transfiguration. He knows that he has not much longer left before his life ends, as Jesus had forecast, and so he is anxious to make sure he leaves behind a message that will sustain them.

Chapter 2 is a long diatribe against the sin of the world, which through the false teaching of certain supposed Christians is invading the Church. It is rather vitriolic, without even a hope that they might repent. It takes delight in the bad end that awaits them in the judgement of God.

Chapter 3 continues in the same strain, rebuking readers for doubting the second coming and affirming that Jesus will return and dissolve the universe before creating a new heaven and a new earth. I take this to be symbolic, a changing of systems, rather than a material burning up of the earth.

The letter finishes with a reference to Paul's difficult letters, which people were misusing. He tells them that now they have been forewarned they should make sure that the false teachers do not seduce them, but that they continue to grow in the grace and knowledge of our Lord and Saviour Jesus Christ.

The letter is a strange mix of good Christian advice and bitter hatred for those who oppose sound teaching. The emphasis on the second coming and the burning up of everything is also unusual in the New Testament context. It is interesting how the writer attributes immorality to the people who are misleading them with false teaching, but he does not go into detail about it.

John's First Letter

There are three letters from John. The second and third are very short self-explanatory ones to individuals. When you have read the first and longer one, you see that he is reinforcing his teaching with warning about certain false teachers.

The first letter is an old man's letter; it rambles a bit, but it has a profound view of the role of Christ. The wandering actually adds to its charm. It circles round its themes and picks them up repeatedly and emphasises the message as it proceeds.

It begins like a spiritual thriller:

> It was there from the beginning; we have heard it; we have seen it with our own eyes; we looked upon it, and felt it with our own hands: our theme is the Word which gives life. This life was made visible; we have seen it and bear our testimony; we declare to you the eternal life which was with the Father and was made visible to us. It is this which we have seen and heard that we declare to you also, in order that you may share with us in the common life, that life which we share with the Father and his Son Jesus Christ.

This is one of the clearest pictures of the relationship between God and Jesus and those who believe in them. There is the life of God which has always existed; it was embodied in the human being, Jesus Christ; through him this life of God flows to the believers. The disciples, of whom John was one, had seen, heard and touched this embodiment of God. He wants his readers to share the joy implicit in this experience, which can be theirs as well, even though less directly.

The Paradox of Sin

John continues with the paradox of sin. He says none of his readers are sinless, but forgiveness comes through the sacrifice of Christ if they confess their sins. If they say they do not sin they are liars and cut themselves off from the light of God which is in Christ. But then he continues that his purpose in writing is that they shall not commit sin. If they do, God accepts them in Christ. There is a kind of see-saw in his argument.

Next he says that you can only know God if you keep his commands. Obedience to God is the only way to show that you love him. You can only dwell in God if you live as Christ lived, which is a high standard indeed. He gives them a new command: if they are to walk truly in the light, they must love their fellow Christians. To hate them is to walk in darkness.

He continues with encouragement to young and old alike and then moves on to tell readers that they should not love the world with its allurements. It is passing away, but those who do God's will remain forever.

False Teachers

John then moves on to false teachers, whom he calls antichrists. They have left the community, but the true believers need to keep alert so as not to be tempted by their blandishments. In some way these antichrists have been denying that Jesus was the Christ, and they have been denying his divine Sonship. The faithful believers must hold fast and so dwell in the Father and in the Son. The anointing of the Spirit would help them to do this.

Then, in Chapter 3, he marvels at the love of God for them, shown in calling them his children and saying that there is more to come; when Jesus appears 'we shall be like him, because we shall see him as he is'. In other words, he declares, being perpetually in the presence of Christ will make them ever more like him.

More About Sin

Then back to the question of sin. Jesus appeared to take away sin and in him there is no sin. No one who abides in Jesus sins, which is a different angle from the earlier claim that if you say you do not sin, you are a liar. No one born of God commits sin, because God's seed lives in him. 'Indeed because he is God's child he cannot sin.'

So we have something of a puzzle, yet no writer would contradict himself so blatantly within the space of a few lines. It must be a deliberate paradox. On the one hand he wants to keep sin as clearly displeasing to God and on the other hand he wants to make it clear that forgiveness of the truly repentant sinner washes away the sin, so that the one who has sinned is no longer a sinner.

It could also be that he has in mind the particular sin of denying that Jesus is the Son who embodies the Father, thereby losing one's connection with God. Also he keeps mentioning that they know they are not sinners when they truly love their fellow Christians. He tells them not to worry. All is well if their hearts do not condemn them. And their hearts will not condemn them if they believe in the name of God's Son and love one another.

And they will know that God dwells in them by the Spirit that he has given them. So there is this intertwining of the Father, the Son, the Spirit and the true believers in a perfect unity based on love.

The Docetists

Then back to the false teachers. The faithful are urged to be careful to test all teachers to be sure that they do acknowledge that Jesus Christ came in the flesh, that he was truly human. He is opposing the gnostic teachers, who claim special mystic knowledge, hence his frequent mention of true knowledge of God. He is also tackling the particular heresy of those who said that Jesus did not really suffer as a man, but only *seem* to suffer. They were called Docetists, from the Greek word for 'seem'. They are not to listen to such teachers, who are not of the Church but of the world. The faithful must learn to distinguish between the Spirit of truth and the spirit of error.

Love of the Brethren

This concern with sound teaching was not merely about theory. John saw it as highly practical, hence his constant reiteration of the theme of love of the brethren, which he now expounds again.

> The source of love is God. Everyone who loves is a child of God and knows God, but the unloving know nothing of God, for *God is love*. This is how he showed his love among us; he sent his only Son into the world that we might have life through him. This is what love really is. Not that we have loved God, but that he loved us and sent his Son as a sacrifice to atone for our sins. If God thus loved us, dear friends, we also must love one another.

He carries on extensively in the same vein. Being a Christian is a matter of believing in the love that God has for us. 'God is love; he who dwells in love is dwelling in God and God in him.' He emphasises that, as our love grows and becomes mature (which is what 'perfect' means), we lose the fear of God in the sense that we are no longer frightened of him and of Judgement Day. Perfect love banishes fear. We love because he first loved us.

Then follows a beautiful piece of teaching, that you cannot hate your fellow Christian, whom you can see, and then say that you love God, whom you cannot see. If you say, 'I love God' but hate your brother, you are a liar. It is not always easy to love people, particularly if they are unlikeable. There is a difference between liking and loving! Yet John says that this command to love the children of God, as the way of showing our love of God, is not burdensome. All it takes is faith in Jesus as the Son of God.

Eternal Life

If you have faith in Jesus in this way, then you have the testimony of God in your heart – in your inward being. He puts it another way by saying that if you 'possess' Jesus as the Son of God then you have his life in you, which he calls eternal life. Eternal life, as he uses the term, doesn't just mean living forever. It includes that, but it is a word of quality, rather than of quantity. He says the whole purpose of his letter is to assure them that they have eternal life.

Prayer

The closing thoughts encourage confident approach to God in prayer, being assured that he listens. He says 'that all we ask of Him *is* ours'. There is some subtlety here. He doesn't say that it *will be* ours, but that it *is*, as if the mood of our asking is such that we have the real intent of our request. As we ask, the meaning of our petition gets straightened out and we are satisfied.

John also suggests prayer for those whom we see are in danger of falling into sin. In this connection he makes a distinction between the fact that all wrong-doing is sin, but not all sin is deadly. Perhaps the only deadly sin is that which becomes so ingrained that it cannot be repented of. Perhaps people like Hitler and Stalin fall into this category and would not want eternal life, God's Kingdom, even if it were offered to them. I believe it is safer to pray for all. How can we judge whether people have committed deadly sin? Had I lived in those days I should have written John a letter to find out exactly what he meant!

Multiple Unity

This epistle is rich in bringing us close to God and to Jesus. In a practical way the circulation of love between the Father, the Son, the Spirit and the believer is made vivid. It is more than a Trinity. It is a multiple unity (a multiplinity!) into which we are invited.

The letter concludes:

> We know that the Son of God has come and given us an understanding to know the true God; indeed we are in him who is true, since we are in his Son Jesus Christ. This is the true God and eternal life.

44

A Christian Opera

Revelation

The Apocalypse

Please call it Revelation, not Revelations, as people often do. It is a translation of a Greek word *apokalypsis*, which means unveiling or revelation, though you may reasonably feel this obscures more than it reveals. It belongs to a genre of writing, familiar in the ancient world, that gave visions and predictions of what the future would be like in highly symbolic form. Such works give special emphasis to the great crisis and end of history, when God would put everything right and overcome all evil. They particularly relish the destructive war on evil.

In the Old Testament, the Book of Daniel is the outstanding example, with its beasts and dragons, which reappear in this Book of Revelation. To some extent the predictions by Jesus of the end of the Jewish commonwealth in Mark 13, Luke 21 and Matthew 24 are in the apocalyptic mode. Then there are many other non-Biblical apocalypses, with more far-fetched scenes than in this Book of Revelation.

Use and Misuse of the Book

Often attributed to John the Apostle, this last book of the Bible relies much on the Old Testament for its images of suffering by the Church followed by ultimate victory. It is so worded that Christians could use it to inspire hope in a number of difficult situations. It can be applied over and over again. Indeed this flexibility has been misused repeatedly by extreme (and sometimes not so extreme) sects to predict the course of history or to describe past events. In the eighteenth and nineteenth centuries people used to work in the Turks, Napoleon, the Roman Catholic Church, the Roman Empire and Russia. Some in the twentieth century have found Hitler, Stalin, the Pope, the two world wars and the nuclear threat – all in the Book of Revelation.

Many of these interpretations have bordered on the absurd, yet people have still found in them some sense of God as the ultimate Lord of history. It was probably written at the time of Emperor Domitian's persecution of the Christians towards the end of the first century. They would have felt that God and the Lord Jesus were on their side in their problems and they would have been encouraged by the plain messages with which the picture language was interspersed.

Too many people have failed to perceive the symbolic and poetic nature of the book and have regarded dragons and demons and lakes of fire literally. In fact much of the now generally rejected view that God will consign all who disobey him to eternal flames has been based on such literalism.

Serious Cartoons and Stupendous Opera

I see much of the book as consisting of serious cartoons of the great battle between good and evil in the world. Some of the characters are caricatures. The action is accompanied with music and vast choirs of the heavenly hosts. I could imagine it being made into a massive operatic movie. Pictorially it would be sensational and the music to accompany it would tax the greatest composers and singers. A good way to read the book is to create such a movie in your mind.

Imagine the larger-than-life figure of Christ, exercising power in Chapter 1. It is a very different picture from the one we have been meeting in John's letters, which is more appealing, yet Jesus is described frequently as sitting at the right hand of God and as upholding everything by the word of his power, so this poet wanted to emphasise this aspect of Christ as judge.

Picture in your mind: the meetings of the heavenly court; the heavenly music festivals; the battles between superhuman beasts, dragons and serpents; flaming abysses, horsemen charging into battle, enormous meteorites falling from heaven; and then finally the pictures of peace, with a new heaven and earth, and a bejewelled New Jerusalem coming down from heaven, Don't try to give precise meaning to everything. Develop a feeling for it as you would for good music, poetry or visual art, and modify it all in the light of the rest of what you know of God and Jesus from the overall picture in the Bible.

The Apocalypse as a Letter

The author begins his book in the style of a letter, with the normal salutations and the seeking of blessings from God and Jesus. These are expressed more vividly than usual, but with emphasis on the death and resurrection of Jesus and the power in developing the Church and the individuals in it.

He says he was in Spirit or in a trance one Sunday and heard a loud voice, which turned out to be that of Jesus, telling him to write to seven churches in Western Turkey. When he saw Jesus with flashing eyes, burning feet and a sword in his mouth he was terrified and fell at his feet, but he was revived by the one who died and is alive for evermore.

The Letters to the Seven Churches

Chapters 2 and 3 then take features of this vision of Jesus and use them in the opening and closing of seven short letters to the seven churches, in places that you can visit in package tours of Turkey, as I have done myself. The letters themselves take hold of features of the collective behaviour of each church and give praise and rebuke in response, with warning and threats about lack of improvement and promises of reward for progress.

One of the main criticisms of most of these churches is their attitude to false teachers. A number of them are characterised as being too tolerant of such people, who appear under strange descriptions, such as the Nicolaitans, that woman Jezebel, the Balaamites. Ephesus has lost its first love and Laodicea is lukewarm. There is a geographical connection in this last description. The cold water of the River Lycus, as it flows from Colosse, joins the warm waters of Hierapolis, in which I have swum, at Laodicea, producing water which was, like its church, neither cold nor hot!

There are only a few faithful people in Sardis; some have not been seduced by Jezebel in Thyatira; most of the people in Pergamum seemed to resist the Balaamites; the church in Smyrna (Izmir) is resisting the synagogue of Satan and false Jews; the Philadelphians seem to have stayed firm and receive no adverse criticism. One feature of these letters is the rich

Old Testament vocabulary employed in describing, often symbolically, the ultimate reward.

The famous words of Jesus – 'Behold I stand at the door and knock; if anyone opens the door I will come in and eat with him' – come in the end of the letter to lukewarm Laodicea. They have been immortalised in Britain by the painting by Holman Hunt, a copy of which is in St Paul's Cathedral in London.

The Unsealing of the Scroll

Chapters 4 and 5 give a vision of the heavenly court, drawing on the twenty-four orders of priesthood in the Jewish temple and the visions of Ezekiel about the cherubim. They also use the vision of Isaiah 6 where the seraphim cry 'Holy! Holy! Holy! Lord God Almighty'. All the heavenly host sing praise to God and Jesus, and then a scroll carrying important information is produced. But no one can unseal it until the lion of the tribe of Judah has conquered and unsealed it. The writer looks to see the lion and sees instead a lamb, which is recovering from having been slain. This is a reinterpretation of the kind of conquest that Jesus achieved, a sacrificial one – not a military one.

Then the scroll is unsealed. Seven seals are removed. The first four cause the four horsemen of the Apocalypse to be let loose; all of the first six seals bring dire distress on the inhabitants of the earth. The nations flee from the anger of the Lamb. The seventh seal brings heavenly peace.

The New Israel

Chapter 7 gives a picture of the Christians being delivered from this wrath as the new Israel, sealed as God's chosen ones, symbolised by the number 144,000, and also as a great multitude out of all nations. They are clothed in white robes, which have been washed in the blood of the Lamb (a strange symbol!). The Lamb (Jesus) is also described as their shepherd who leads them to living waters (echoes of the well-known Psalm 23 'The Lord is my shepherd').

The Seven Trumpets

In Chapters 8 and 9 we have seven trumpets being blown to call forth more plagues upon the whole of humanity, yet people do not repent of their idolatry, immorality and violence. The sixth trumpet leads to seven thunderstorms, in Chapter 10. These are not detailed but remain sealed up. But, like Ezekiel, the author is given a little scroll from which, after eating it, he is to prophesy woe on the nations.

The Beasts

Chapter 11 gives us the faithful as witnesses against the nations. They suffer for it, but in the end are rewarded and triumphant. Temple symbolism and numerical symbols from the Book of Daniel are used in describing them. The Book of Daniel gives rise to the beast symbols of Chapters 12 and 13. Various strange animals arise to persecute the people of God. One incorporates Daniel's four beasts in one composite animal, with the body of a leopard, the feet of a bear, the mouth of a lion, seven heads and ten horns.

The Celebratory Concert

Chapter 14 is a picture of the ultimate happy end of the faithful — the 144,000 upon Mount Zion, who have the Father's name written in their foreheads. They are holding a wonderful concert to celebrate the downfall of the world's forces, described as Babylon and as the worshippers of the beast.

The Wine Press of God's Wrath

Then there is a harvest scene where the wicked are being cut off like bunches of grapes and a wine press gives rise to a 200-mile flow of human blood as high as a horse's bridle. (I admit I find this image quite repulsive, and not at the same level as most of the New Testament.)

Pictures of Joy and Bowls of Wrath

Chapter 15 gives us a picture of peace and harmony on the earth, with the faithful singing the praises of God. But then it goes on to prepare us for the pouring out of God's anger from seven bowls. The angels are standing ready for the task. The structure of these chapters seems to be that of a picture of the ultimate harmony of the Kingdom of God followed by a history of more of God's judgements on a wicked world, said to be necessary before the peace can be reached.

Chapter 16 gives us the pouring out of the bowls of wrath, with emphasis on the fact that they are punishment for the way in which God's servants have been persecuted. It is impossible to fit this in with the teaching of Jesus that we should love our enemies. It seems to encourage the acceptance of persecution in the spirit of 'Ah, well, never mind, they will get what's coming to them from the anger of God.' Contrast it with 'Father forgive them for they know not what to do'.

The seventh bowl of God's anger is the end of history, after the Armageddon of the sixth bowl. (This is where the name Armageddon comes from.) As people are tortured by enormous hailstones and Babylon is made to drink the cup of God's wrath a voice cries, 'It is over.'

The Fall of Symbolic Babylon

Chapter 17 gives us a terrible picture of a queenly prostitute sitting on one of the beasts we have met earlier. The kings of the earth are gathered together to make war on the Lamb (Jesus). The Lamb wins and they proclaim him King of Kings and Lord of Lords.

Chapters 18 and 19 provide more songs of victorious gloating over the defeat of the enemies, now again described as Babylon. Many Old Testament references are picked up. Chapter 19, a song to celebrate the vengeance of God, actually contains the basis of the 'Hallelujah' chorus. Jesus as the Word of God leads the armies of heaven into this victory and at one stage the prayer is 'give them blood to drink for they are worthy'.

The Millennium

Chapter 20 gives us the origin of the idea of a 1,000-year rule of Christ, during which he will tame the nations. In common speech it is spoken of as the millennium. At the end of it rebel forces try to reverse the work of Christ and are finally obliterated.

New Heaven and New Earth

Finally in Chapters 21 and 22 we enter more peaceful territory. Wonderful symbols are poetically expressed in words often used at funerals. A new heaven and a new earth are created and the new Jerusalem comes down as a bride adorned for her husband. This mixed metaphor represents the Church in its perfection. God wipes away tears from all eyes; death shall be no more; there will never be sorrow or mourning or pain again.

Perhaps all the horrible pictures are a comment on the basic rebelliousness of the human race, which in the end gets cured and God achieves his benevolent purposes. We need to have the darkness before we can have the light. However it is still difficult to see why God's judgements are portrayed in such bloodthirsty terms. It is almost as if the writer had not caught up with the love of Christ.

Also the idea that the human heart can be changed by bloody compulsion does not fit with the idea that God seeks willing hearts. He doesn't say 'Love me or I will kill you', though that is how some Old Testament writers saw him, and the Book of Revelation seems to go backwards to those perspectives.

Could it be that in the providence of God we are being shown how easily the Church has repeatedly gone backwards? In our own time we have had sections of the Church blessing armies and battleships and praying for the victory of their side. Is the Book of Revelation given to show us how *not* to think of God? In this case the last few chapters and the peaceful pictures scattered throughout the book are saying, 'This is what God is really like.'

The Beauty of the New Jerusalem

Certainly the poetry of the last two chapters contrasts with the warlike tone of so much we read in this book. The New Jerusalem represents the glorified Church and is bedecked with jewels in its walls and gates. Streams of living waters flow out of it, with fruit-bearing forests on their banks. Only purity will dwell there and they shall see the face of God! No falsehood will find a place there and 'they shall reign forever and ever'.

Warning and Encouragement

The very end of the book warns Christians that when Jesus comes they will be rewarded for their behaviour. If this is not satisfactory there is not much time to change, so they had better act fast and drink of the water of life.

There is a special warning not to tamper with the words of this prophecy, either to add to it or take away from it. This seems to reflect the fact that the writer was having difficulty in getting his message accepted as authentic. In fact the Church nearly excluded it from the New Testament when the final recognition was being made of what was scripture and what was not. In spite of the difficulties the book creates, it has also contributed much to Christian hymns and worship. We should be poorer without these contributions, even if they are used out of context sometimes.

The writer finishes on a note of expecting the second coming of Christ very soon. His expectations have not been fulfilled, but there is a note of confidence that ultimately God will have his dwelling with mankind. So there is hope and light shining through all the gloom and terror of so many of Revelation's images.

Even the last words provide it: 'Amen, Come Lord Jesus'!

Afterword

We have now travelled from Genesis to Revelation, through all sixty-six books of the Bible. We have seen how in all of them there is scope for learning something about God and Jesus Christ, who shows us what God is like. We have not suggested a simplistic acceptance of every verse of the Bible as a direct instruction from God or presenting a literal scientific fact. We have seen how there is a development of understanding as men and women are moved to share their insights into the authority of God with the human race.

Thus the Old Testament is able to make us 'wise unto salvation' only through 'faith in Jesus Christ (2 Timothy, 3:15). Without the New Testament revelation of Jesus, the Old is limited; with this revelation the jewels in the Old begin to sparkle.

The aim of it all is 'salvation', bringing human beings into fellowship with God, with a deeper sense of the meaning of life and how to live it. We have seen how even the follies and absurdities of people as well as the great deeds of righteousness contribute to this understanding. As Michael Ramsay wrote in *The Anglican Spirit*: 'In the whole drama of the Bible, with all its ups and downs, God is manifesting Himself as the righteous saviour God in a way that points to Christ, and is incomplete without Christ.' He also describes what we have been learning, that 'the Bible is not diminished, but enhanced if God's revelation is not limited to prosaic literal statements, but able to use poetry, drama, symbol, imagery and a whole wealth of literary forms of speech and thought in showing [God's] existence, His graciousness and His purposes to humanity'.

Edgar Wille
August 1999

Further Reading

These books are just a small selection written from different perspectives. The reader will have to decide what he or she accepts, what is rejected and what is left for further reflection. If the books are out of print a public library may be able to lend them to you.

J. Drane, *Introducing the New Testament* (1986: Lion, Oxford)
——, *Introducing the Old Testament* (1987: Lion, Oxford)
J.A.T. Robinson, *Redating the New Testament* (1976: SCM, Westminster)
P.S. Fiddes, *Past Events and Present Salvation* (1976: Darton, Longman & Todd, London)
G.E. Ladd, *The Presence of the Future* (second edition, 1980: SPCK, London)
C.H. Dodd, *The Apostolic Preaching and Its Development* (third edition, 1963: Hodder and Stoughton, London)
J.D.G. Dunn, *The Evidence for Jesus* (1985: SCM, London)

N.T. Wright, *Following Jesus* (1994: SPCK, London)
T. Wright, *The Original Jesus* (1996: Lion, Oxford)
(Tom Wright writes under both of these names.)
G.B. Caird, *The Language and Imagery of the Bible* (1980: Duckworth, London)
J. Bright, *A History of Israel* (1980: SCM, London)
——, *The Authority of the Old Testament* (1967: SCM, London)
H.H. Rowley, *The Faith of Israel* (1956: SCM, London)
D.F. Henson, *History of the Israel – Old Testament Introduction Part 1* (1990: SPCK, London; all of the SPCK International Study Guides are valuable)
B.W. Anderson, *The Living World of the Old Testament* (1978: Longman, London)
J.P. Prévost, *How to Read the Prophets* (1995: SCM, London)

There are many commentaries on individual books of the Bible (Old Testament and New Testament). Among them are:

The Daily Study Bible (The Saint Andrew Press, Edinburgh)
The Anchor Bible (Doubleday)
The New Century Bible (Oliphants/Eardmans)

Key Dates

We cannot be sure of precise accuracy, but these traditional dates are offered to give some kind of a time frame for events in the Bible. There is plenty of scope for detailed debate, but this list will help you to place events in context.

BC
2166	Abraham born
2066	Isaac born
2006	Jacob and Esau born
1915	Joseph born
1526	Moses born
1446	Israel crosses the Red Sea – the Exodus
1406	Moses dies. Joshua takes over
1375–1050	The Judges
1105	Samuel
1050–1010	Saul
1010–970	David

970–930   Solomon

930   The division of the Kingdom into Judah (two tribes, south) and Israel (ten tribes, north)

Israel: Some Key Kings
874–853   Ahab
793–753   Jeroboam II
722   Fall of Israel

Judah: Some Key Kings
910–869   Asa
872–848   Jehoshaphat
848–735   Jehoram, Athaliah, Joash, Uzzrah, Jotham
735–715   Ahaz
715–686   Hezekiah
640–609   Josiah
609–598   Jehoiakim
597–586   Zedekiah. Jerusalem falls. Babylonian exile starts

Prophets of Israel
875–848   Elijah
848–797   Elisha
760–750   Amos
750–715   Hosea

Prophets of Judah
740–681   Isaiah
626–585   Jeremiah

Prophets of Exile

593–571	Ezekiel
605–530	Daniel (period allocated to the story even if the prophecy was written later)
538	Return from exile under Zerubbabel and Joshua
455	Further return under Ezra
432	Last return under Nehemiah

Prophets of the Return

520–480	Zechariah and Haggai
440–430	Malachi
	Isaiah 40-66 emerges in the period of the return probably from the School of Isaiah, often referred to as Deutero–Isaiah (Second Isaiah) and Trito–Isaiah (Third Isaiah)

Period between the Testaments

430–birth of Jesus	Events include the struggles of the Maccabees and the takeover by the Romans

New Testament

5 (?)	Jesus born

AD

26–30	Ministry of Christ, crucifixion, resurrection and ascension
30	Pentecost
35	Paul's conversion
46–48	Paul's First Missionary Journey
50–52	Paul's Second Missionary Journey
53–57	Paul's Third Missionary Journey

59–62	Paul imprisoned in Rome
67/68	Paul's execution
70	Jerusalem destroyed by the Romans
90–95	John exiled to Patmos; receives the vision recorded in the Book of Revelation